MW00856794

THE LAWYER'S ESSENTIAL GUIDE TO WRITING

Proven Tools and Techniques

MARIE BUCKLEY

LawPractice ManagementSection
MARKETING • MANAGEMENT • TECHNOLOGY • FINANCE

Commitment to Quality: The Law Practice Management Section is committed to quality in our publications. Our authors are experienced practitioners in their fields. Prior to publication, the contents of all our books are rigorously reviewed by experts to ensure the highest quality product and presentation. Because we are committed to serving our readers' needs, we welcome your feedback on how we can improve future editions of this book.

Cover design by Elmarie Jara, ABA Publishing.

Nothing contained in this book is to be considered as the rendering of legal advice for specific cases, and readers are responsible for obtaining such advice from their own legal counsel. This book and any forms and agreements herein are intended for educational and informational purposes only.

The products and services mentioned in this publication are under or may be under trademark or service mark protection. Product and service names and terms are used throughout only in an editorial fashion, to the benefit of the product manufacturer or service provider, with no intention of infringement. Use of a product or service name or term in this publication should not be regarded as affecting the validity of any trademark or service mark.

The Law Practice Management Section of the American Bar Association offers an educational program for lawyers in practice. Books and other materials are published in furtherance of that program. Authors and editors of publications may express their own legal interpretations and opinions, which are not necessarily those of either the American Bar Association or the Law Practice Management Section unless adopted pursuant to the bylaws of the Association. The opinions expressed do not reflect in any way a position of the Section or the American Bar Association.

© 2011 American Bar Association. All rights reserved.
Printed in the United States of America.

Library of Congress Cataloging-in-Publication Data

Buckley, Marie P.
  The lawyer's essential guide to writing : proven tools and techniques /
Marie P. Buckley ; with tips for transactional attorneys by Ilissa K. Povich.
     p. cm.
  Includes a usage and punctuation guide, bibliographical references and index.
  ISBN 978-1-61632-965-5
  1. Legal composition. 2. Law—United States—Language. I. Povich, Ilissa K.
II. Title.
  KF250.B83   2011
  808′.06634—dc23

                                                                    2011022337

14 13 12   5 4 3

Discounts are available for books ordered in bulk. Special consideration is given to state bars, CLE programs, and other bar-related organizations. Inquire at Book Publishing, American Bar Association, 321 N. Clark Street, Chicago, Illinois 60654.

Dedication

For Charles, who edits me.

Table of Contents

About the Authors vii

Acknowledgments ix

Preface xi

Conventions and Other Details xiii

Chapter 1: Why Writing Matters 1

Chapter 2: Winning the Battle for Your
            Readers' Attention 5

Chapter 3: The Three Essential Principles for
            Powerful Writing 9

Chapter 4: Plain English and Other Tricks to Help
            You Sound Human 13

Chapter 5: The Question of Voice and Tone 33

Chapter 6: The Transition from Academic to
            Professional Writing 39

Chapter 7: Understanding the Big Picture 43

Chapter 8: Research: Finding and Understanding
            the Cases 47

Chapter 9: Organizing Your Research for
            Efficient Writing 51

Chapter 10: Beyond Research: Seeing the
            Big Picture in the Cases 55

Chapter 11: Brainstorming 57

Chapter 12: The Process of Writing and Overcoming
Writer's Block 61

Chapter 13: Honesty and Authorship 69

Chapter 14: The Distinction Between a Memorandum
and a Brief 75

Chapter 15: Using Structure to Lead from the Top 77

Chapter 16: Memorandum Structure 83

Chapter 17: The Story or *Facts* 87

Chapter 18: The Issue 95

Chapter 19: The Conclusion or Brief Answer 99

Chapter 20: Substantive Headings in the *Analysis* or *Argument* . . 103

Chapter 21: The Analysis or Argument: General Thoughts 109

Chapter 22: Talking About Cases and Other Authority 119

Chapter 23: The Truth About Transitions 127

Chapter 24: Tell Your Reader What to Do Next 133

Chapter 25: Citations 135

Chapter 26: Deep Editing 143

Chapter 27: Proofreading and Finalizing Your Work 147

Chapter 28: Using Design As a Writing Tool 153

Chapter 29: Working with Junior Colleagues 161

Chapter 30: Tips for Transactional Attorneys
by Ilissa K. Povich 171

Chapter 31: Letters 175

Chapter 32: E-mail 185

Chapter 33: Blogging 203

Chapter 34: Housekeeping 213

Chapter 35: The Nutshell Summary of This Book 215

A Usage and Punctuation Guide 219

Bibliography 245

Index 251

About the Authors

Marie Buckley is the founder of Legal Advocacy Workshops and has been training lawyers at major firms for over a decade. She has worked individually with over one thousand lawyers and lectures regularly on legal writing at law firms.

Marie was a litigator at a major Boston law firm and handled a wide variety of cases, including multi-million dollar contract disputes, failed acquisitions, pension disputes, anti-trust defenses, toxic torts, white-collar crime, SEC investigations and insurance fraud. She was also appointed Special Counsel to the Board of Bar Overseers. She has tried cases and argued in many courts, including the United States Court of Appeals for the First Circuit.

Marie graduated from Bowdoin College, *magna cum laude*, and from Boston University School of Law. At B. U. Law, she won the Albers Second Year Invitational Moot Court Competition, including the Tauro Award for Outstanding Oral Advocacy (Best Speaker) and Best Brief.

Marie blogs about legal writing at "A Lawyer's Guide to Writing" (**www.mariebuckley.com**).

Ilissa Povich (Chapter 30, *Tips for Transactional Attorneys*) is a consultant at Legal Advocacy Workshops and focuses on transactional writing. She practiced business law at a major Boston law firm and has played a lead role in negotiating and drafting documents for public offerings, secured lending transactions, venture capital financings and private placements. Following her years in private practice, Ilissa spent four years as Vice President and General Counsel for Interactive Data Corporation in Bedford, Massachusetts. Ilissa has also been a writer for Brumberg Publications.

Ilissa Povich graduated *summa cum laude* from Duke University, where she was elected to *Phi Beta Kappa*, and from Harvard Law School.

Acknowledgments

It may take a village to raise a child, but it took a small city to write this book and I owe my heartfelt thanks to many people.

My sister, Elaine Buckley, was my muse. She edited chapters, answered substantive questions on technology issues and encouraged me throughout. Her advice was always sharp and wise. My sister, Kathleen McMorrow, was also a source of support and encouragement and her advice steered me through many a writing slump. During this project, the three of us exchanged at least a thousand e-mails and I consider myself lucky indeed to have a group called "sisters" in my contacts.

My colleague, Ilissa Povich, wrote the chapter on transactional editing and was always insightful and supportive. Sharing this project with Ilissa made the work almost fun and she is simply the best of partners. Thank you also to Barbara Gruenthal for her penetrating thoughts on research questions and, even more, for her long and constant friendship. In the great battle of law and life, I have been blessed to have her on my team. My thanks also to Tony Feeherry for encouraging me to begin teaching writing so long ago and to Bob Ambrogi for kick-starting this project.

My warmest thanks to the many helping hands at the American Bar Association. My editor, Tim Johnson, was a delight to work with and a wise advisor. He has a unique gift for seeing the big picture and that gift helped me focus and sharpen my own thoughts as I wrote. This book is far stronger for his input. Many thanks to Timothy White, who reviewed the manuscript in its early stages—a selfless, thankless task, for which I will always be grateful.

And I am deeply grateful to the many lawyers whom I have coached over the years. I am always inspired by the talent of my young colleagues and touched by their enthusiasm for writing and for their chosen profession. They represent everything that is good about our profession. My students have taught me far more about writing than I could ever teach them and they have made teaching fun.

Finally, to my husband, Charles. Thank you for being my help desk, my crisis-management team, my therapist, my proofreader, my sounding board, my gofer, my cheerleader, and my friend. You are a kind husband and a mean editor. I needed both. This book would never have happened without you.

While many people contributed to this book, any mistakes belong to me alone. In spite of the mountains of support that I receive from my family, my friends and my colleagues, I remain far from perfect. My friends and family know this so I thank them, above all, for putting up with me.

Preface

When a major Boston law firm first asked me to teach writing to young lawyers, I eagerly agreed. I loved the intellectual rigor of legal argument and the symmetry of a finely crafted brief. How hard could teaching writing to talented young lawyers be? I had surely found the easiest law-related job in town.

Then I confronted my first paper. It was a research memorandum on a contract issue and a dense and tangled web. In other words, typical lawyer stuff—much like the dense prose I myself had often written as a young lawyer. So just as I once struggled to correct my own bad habits, I now struggled with my student's paper. I cut the clutter, rewrote paragraphs in plain English, crafted lead sentences, reorganized thoughts, and deciphered a conclusion. The editing took hours—far more time than it would have taken to write the paper from scratch. I was exhausted, but the paper was much improved.

The next day, the earnest young lawyer who had written the paper sat down for a review session. As I walked him through my suggestions, I found myself struggling to explain *why* I had suggested those changes. I realized then that my new role required me to work with the writer, not just the writing— to teach, rather than simply edit. What could I offer my student that would enable him to improve not just this paper, but the hundreds of papers he would write in his legal career?

Indeed, what is good legal writing? We all know it when we see it, but are there rules or best practices? Or is writing too personal and complex for rules?

So I began to study the papers I reviewed. I deconstructed papers that worked to determine why they worked. I searched for best practices. I noted common pitfalls. And I tried to look beyond the common admonition to "use plain English" and to focus instead on the structure and substance of legal writing.

Since that long-ago meeting with my first student, I have coached over a thousand lawyers. I have learned that I must explain not just *what* changes I suggest, but *why* I suggest those changes. My years of coaching have left me with strong convictions about what makes for powerful legal writing and an even stronger belief that legal writing is a skill that can be taught and learned.

This book shares the many lessons my students have taught me—lessons that should guide others lawyers, whether they are solo practitioners, government prosecutors or globe-trotting international lawyers. I hope these lessons nurture your talent for writing and encourage you to nurture that talent in others.

May this book help you find your own voice.

Conventions and Other Details

Since this is a book about language, I have needed to talk about words and phrases and to provide examples to illustrate various points. I have set off most examples in italics, rather than quotations, because the italics seemed less cumbersome. These italicized examples represent common words, phrases or sentences or my own suggestions for rewriting those passages. Some of these examples are based on common phrases or constructions that I have seen in my students' writing. Because the examples represent common usage and because I do not want to embarrass anyone, I have not attributed these examples. When I have quoted an example from a case or other source, I have put that example in quotations and cited to the source.

In citing to cases, I have included a vendor-neutral citation wherever possible. Since this book is not a law review article or a brief, I have not followed strict citation conventions, but have simply aimed for readable, informative references. You will not find an *id.* or a *supra* in these pages.

I have also explained how to do some of the mysterious word-processing tasks that often befuddle lawyers. Those references are to Microsoft Word 2007. My apologies to other vendors.

Why Writing Matters 1

For I am a bear of very little brain and long words bother me.

—A. A. Milne, *Winnie the Pooh*

NOBODY UNDERSTANDS US. We lawyers are the topic of late-night jokes, the species most frequently compared to sharks, the supplicants least likely to pass through the pearly gates. We make too much money. We bill for breathing. And we dress like clones.

But the bigger problem, or perhaps the root of our problem, is that nobody can *understand* us. We speak in code or, as the columnist Dave Barry has written, in Martian. Our writing sounds pompous and superior. While the civilian world tweets away, we run on and on in circular marathons of words. We write documents, not papers. And those documents are not just baffling. They are ugly too.

Lawyers have always lived and died through their words. But today, those words are almost always written. Virtually everything we do—our negotiations, our legal arguments, our advice to clients, even our exchanges with colleagues—we now do in writing. Yet we often belittle the skill required to write masterfully. How often have we suggested that something be "*reduced* to writing?" But now that all lawyers are essentially in the writing business, the ability to write clearly and efficiently has become a survival skill. You cannot be an effective lawyer today if you cannot write.

Why is legal writing so important? Because legal writing drives deals, molds thought, sets rules, and governs relationships. Because once legal thought is *promoted* to writing, it becomes a permanent guide and reference. Because our writing represents both our clients and our firm. And because our writing reflects on each of us as an advocate and a person. Our writing defines who we are.

Writing skills are particularly essential for young lawyers. Young lawyers' careers often rise—or fall—based on their ability to write. Therefore, writing is any young lawyer's best tool for advocating for his or her own skills. Writing is the way young lawyers build their reputations and begin to create their own story as sharp legal thinkers and promising advocates.

Our poor writing costs us dearly in both time and results. Indeed, it often seems contagious. New lawyers agonize over their writing. Senior lawyers waste years of their lives revising poorly written work from those junior attorneys. Clients struggle to decode their own lawyers' missives. Meanwhile, judges turn gray deciphering convoluted briefs, while lawyers struggle to make sense of dense judicial opinions.

And we haven't even mentioned the plight of the public. The people of a nation founded on the rule of law are entitled to understand the laws and rules that govern their society. Poor legal writing leads to poor decision making. So the least we can do for a nation that often questions the value of lawyers is to try to speak in a language that adds value—a language that makes legal thought accessible and that regular folks can understand. Open, readable language promotes justice and order.

We lawyers are not alone in our writing woes. The plague of poor writing infects the business world, as well. The recent National Commission on Writing reports that American businesses spend as much as $3.1 billion annually to address writing problems in the workforce.

In the legal profession—where anxiety seems to run in our blood—we are particularly anxious about writing. But when lawyers fret about legal writing to me, they often focus only on the obvious concerns: the typographical errors, the occasional grammatical mistake, or the failure to proofread. But the real factors that drive excellence in legal writing are much more substantive.

What is excellent legal writing? Strong legal writing speaks a modern language—plain English. It respects our readers' time and intelligence by being concise but thorough. It takes complex ideas and makes them clear. It leads from the top. It builds on the mind's innate love of pattern and it tells our readers what to do next. The best legal writing earns both the readers' trust and the right to the readers' time. Above all, strong writing leads to easy reading.

Today, technology and the emergence of the Internet challenge us to find new ways to keep legal writing relevant and meaningful. Information now moves instantaneously. E-mail has become the engine for business communication, and PowerPoint has emerged as the leading medium for presenting information. But while information on the Internet has become faster, flashier and more visual, legal writing often remains stuck on paper—even though that paper may be filed electronically—and mired in its ancient forms.

It is long past time for change. The same technologies that challenge our old ways of writing also provide the opportunity to bring legal writing into the modern age. Technology should make it possible to abolish cumbersome citation formats, to deep link to relevant information, and to redesign legal documents in new mediums that have the functionality of web pages and read like letters, rather than term papers.

But we must do more than simply adapt our traditional forms to take advantage of modern technology. The modern lawyer must also be fluent in modern mediums, such as newsletters, blogs, e-mail and PowerPoint. Fortunately, the techniques that make for powerful writing apply to all our forms of communication, from the lowly e-mail, to a casual blog or newsletter, to a weighty appellate brief.

It's a fast, loud world—a world in which virtually everyone has a voice in the collective conversation that is the Internet. Our fancy law degrees are no longer enough to make people listen to us, so we may no longer hide behind time-worn conventions of legal writing. We lawyers will forfeit our voice in the collective conversation—and much of our influence—if we don't learn to communicate more clearly.

Because English is the language of the Internet and international business, we English speakers are uniquely positioned to flourish in our Information Age if we can make ourselves heard through the noise. But we will be heard only if we speak clearly and with confidence, authority and integrity. Today more than ever, our times challenge us to be lawyerly—to play a thoughtful, useful role in our changing world and to be advocates for our clients and our causes, even when a cause may be as mundane as writing a clean, crisp motion or drafting an easily understood contract.

And if we can learn to communicate clearly, people may begin to understand us. If they understand us, they may begin to trust us more and, perhaps, even listen to and learn from what we say. We will have joined the conversation.

After all, communication, at its best, is about community.

Winning the Battle for Your Readers' Attention 2

I leave out the parts that most people skip.
—Elmore Leonard

Pity Your Poor Readers

No matter how poetic your prose or rational your reasoning, you will never find a reader eager to curl up in front of the fire on a Saturday night with your latest brief or contract. *The New York Times'* website, your old flame's blog, Malcolm Gladwell's latest book and even your brother's Twitter feed all have one huge advantage over legal writing. People read civilian writing because they *want* to. But sane people don't read briefs, contracts or statutes for pleasure. They read briefs, contracts and statutes because they are being paid to read them or because they have a problem and need to read them. Reading legal writing is *work*.

So face facts. You are not writing the great American novel, and no one will ever quote from one of your briefs when they deliver your eulogy at your funeral. All legal writing is technical writing and our readers are all unwilling captives to our writing.

Understand Your Readers' Environment

Not only are your readers reluctant, they also bombarded by information and competing demands on their time. A large law firm sees hundreds of thousands of e-mails each day, as well as a blizzard of paperwork. A judge usually has hundreds of cases on his docket and reads thousands of pages each month. A senior lawyer may be managing dozens of cases and supervising a dozen other attorneys. A junior lawyer may work for several partners who each think they have the exclusive lock on that young lawyer's time. Clients expect round-the-clock availability. The administrative aspects of practice demand care and feeding. Add in hand-held devices, Skype, e-mail and social networking and the racket of today's workplace becomes deafening.

Be Kind to Your Readers

Your job, as a writer, is to earn the right to your readers' time and to speak clearly through the noise of modern life. Because our subject matter is so dry and our readers are so busy, every legal writer has a challenging relationship with readers—even before they begin reading.

Before your readers will listen to you, they need to know that you have listened to them by understanding their challenges and needs. So before we discuss the techniques for powerful writing, let's focus on our readers, because respect for our readers is the basis for all strong writing techniques.

- ♦ **Respect your readers' time.** Be merciful. Don't take up any more of your readers' time than necessary. A judge will probably read only the first paragraph of your brief. Your colleague may have mere moments to marvel at your memorandum. Your job is to answer the question, argue the point, or lay out the deal as concisely, but as completely, as possible.
- ♦ **Respect your readers' intelligence.** Yes, your readers crave brevity. But your readers are also highly trained and intelligent, so they expect thoughtful, deep analysis. While you must be brief, it is more important to be thorough. Your readers will give you their time if you reward their effort with deep knowledge.
- ♦ **Make it as easy as possible for your readers.** Since your readers would rather be doing something else, don't make them work any harder than necessary to understand your paper. Write in the language your readers already know and love—plain English.
- ♦ **Satisfy your readers' curiosity.** Your readers are deeply curious. But they are more curious about you as a writer than they are about your topic. Do you know your subject? Are you masterful or just workmanlike? Are you reasonable and worth working with? Are you easily lost in the details? Use your writing to convey who you are as

a lawyer and to set the tone for your advocacy. Let your style suggest confidence and authority and show that you have mastered your topic.

◆ **Focus your readers.** Given the competition for your readers' time, you must focus your readers' attention for them by leading from the top—the key to effective professional writing and the principle this book focuses on. Leading from the top means that each part of your paper must open with a lead—a few paragraphs, a heading or a sentence—that summarizes the point of each section. (The next chapter, *The Three Essential Principles for Legal Writing*, provides an overview of leading from the top. Chapter 15, *Using Structure to Lead from the Top*, discusses leading from the top in detail.)

◆ **Give your readers choices.** Headings and introductory sentences also allow your readers to choose *not* to read a section or to mark a section for reading later. Give your readers the option to just say *no* or *later*.

◆ **Keep your readers' eyes moving.** Legal reading may never be easy, but it does not need to be an athletic event. Your readers should be able to move seamlessly from the beginning to the end of your paper. Establish a measured pace and maintain that pace throughout the paper. Your logic must flow smoothly. Begin with the most important points and work from general to specific. Transition your reader between thoughts. Avoid repetition within the body of your paper because repetition breaks the forward momentum of reading. Let your reader know when you are taking a brief detour by using signal words or phrases, such as *by contrast*, *similarly*, or *but*. Above all, keep your readers' eyes moving—because if their eyes are moving, so is the flow of your paper. Any style that halts that forward momentum destroys your readers' trust in you as a writer.

In legal writing, empathy for our readers simply means that we respect our readers and understand their needs. This consideration for our readers is the *why* that informs all techniques for powerful legal writing.

The Three Essential Principles for Powerful Writing

3

The beginning is the most important part of the work.
—Plato, *The Republic*

ALL MY SUGGESTIONS for powerful writing boil down to three guiding principles. And these principles apply not only to briefs and memoranda, but to the many mediums in which lawyers work today, including letters, e-mail, blogs, client advisories, newsletters, and even PowerPoint.

Principle One: Use Plain English

Let your readers know that you speak a modern language. Our clients speak plain English and you should too. If you would not use a word or phrase when speaking with a colleague, don't use it in your writing. Say your sentences aloud to edit for plain English and to cure clutter. Your prose must be crisp and clean. Speak human. (Chapter 4, *Plain English and Other Tricks to Help You Sound Human*, discusses plain English.)

Principle Two: Lead from the Top

Leading from the top is the single most effective tool for strong, persuasive writing. News editors know this and push their reporters to write the perfect lead. All my suggestions on how to structure a paper boil down to this one rule: lead from the top.

Why is leading from the top so important? Because leading from the top primes your reader about what to look for in the rest of the paper. If you begin your paper by telling your reader what is important, they will look for that information as they read. When you present that information later, the reader will seize on it and it will click quickly, like a puzzle piece snapping into the space that you have already prepared for it. Leading from the top is like the literary technique of foreshadowing. It prepares the reader for what happens later.

And the principle of leading from the top is like a fractal because it applies on large and small scales. Leading from the top means that your paper as a whole—and each part of your paper, as well—must begin with a "lead" that summarizes the point of that section. We'll discuss the techniques for leading from the top throughout this book, but let's begin with an overview of those techniques. (Again, Chapter 15, *Using Structure to Lead from the Top*, explains the principle of leading from the top in detail.)

- **Lead with a clear descriptive title.** Your title must explain the purpose of your paper in plain English. The title is also the key to finding the paper later. Choose a strong, working title or your paper may never be read. And if your work will be posted on-line, consider the terms someone might use to search for your topic. Include those terms in the title to improve the paper's rankings in search engines.

- **Lead your paper with a strong opening.** You will win or lose your readers in the first one or one-and-a-half pages of your work, often in the first paragraph. Therefore, your opening paragraph or paragraphs are the most important part of your paper and must lead for the whole paper. An opening must explain three things: the background facts, the issue and the conclusion.

- **Lead your paper with your conclusion.** Put your conclusion on your first page, if possible. Better yet, put the conclusion in the first paragraph, write it in neon lights, or tattoo it on your forehead. Readers—particularly lawyers—are not known for their patience. (Chapter 19, *The Conclusion or Brief Answer*, discusses how to write conclusions.)

- **Lead each section with a substantive heading.** Substantive headings break your paper into workable pieces and allow your readers to choose whether to even read a section. Even an eager reader will appreciate headings as a roadmap for your paper. (Chapter 20, *Substantive Headings in the Analysis or Argument*, discusses headings.)

- **Lead each paragraph with a short, introductory sentence.** Within each paragraph, lead from the top by beginning with an original, topic sentence. Although the body of the paragraph may simply refer to case law, statutes, or documents, the first sentence must be your *original* writing and it should summarize the paragraph completely. Your readers should be able to understand your paper by reading only the first sentence of each paragraph. (Chapter 21, *The Analysis or Argument: General Thoughts*, discusses how to structure paragraphs in the body of your paper.)

Principle Three: Tell Your Readers What to Do Next

Most professional writing, including legal writing, is meant to help your readers decide what to do next. Ask yourself, why did your colleague ask you to write the memorandum? What is your reader going to use the information for? What should the client do next? Does your research or analysis suggest specific discovery? What are you asking the court to do? Always finish by telling your readers what to do next.

Plain English and Other Tricks to Help You Sound Human

4

> *"Rabbit," said Pooh to himself. "I like talking to Rabbit. He talks about sensible things. He doesn't use long, difficult words, like Owl. He uses short, easy words, like 'what about lunch?' and 'Help yourself, Pooh.'"*
>
> —A. A. Milne, *Winnie the Pooh*

STRONG WRITING BEGINS with our choice of words and a knack for writing clean, crisp sentences, so let's begin with plain English and other sentence-level issues. (The *Usage and Punctuation Guide* at the end of this book addresses the common grammar, punctuation, and usage issues that arise in legal writing.)

Use Plain English

If you would not use a word or phrase when speaking with a colleague, don't use it in your writing. Write in modern, conversational English. Using plain English establishes your credibility because it tells the reader that you are speaking a language they already know. Plain English is not only clear and transparent, it also shows your humanity and, therefore, promotes trust. It is the springboard for powerful writing.

13

Write for Aunt Agatha

Any slightly above-average bear should be able to understand your paper. Imagine you are writing for your Aunt Agatha, your neighbor, or your friends on the train. These people will keep you real because they are very, very smart, and they will not tolerate fussy, impenetrable sentences.

Say Your Sentences Aloud

Say each sentence aloud to edit for plain English and to cure clutter and grammatical errors. If you are smart enough to make it through law school, the grammatical rules of modern English are embedded in your brain and ear. Saying your sentences aloud is the only tool an educated writer needs for effective sentence-level editing. So read through your paper sentence by sentence and rely on your well trained and unforgiving ear to weed out clutter and confusion.

Choose Familiar, Concrete Words

Use the Editing Workshop, rather than *utilize* it. Would you rather *talk with someone* or *reach a human interface*? *Begin* your argument rather than *commence* it. Focus on the *beginning*, rather than the *inception*. *Explain* your thoughts rather than *elucidate* them. *End* your memorandum rather than *terminate* it. Let your argument *show* rather than *evidence* your convictions. Use a *term* but avoid *terminology*. Follow the *signs* but ignore the *signage*. *Get out of the car* but don't *exit the vehicle*. *Go inside* the *house*, but don't *enter* the *residence*. Remember that courts *hold, explain*, and *state*, but they do not *indicate*. If a proposal is *feasible*, it also *doable*. A statute that *prohibits* conduct also *bans* it. *Additionally* should be pared down to *also*. And would you ever voluntarily read a sentence that begins with *Also of import to the arguments made. . . ?*

Be Brief

Brevity is the golden rule of professional writing because it lends confidence and authority to your presentation. Even if you are not feeling confident about your writing, writing briefly can make you briefly brave. Avoid falling in love with your own words. Edit and cut, cut, cut. Then cut some more. But always balance the wisdom of brevity against the often-more-important need for thoroughness.

Write Memorable Sentences

The most talented writers craft sentences the rest of us can only envy. In a decision overturning Seattle's voluntary student assignment plan, Justice Roberts concluded his majority opinion in a pithy, memorable sentence: "The way to stop discrimination on the basis of race is to stop discriminating on the basis of race." *Parents Involved in Community Schools v. Seattle School Dist. No. 1*, 551 U.S. 701, 748 (2007). Justice Breyer dissented and sparred with Justice Roberts in equally succinct language: "This is a decision that the Court and the Nation will come to regret." 551 U.S. at 868.

Keep Your Sentences Short

Short sentences are simple, clean—and often inspirational:

- "Let there be light."
    —2 Corinthians. 4.6
- "I have a dream."
    —Martin Luther King, August 28, 1963
- "But let us begin."
    —John F. Kennedy, Jan. 20, 1961 (Inauguration speech)

Even if you are not seeding a universe or changing the course of history, you should still keep your sentences short. Justice Roberts, for example, is a master of the art of short sentences:

- "Nor could it."
    —*Parents Involved in Community Schools*, 551 U.S. at 721.
- "The FEC asks for too much."
    —*Federal Election Com'n v. Wisconsin Right to Life, Inc.*, 551 U. S. 449, 463 (2007).
- "These cases are about political speech."
    —*Federal Election Com'n*, 551 U. S. at 481.
- "Not all students waited patiently."
    —*Morse v. Frederick*, 551 U.S. 393, 397 (2007).
- "The message on Frederick's banner is cryptic."
    —*Morse*, 551 U.S. at 401.
- "The problem remains serious today."
    —*Morse*, 551 U.S. at 407

Short, punchy sentences are a particularly powerful technique for beginning paragraphs. But even your sentences within paragraphs should not exceed two or three lines.

But Occasionally Vary the Length of Your Sentences

A long string of short sentences can sound choppy. Strive for rhythm and cadence. Vary your short sentences with an occasional longer sentence. Simply combine two short sentences in the middle of your paragraph to relieve the tedium of too many choppy sentences.

Put Two or Three Paragraphs on a Page

Break up any paragraph that wants to fill a whole page. White space is eye candy for your readers so shoot for at least two paragraph breaks on each page.

Use the Passive Voice Sparingly, but Artfully

Passive voice is effective when you want to disguise the actor (*Mistakes were made* is more persuasive than *Our client made mistakes*), when the actor is hard to describe (such as when describing the legislative history of a statute), when dealing in abstractions (as in *All men are created equal*), when discussing many actors (as in *The legislation was signed*), or when you don't know the actor (as in *The building was vandalized*).

But most passive constructions are simply wordy and impotent. Imagine if the anti-drug campaign *Just Say No* had been written in passive voice, as *No Should Just Be Said*. Contract language requiring that *Notice must be given* is ambiguous. Who should give the notice? *The proceeds shall be used to create a sign to be prominently displayed* is wordy and unclear. Rewrite it as *The owner must use the proceeds to create and display a prominent sign.*

Search for *by* and *of* to weed out passive voice. Set *Grammar Check* on your word-processing software to flag passive-voice constructions.

Use Your Massive Vocabulary

Plain English does not mean simple English. Use your well-earned vocabulary to achieve precision and convey nuance. Write about a *seminal* case, a *pivotal* event, a *bare* declaration, a *cascade* of events, a *vital* resource, a *critical* need, a *haphazard* response, *escalating* hostilities, or a *perfunctory* answer. Explain how the company *parsed* its words or tried to *mollify* its customers through a *pervasive* campaign. A letter may be *lucid*, a speaker *articulate* and a visitor *urbane*. A defendant's action may *frustrate* the parties' agreement and poorly written briefs may *confuse* the issue. An outdated case may be a *relic* from a bygone era. A message may be *cryptic* and a building may be a *fortress*. Unruly students don't *have altercations*. As Justice Roberts explains, they *scuffle*.

An artful choice of words marks a deft, confident writer. Fancy words chosen only to impress—such as legalese—mark the amateur.

Cut the Clutter

Don't use five words if three will do. Glue words, such as *of, by* and *or*, usually mean you can pare your sentence down. For example, *The orders of the shipping department were produced by Widget Company* should be rewritten as *Widget Company produced its shipping department's orders.* (*By* and *of* are glue words that should come out.) *The crux of the argument turns on* should become *The argument turns on. By virtue of his ownership of the land* should be pared down to *Because he owned the land.* Don't *state by way of explanation.* Just *explain. Whether or not* should be unknotted down to plain old *whether.* This *point in time* means *now.* An *ongoing problem* is just a plain old *problem.* A *workable solution* is simply a *solution* and a *fellow colleague* is just a *colleague.*

Lose the Legalese

In particular, avoid legal jargon, such as *in connection with, with respect to, on or about, the present* or *instant case* (use *here* instead), *pursuant to, said* (as in *said contract*), *same* (as in *paragraph 6 of the same*), and *such* used as an adjective (as in *such contract*). If you find yourself stringing many words into one, as in *heretofore, hereinafter, aforementioned, herewith,* or *whereas,* you have lapsed into legalese. (*The Usage and Punctuation Guide* suggests alternatives to legalese.)

Avoid All Jargon

Every profession has its jargon. Your job is to rewrite that jargon in plain English. Clients, colleagues and even judges want it out. Judge Posner recently lamented the use of jargon:

> A note finally, on advocacy in this court. The lawyers' oral arguments were excellent. But their briefs, although well written and professionally competent, were difficult for us judges to understand because of the density of the reinsurance jargon in them. There is nothing wrong

with a specialized vocabulary—for use by specialists. Federal district and court circuit judges, however, with the partial exception of the judges of the court of appeals for the Federal Circuit (which is semi-specialized), are generalists. We hear very few cases involving rein-surance, and cannot possibly achieve expertise in reinsurance prac-tices except by the happenstance of having practiced in that area before becoming a judge, as none of us has. Lawyers should under-stand the judges' limited knowledge of specialized fields and choose their vocabulary accordingly.

Indiana Lumbermens Mut. Ins. Co. v. Reinsurance Results, Inc., 513 F. 3d 652, 658 (7th Cir. 2008) (available in PDF by link at **http://blogs.wsj.com/law/2008/01/17/the-inimitable-judge-posner-strikes-again/**).

Lose the Latin

You are living in the modern world, not ancient Rome. If you would not use a word when speaking with a colleague in the hall, it is probably legalese. Therefore, resist any Latin word or phrase that can be written in modern English. (And if you do use Latin or other legalese in conversation, your problems are far beyond the scope of this book.)

Many commonly used phrases, such as *i.e.* and *e.g.* are Latin—and legalese. *E.g.* stands for *exempli gratia* and means *for example. I.e.* stands for *id est* and means *that is* or *in other words.* So why not just say *for exam-ple* or *that is?* But do use *e.g.*, rather than *for example*, in introductory sig-nals that cite to cases, such as *see, e.g., Smith v. Jones.* (Again, the *Usage and Punctuation Guide* suggests alternatives to common legalese.)

However, foreign phrases that are terms of art, such as res ipsa lo-quitur, habeas corpus or res judicata, are permissible. (These phrases are considered common usage in legal writing, so they do not need to be itali-cized.)

Choose Words for Their Sound

Write as if your paper were going to be read out loud and choose words for their spoken impact. The same techniques that work for poets often work in prose, as well. Your words should have rhythm—a pleasing cadence of stressed and unstressed syllables within sentences and an appealing varia-tion between short and long sentences.

For example, alliteration puts punch in your writing if you keep it subtle and don't overuse it. Consider the famous brief for the school children in *Brown v. Board of Ed. of Topeka*, 347 U.S. 483 (1954) (also cited in Steven Stark's *Writing to Win*). There, Thurgood Marshall and his colleagues used alliteration to summarily distinguish the other side's cases. In *Brown*, the Board of Education's brief cited equal protection cases that raised common nuisance issues, such as noise or overhanging cornices. Marshall and his colleagues masterfully dismissed that precedent with a memorable alliteration by explaining that those cases involved a mere "cautious calculation of conveniences" that had no bearing on the essential rights undermined by segregated education. The phrase "a cautious calculation of conveniences" is a pithy sound-bite—made memorable through alliteration—that effectively distinguishes all the opposing authority Marshall faced.

Choose Descriptive, Picturesque Verbs

Colorful verbs convey images. Babies *wail*. Toddlers *whine*. Children *fidget*. Teenagers *flirt*. Hearts *flutter*. Later in life, traffic *crawls*, markets *seize* or *melt* and the right cars *sip* gas.

Colorful verbs can convey passion, indignation, outrage and a strong sense of right and wrong. In the Declaration of Independence, for example, our founding fathers chose Biblical verbs to convey the depth of their oppression by the King of England: "He has *plundered* our seas, *ravaged* our coasts, *burnt* our towns, and *destroyed* the lives of our people." Declaration of Independence, paragraph 25. With verbs like that, who would doubt the justice of their cause?

How powerful can verbs be? In Exodus 8.7, Moses "*smote* the waters of the river"—and *smote* them so powerfully that "all the rivers that were in the water turned to blood." Without a verb like *smote*, Moses might never have been able to inflict a plague on Egypt. In more recent times, great leaders like Lincoln have *bent* history with their verbs. Consider the Gettysburg address, in which Lincoln lamented that "we cannot *dedicate* . . . we cannot *consecrate* . . . we cannot *hallow* . . . this ground." In his great speech, Lincoln committed a nation to its future with presidential verbs: "we here highly *resolve* that these dead shall not have died in vain; that this nation, under God, shall have a new birth of freedom; and that government of the people, by the people, for the people, shall not *perish* from the earth."

Many of your favorite childhood friends also depended on strong verbs. Remember when the wild things "*roared* their terrible roars and *gnashed* their terrible teeth and *rolled* their terrible eyes" until Max (the king of all wild things) "*tamed* them with the magic trick of *staring* into all their yellow eyes. . . ."? Of course you remember. You remember so well that I don't need to remind you that this passage comes from Maurice Sendak's *Where the Wild Things Are*. Strong verbs *cement* themselves in memory.

And there are descriptive verbs for every phase in your life, including your years practicing law. Legislation may *falter* in the House or *sail* through Congress. Plaintiffs *malinger*. Defendants *plead*. Witnesses *mumble*, *squirm*, and *duck* questions. Other questions *elicit* responses. Courts *admonish*. Companies don't simply *fail to disclose* losses. They *hide* those losses. And those losses then *propel* companies into dangerous financial positions, where they *teeter* on the verge of bankruptcy.

Colorful verbs can bring passion to judicial opinions, as well. Consider Justice Stevens's dissent from the recent Supreme Court decision allowing campaign spending by corporations. There, Stevens lamented that "the majority *blazes* through our precedents. . . ." *Citizens United v. Federal Election Com'n*, 130 S. Ct. 876, 930 (2010) (Stevens dissenting) (also available at **http://www.supremecourt.gov**).

Both life and the law happen in color so never settle for black and white verbs.

Rather Than Use an Adverb, Choose a Strong Verb

My grandmother-in-law—an accomplished poet and a wise woman—once advised me that "Adverbs are not your friend, Dearie." She's right. Adverbs don't belong in your writing because they add little and often backfire. For example, *The defendant actively disputes that claim* simply means that *The defendant disputes that claim*. *The company strongly cautioned* is hesitant and bureaucratic. *The company banned* is stronger and more believable. Avoid adverbs by describing conduct more specifically. For example, replace *The company thoroughly met its obligations to warn* with *The company explained the risk of nerve impairment.*

Adverbs can also be evasive. Avoid hedging words such as *generally*, *usually, customarily,* or *basic*. An assertion that *Client X usually honored gift certificates* will translate as *But Client X didn't honor this gift certificate. The contract is absolutely clear* simply means that *The contract is clear* or—more likely—that *The contract is not clear at all. The defendant arguably met its obligations* means that *The defendant did not meet its obligations this time.*

Search for *ly* as part of your proofreading edit to weed out pesky adverbs, such as *plainly, clearly,* or *patently*.

Avoid Turning Strong Verbs into Fussy Nouns

Avoid nominalizations. Do not *offer an explanation* if you can simply *explain*. Don't *make a statement* when you can simply *state*. Hunt down wordy nominalizations by searching for their common endings: *ment* and *ion*. (*The Usage and Punctuation Guide* collects common nominalizations and suggests plain-English alternatives.)

Avoid Qualifying Adjectives

A *rather strong case* is a *strong case*. A *relatively sane defendant* is a *sane defendant*. A *somewhat unexpected development* is an *unexpected development*. And a *genuinely intelligent writer* is an *intelligent writer.*

Avoid Pompous Words

Stay away from words that sink under the weight of their own importance and aim only to impress. *Pusillanimous* shows that you took an AP Latin course, but it has little meaning to a modern reader. What is a *baroque* argument? Is it like a *pellucid* argument? What does it mean if something is *axiomatic*? Avoid sounding like a thesaurus. Again, speak human.

Avoid Clichés

Clichés are a writer's copout. Using clichés suggests that you can't find your own words. You know the common legal clichés all too well: *within the purview of; slippery slope; cut to the chase; Achilles' heel; Pandora's box; lodestar; fishing expedition; part and parcel; lion's share; pulled out of whole cloth; can't see the forest for the trees; the devil is in the details; of particular concern; all fours; fraught with peril; second bite at the apple; cut to the chase; it is axiomatic that; eminently qualified; incumbent upon; dilatory tactics; begs the question* and so on *ad nauseum.*

Indeed, clichés seem to have infiltrated most professions. Police fear the word *now* and jazz it up to *at this point in time* and their investigations are always *ongoing*. In the business world, all job applicants are *innovative, results-oriented, dynamic team players* with a *proven track record*. Once those *team players* are hired, they are at the mercy of human resources departments that are always magnanimously *reaching out* to someone or, less magnanimously, *downsizing* or *reallocating resources*. The business world is relentlessly *proactive* and so cheerily focused on *optimizing results* and *utilizing resources*. In those hallowed halls of business, someone always wants to *dialogue*, to *circle back*, or to get *face time*. There are *matrixes* to build and *paradigm shifts* to navigate. To be a *valued employee*, you must *row in the same direction, hit the ground running*, and *get your ducks in a row*. And once your *ducks are in a row*, you must *be on your game* so that you can run a *smell test* to discern when someone has *put lipstick on a pig*.

If your husbandry skills are lacking, you can always leave the business world for academia where students must *demonstrate competency* or *proficiency* and avoid *risky behaviors*. But *educators* are ready to help by providing *support services*, by nurturing *life-long learners*, and by encouraging *emerging readers*. And when those *emerging readers* finish emerging, they can learn about books from literary critics, who always seem to find the books that are *translucent, gripping, haunting, riveting, compelling, lyrical* and *evocative*.

Admittedly, some professional clichés serve a real purpose in spoken language. They are picturesque or funny and the shared language may encourage bonding among enslaved tribes. But clichés never belong in written language because written language should be slightly more formal than speech. Let your writing identify you as a member of the human race, rather than as a member of a particular profession.

Write in the 21st Century, Not the 18th

Legal writing is often filled with archaic sayings, such as *per your request, pursuant to our conversation, in accordance with your instructions, please be advised that*, and the ubiquitous *enclosed please find*. Dare to write as if you really do live in the 21st century. Write the way you speak. Use phrases such as *as you asked, as we discussed* and *I have enclosed*. Similarly, unless you are rewriting the Ten Commandments, avoid the archaic *shall*. Use *will* instead. And purge your pleadings of pompous phrases such as *Now comes the plaintiff*.

Keep It Formal

Legal writing, like all written work, should be slightly more formal than spoken language. Avoid slang and colloquialisms.

Avoid Grammatically-Correct-but-Tortured Constructions

Stay away from sentences that are grammatically correct but sound as if they were written by the grammar police. Avoid constructions such as *I do not trust the boy with whom I traveled.* Say *I don't trust that boy* or *I don't trust him.*

Keep Punctuation Simple and Use Modern Forms

Colons and semi-colons often signal complicated constructions and you should use them as little as possible. The dash—also known as the double dash or the em dash (and discussed in more detail next)—is standard modern English, although some of your colleagues may have missed the bulletin allowing the use of em dashes. Never use exclamation points in legal writing because exclamation points look angry and childish. Really!!!

Use Punctuation Artfully to Set Off Clauses Within a Sentence

There are three ways to set off clauses or any material that interrupts a sentence:

- **Commas.** Commas are neutral.
- **Dashes.** The long dash—formally known as the em dash—adds emphasis and isolates material within a sentence.
- **Parentheses.** Parentheses take away emphasis.

Although em dashes are standard modern usage, you don't want to overdo them. Try not to use more than two sets of em dashes on any page. A third set suggests an unhealthy addiction. Bring the text right up to the dash, without putting a space before and after the dash. (To make an em dash, use the shortcut *alt0151* or click *Insert/*click *symbols* on the far right/ select *more symbols, special characters* and *em dash.* Simplify your life by assigning a shortcut key to the em dash and any other symbols that you use frequently.)

Save parentheses for references to outside material, such as exhibits, or for very minor points. In our hierarchy of writing—where we led from the top with our key points—parentheses suggest a lower layer of importance than ordinary text, so they often disrupt the flow of reading within a paragraph. Therefore, don't use parentheses unless you really mean to de-emphasize the material in the parentheses.

(The *Usage and Punctuation Guide* explains how to use these marks in more detail and provides examples.)

Limit Your Commas

A long series of commas within a sentence makes for choppy reading. Try to write short sentences that need no more than two commas. Indeed, one comma is better than two commas, and no commas are best of all. (If you have a clause within a clause, consider replacing the outside commas with a dash. Setting the larger clause off in dashes shows that the internal phrase is subsidiary to the larger phrase.)

Do Not Quote Literary Sources

Save Shakespeare for the stage. Quoting literary sources in a brief or memorandum is arrogant and cliché. It just doesn't fit the medium.

Use Three-Letter Words to Kick-Start Sentences

Certain four-letter words never belong in writing. But why are lawyers so afraid of starting sentences with three-letter words such as *but*, *and*, *yet* or *nor*? Three-letter words are strong sentence starters because they help you control the pace and rhythm of your sentences. Using them will liberate your style.

Supreme Court justices routinely begin sentences with *but*, *and*, *yet* and *nor*. Indeed, they slip into three-letter sentence starters once they are deep into their argument and their writing is at its most earnest. Consider these examples from various justices writing in *Parents Involved in Community Schools*:

- "But I am quite comfortable in the company I keep."
  —551 U.S. at 772 (Justice Thomas, concurring)
- "But the district vigorously defends the constitutionality of its race-based program."
  —551 U.S. at 719 (Justice Roberts, writing for majority)
- "And my view was the rallying cry for the lawyers who litigated *Brown*."
  —551 U.S. at 772 (Justice Kennedy, concurring)

- "And appropriately so."
  —551 U. S. at 752 (Justice Thomas, concurring).
- "Yet our tradition is to go beyond present achievements, however insignificant. . . ."
  —551 U. S. at 787 (Justice Kennedy, concurring).
- "Yet the plurality would deprive them of at least one tool that some districts now consider vital. . . ."
  —551 U.S. at 862 (Justice Breyer, dissenting).
- "Nor could it."
  —551 U.S. at 721 (Justice Roberts, writing for majority).
- "Nor is it likely to find such a case."
  —551 U.S. at 851 (Justice Breyer, dissenting).

Put the Most Important Part of the Sentence at Either End of the Sentence

Consider the sentence: *Until the court makes its ruling, the client's exposure remains uncertain.* Here, the concern is the client's exposure so that phrase should come first: *The client's exposure remains uncertain until the court makes its ruling.* Alternatively, in a longer sentence, put the important phrase last in the sentence to add emphasis.

Work from General to Specific Within a Sentence

When using names or proper nouns, put the explanatory information about the party before the name itself. Consider the sentence *The Company reached an agreement with Local 200, our client's union.* The sentence leaves the reader wondering for a brief second what role Local 200 plays in the case. So put the general phrase, *our client's union*, before the specific identification, *Local 200*, and say *The Company reached an agreement with our client's union, Local 200.*

Put Modifying Words Close to the Word They Modify

Misplaced words and phrases create confusion. Consider the sentence: *A judge who falls asleep often is not suited for the bench.* Does it mean that a judge is not suited for the bench if he or she often falls asleep? Or does it mean that a judge who falls asleep may not always be suited for the bench—leaving open the possibility that our sleepy judge might sometimes be suited for the bench.

Only is also misleading if it is not placed next to the word it modifies. For example, *Only Paul brought his books* means that nobody but Paul brought books. *Paul only brought his books* means that Paul brought his books but didn't do anything else with them—such as read them. And *Paul brought only his books* means that Paul didn't bring anything but his books.

Avoid Sayings Beginning with Phrases Such As *It Is Clear That*

Delete throat-clearing sayings that begin with *it is*, such *as it is clear that, it is likely that, it is mere speculation to suggest that,* or *it is axiomatic that.* Also delete phrases such as *there is a possibility that.*

If deleting the phrase would sacrifice some meaning, rephrase those sayings with an adverb. For example, rewrite *It appears that Mr. Jones never received notice* as *Mr. Jones apparently never received notice.* Only a few *it is* phrases are worth keeping, including the ubiquitous *It is well established that.*

Avoid Beginning Sentences with *It* and *There*

A sentence beginning with *it* or *there* is usually clutter. If *It goes without saying that the sun is shining,* why are you saying it? If *It is clear that it is a cloudy day,* why must you point it out? Some *it is* sentences have become clichés, such as *It is with a heavy heart (or great glee) that I announce. . . .* Similarly, *There are many possibilities* should be pared down to *possibly.*

Do Not Use *This, That* or *These* As a Subject

This, that or *these* should be used only as an adjective and not as a subject. Say *I love these books,* rather than *These are the books I love.* Instead of using *this* or *that* as the subject of your sentence, spell out what *this* or *that* refers to. For example, don't begin a sentence with *This means that. . . .* Instead, say *The defendant's refusal to honor the contract means that. . . .* Using *this* or *that* as a subject requires your readers to look back to the previous sentence to determine what *this* or *that* refers to and defeats the goal of keeping the readers' eyes moving.

But you may use *this* or *that* as an adjective. Indeed, using phrases such as *this theory* or *that contract* to refer to material in the preceding sentence is a helpful transition technique. Thus, *the theory of the corporate veil* in one sentence can become *that theory* in the next sentence.

Avoid *the Former* and *the Latter*

The former and *the latter* also require the reader to look back in the sentence or paragraph to determine what *the former* or *the latter* refers to. Just restate the original words to which *former* and *latter* refer. Restating the concept is more work for the writer but less work for the reader.

Avoid the Verb *to Be*

Choose a strong verb over constructions that use the verb *to be*. For example, *The rule applies* is stronger than *The rule is applicable. It is undisputed* should be rewritten as *The plaintiff does not dispute.*

Avoid the Subjunctive *Would* and *Could*

The subjunctive *would* and *could* are so sloppy and imprecise that courts routinely sustain objections to direct questions of a witness that are phrased in the subjunctive. Whether a person *would* take action is irrelevant. Whether the person actually took action matters. Lose the subjunctive *would* and *could* except where you are dealing with a genuine hypothetical, as in *If the District Court requires evidence of intent, the government would be required to. . . .*

Keep the Articles *the* and *a*

You'll sound like robot if you drop article. (Indeed, the failure to use articles may suggest that English is not your first language. Many other languages, such as Chinese, do not use articles.)

Avoid Ambiguous Uses of *It*

Spell out what *it* refers to if the meaning of *it* would otherwise be ambiguous. For example, a sentence that states *Despite its origins in the 9th Circuit, the Supreme Court held that . . . .* suggests that the Supreme Court itself originated in the 9th Circuit. Instead, be clear and spell out what *it* refers to by saying *Despite this case's origins in the 9th Circuit, the Supreme Court held that. . . .*

Avoid Putting Dependent Clauses in the Middle of a Sentence

Move dependent clauses to the beginning or end of the sentence to make your writing sound less choppy. For example, do not say *The Court, when it granted sanctions, did not understand the facts.* Instead, say *When the court granted sanctions, it did not understand the facts.*

Avoid Multiple Negative Concepts

We all know to avoid double negatives, such as *He is not bringing no bananas.* But we should be equally wary of the double or triple conceptual negative, in which one negative concept cancels out another negative concept, which cancels out the original negative concept. For example, what is *a decision vacating an injunction prohibiting the state from requiring a sex offender to register?* Think positively and simply say *The decision allows the state to require a sex offender to register.* (If you must explain the procedure more precisely, do so in a follow up sentence: *Specifically, the court vacated an injunction. . . .*) What does it mean if *A court reversed a decision enjoining the enforcement of a regulation that prohibited the use of alcohol?* Simply say that *The Appellate court allowed the town to prohibit the use of alcohol* and follow up with a sentence detailing the procedural history, if necessary. Similarly, *The speech would not be an unprotected expression under the First Amendment* means that *The speech would be a protected expression. The court voted not to allow* means that *The court voted to prohibit. It is unlikely to be inaccurate* means *It is likely accurate.*

Avoid Complicated Acronyms

How is a mere mortal to remember that *UCCIWOM* means *Uniform Commercial Code claims for implied warranty of merchantability?* Simply refer to the concept as *the Warranty.*

Do Not Refer to Your Client As *We*

Your client is buying your objectivity and reputation as an independent advocate. Keep your distance. You may need it later.

Use the Terms *Plaintiff* and *Defendant* Once and Once Only

Identify the parties as *plaintiff* or *defendant* once and then use the parties' names after that initial reference. Similarly, the terms *appellant* and *appellee* are so confusing that many jurisdictions' local rules prohibit their use after the initial identification of the parties.

Use Surnames

Using surnames is polite. Say *John Goodfellow* the first time and use *Mr. Goodfellow* for later references. Never write an identifier explaining the common use of the terms *Mr., Mrs.,* or *Ms.,* as in *John Goodfellow ("Mr. Goodfellow")*. *Mr., Mrs.* and *Ms.* are common usage so putting those terms in identifiers suggests that you don't get out much.

Avoid the Gender Minefield by Using Plurals

Rewrite *A student may leave his or her books on the tables* as *Students may leave their books on the tables.* Plurals will also enable you to avoid awkward but politically correct constructions, such as *his/her. His/her* fails the test for plain English because it is not even pronounceable. If you cannot rewrite the sentence with plurals, use *his or her.*

Remember That a Corporation Is an *It*, Not a *They*

If you must personalize a corporation, do so with a glowing description of its activities rather than by an incorrect use of pronouns.

Use Italics to Clarify

In a long and complicated sentence, *italicize* the operative words. Italics tell your reader where to focus and cut reading time significantly. For example, if you explain that "The court should not grant an injunction here because the plaintiff has not suffered *irreparable* harm," your reader will know that you are turning your focus to the nature of the harm. But don't overuse italics. If every other word is emphasized, your italics will have no impact because they are ubiquitous.

Use Modern Constructions

Ignore archaic usage rules enforced by self-appointed and often ill-informed grammar police.

- **You may put *however* at the beginning of a sentence.** Many lawyers refuse to put *however* at the beginning of a sentence because they learned long ago that some "rule" required that *however* be placed in the middle of a sentence. The "rule" requiring that *however* be placed in the middle of a sentence originated in Strunk and White's *The Elements of Style* and is now considered outdated. (Trust me on this.) The word *however*—like its modern alternative, *but*—can certainly go at the beginning of a sentence. Indeed, placing *however* in the middle of a sentence often leads to clunky constructions, in which the word *however* commits the unpardonable sin of separating a subject from its verb, as in *The court, however, denied the motion.*

    However (note my courageous placement!), even though modern usage allows you to put *however* at the beginning of a sentence, many lawyers still swear by the old rule on the grounds that putting *however* in the middle of the sentence is "softer." But who wants a soft lawyer? So if you are writing for a curmudgeon, indulge that lawyer's neuroses and move *however* to the middle of your sentences. Otherwise, feel free to begin your sentences with *however.*

- **You may also begin your sentences with *but*.** *But* is the modern alternative to *however*. Again, Supreme Court justices routinely begin sentences with *but*. Indeed, our founding fathers used a beginning *but* in the Constitution: "*But* neither the United States nor any State shall assume or pay any debt or obligation incurred in aid of insurrection. . . ." Amendment XIV, § 4.

- **And you may begin a sentence with *and*.** Using *and* at the beginning of a sentence is modern usage, although it may sometimes seem too artsy for formal writing. But then again, Supreme Court justices use *and* to kick-start sentences, so why shouldn't we? Beginning sentences with *and* allows you to pace your sentences to follow the rhythms of spoken language.

- **You may begin a sentence with *because*.** Why? Because beginning a sentence with *because* adds emphasis and is standard modern usage.

◆ **You may split your infinitives.** The admonition against splitting infinitives arose because English is derived from Latin, in which the infinitive is a single word, such as *amore* for *to love*. Because Latin infinitives were one word, they could not be split. But the admonition against splitting infinitives has less force in English because the infinitive form is two words practically begging to be split. So, if you cannot find a reasonable alternative to a split infinitive, feel free *to boldly go* where grammar police fear *to even tread*.

Keep a Modern Usage Guide on Your Desk

I live by *The New York Times Manual of Style and Usage* and I have suggested several other resources in the bibliography. Whatever guide you choose, keep that guide on your desk. It will keep you clean.

The Question of Voice and Tone

. . . they roared their terrible roars and gnashed their terrible teeth and rolled their terrible eyes and showed their terrible claws.
—Maurice Sendak, *Where the Wild Things Are*

Find Your Own Voice

Although lawyers may not always be free to vary the form of legal writing, you will be a powerful writer if you have the confidence to speak in your own voice. Be interesting and honest. Choose words with meaning. Avoid sermonizing. Emphasize themes. Search for the artful turn of phrase. Be succinct where others are windy. Focus on fact when others are bogged down in theory. Establish a clean, trustworthy tone and pitch. Use your early years as a writer to establish your own style of lawyering and to build your own story about who you are as an advocate and a professional.

Put Your Name on It

Even as a young lawyer, insist on authorship. Ask that your name stay on work you author. Do not let yourself be reduced to ghostwriting. No name means no credit and you cannot have a voice if you do not have a name.

But recognize that limiting recognition to only a few authors is frequently justified. If a client is already concerned about mounting fees, it may not be wise to list the names of every junior attorney who worked on a memorandum. And listing 20 contributing lawyers on a major brief is never a wise idea.

Choose a Tempered, Balanced Tone

Spare the vitriol and accusations. Wisdom and reason speak for themselves and need not hide behind fighting words. Let your pitch and tone suggest your integrity and show the court that you are reasonable and worth dealing with. A shrill writer simply can't be trusted.

But Keep Your Passion

Keeping a balanced tone should not mean that you sacrifice passion and zeal. For example, in his dissent from the Supreme Court's recent decision allowing corporate spending in campaigns, Justice Stevens finished his dissent with a biting comment that nailed his thoughts in history. Showing that his ninety years have not diminished his convictions, Justice Stevens concluded: "While American democracy is imperfect, few outside the majority of this Court would have thought its flaws included a dearth of corporate money in politics." *Citizens United*, 130 S. Ct. at 979 (Justice Stevens, dissenting) (also available at **http://www.supremecourt.gov**). Words are an advocate's sharpest tool so let your convictions inspire your language.

Be Honest

Your tone is also the first signal for conveying your honesty and candor. Tell the truth whenever you can. If you must slant the truth, slant it truthfully.

Avoid Sarcasm and Ridicule

Sarcasm and ridicule detract from your advocacy and make you look desperate. Only little lawyers are sarcastic.

Avoid Both Euphemisms and Hyperbole

Be neither dainty nor deranged. Your readers will distrust both. If you treat words like smoke and mirrors that can disguise the truth, you will lose credibility. Avoid terms like *downsizing* or *resource allocation*. Exaggeration is equally dangerous. Do not argue that *Client X has gone out of his way to fulfill the contract* if Client X did nothing of the sort.

Avoid Excessive Detail

We lawyers sometimes go to ridiculous lengths to avoid stating the obvious. Consider the following passage from an ordinance in Manatee County, Florida that outlawed nude dancing and required pasties and G-strings to protect the modesty of its dancers and the sensibilities of its citizens. Lest its dancers question the law's sartorial requirements, the statute described the minimally required coverage with maximum precision:

> The area at the rear of the human body (sometimes referred to as the glutaeus maximus) which lies between two imaginary lines running parallel to the ground when a person is standing, the first or top of such line being one-half inch below the top of the vertical cleavage of the nates (i.e., the prominence formed by the muscles running from the back of the hip to the back of the leg) and the second or bottom line being one-half inch above the lowest point of the curvature of the fleshy protuberance (sometimes referred to as the gluteal fold), and between two imaginary lines, one on each side of the body (the 'outside lines'), which out-side lines are perpendicular to the ground and to the horizontal lines described above and which perpendicular outside lines pass through the outermost points at which each nate meets the outside of each leg.
>
> Notwithstanding the above, buttocks shall not include the leg, the hamstring muscle below the gluteal fold, the tensor fasciae latae muscle of any of the above-described portion of the human body that is between either the left inside perpendicular line and the left outside perpendicular line or the right inside perpendicular line and the right outside perpendicular line. For the purpose of the previous sentence the left inside perpendicular line shall be an imaginary line on the left side of the anus that is perpendicular to the ground and to the horizontal lines described above and that is one-third the distance from

the anus to the left outside line, and the right inside perpendicular line shall be an imaginary line on the right side of the anus that is perpendicular to the ground and to the horizontal lines described above and that is one-third of the distance from the anus to the right outside line. (The above description can generally be described as covering one-third of the buttocks centered over the cleavage for the length of the cleavage.)

Manatee County, Florida, Code § 2-21-133(b). In Manatee County, and the several other counties that have drafted identical ordinances, less does indeed seem to be more or, at least, to require more words. And the good citizens of those careful counties now need both an anatomy textbook and a tape measure to interpret the law.

Avoid Mudslinging

Legal argument should be a battle of ideas, not a clash of characters. Consider this introduction to a brief in a case involving a spoon-bending psychic:

> After reviewing Plaintiff's opposition to the Defendant's Motion to Dismiss it becomes *painfully clear* that the Plaintiff and his lawyers will *stop at nothing* to keep this frivolous lawsuit alive. As the Court will see, they *twist* the law, the facts and the rules of procedure *to the breaking point*. If they can't respond to an argument, they *ignore* it. When faced with the actual (and truthful) language of the March 23, 2007 e-mail (which they continue to hide from the Court) *they turn a blind eye* to it and claim instead (both here and for their multiple press releases) that it is somehow an illegal misrepresentation. Plaintiff also uses the Defendants interchangeably *in a clumsy attempt* to establish personal jurisdiction that simply does not exist.

Reply Brief to Plaintiff's Opposition to Motion to Dismiss at 1, *Sapient v. Geller*, No. 3.07-cv-02478 VRW (N. Dist. Cal. December 6, 2007) (emphasis added) (available at **http://docs.justia.com/cases/federal/district-courts/ california/candce/3:2007cv02478/191883/33/**). This passage tells us one thing: the lawyers will not be having lunch together anytime soon. The legal arguments, whatever their merit, are lost.

Avoid Disparaging Comments About Your Opponents or Their Work

Phrases such as *The defendant leaps to the conclusion that* or *Defendant baldly asserts that* suggest an inappropriate warrior mentality. Stay away from words that antagonize, such *as plaintiff's unproven claim* or *defendant's distorted interpretation.*

If opposing counsel has misread the law, give them a gracious way out. Don't accuse opposing counsel of *incorrectly citing Smith v. Jones for the proposition that.* . . . Instead, simply explain that *Smith v. Jones involved quite different facts.* The court will still get your point.

Be Confident

Phrases such as *we submit, we believe* or *we contend* suggest that you don't really believe your own argument and they don't belong in your argument. Phrases such as *I could find no cases* and *based on my understanding of the facts* also make you sound unsure. Why couldn't you find any relevant cases? Did you not have enough time? Did the Westlaw or LexisNexis self-destruct while you were researching? Where did you look? If you didn't find it, it's probably not out there. Since you are responsible for only the reported case law, simply say *No reported cases hold that.* . . .

Do Not Hedge Your Research with *Appears to* or *Apparently*

New lawyers often qualify their research by saying *The case law appears to hold that.* . . . Never use *appears to* or *apparently* if you have access to all the information you need to make your decision. Because you have access to all reported cases, *apparently* is rarely appropriate to hedge your conclusion about the case law. Reach a conclusion and stand behind it, even if you can only identify the trends in the case law or the weight of authority.

Avoid the First Person

First person phrases, such as *we submit, we believe* and *we contend,* also shift the focus towards the lawyer and away from your ideas. Constructions such as *I will now turn my attention to* or *I will now briefly address* also insert the lawyer into the discussion. Banish that bothersome lawyer now.

Avoid Sharing Your Stream of Conscience

Your readers do not need to know how you arrived at your conclusion. They simply need to know what your conclusion is, so avoid sharing your thought process. Phrases such *as I will now turn my attention to, we will next review,* or *this memorandum will then address* bog your readers down in your thought process and obscure your actual conclusion.

Avoid the Mysterious *One*

Similarly, steer clear of the third person *one*, as in *one could argue.* Too many *ones* arguing lead to ball bouncing—a distracting batting back and forth of ideas. Chances are that enough parties are already involved in your case so you don't need to add an invisible player. Also avoid *on the one hand* because it leaves the reader waiting for you to talk about *the other hand*—which is like leaving your reader to wait for an invisible shoe to drop.

Avoid Characterizing Your Own Work

Avoid phrases such as *after an exhaustive review of the case law* or *this memorandum provides an in-depth discussion of.* Let the quality of your work, rather than your own characterization, leave your reader convinced that your work is exhaustive or clear. Even some common introductory phrases, such as *stated more plainly,* are self-aggrandizing. What if your reader finds your restatement more confusing than the first telling? Similarly, seemingly apologetic phrases, such as *out of an abundance of caution,* may also backfire if your reader ultimately decides your work is sloppy or careless.

The Transition from Academic to Professional Writing

6

The only thing worse than being blind is having sight but no vision.

—Helen Keller

Embrace the Brave New World

As you make the transition from law school to the professional world, the impartiality you were taught in law school may hobble your ability to be a bold, creative lawyer. Even early in your career, effective advocacy requires that you go beyond a slavish repetition of precedent and that you take a position and think originally. Your colleagues and clients are paying you to tell them what you think. Give them their money's worth.

Dare to Reach a Conclusion

In particular, new lawyers are often so trained to analyze both sides of a question that they may be reluctant to reach a firm conclusion on an issue. A conclusion that simply says *maybe* is timid and not worth the cost of your research. Qualify your conclusion if you must. But you must reach a firm conclusion.

Avoid Hedging Language in Your Conclusions

Hedging language betrays your fear of reaching a conclusion and a troubling lack of confidence in your own skills. Again, avoid language such as *I could find no cases on point, it is difficult to determine whether, it is far from certain whether,* or *it is possible that.*

Write Originally

Again, clients, colleagues and judges want to know *your* original ideas about a topic. Although we must base arguments on precedent, a memorandum or brief should not be a simple précis of the cases but must include *your* thoughts about those cases.

For example, careful organization of the research by fact pattern shows that you have thought deeply about the cases, rather than simply organized them chronologically or by jurisdiction. Headings should represent *your* conclusion or argument about the law in that section. Most important, the opening sentence of each paragraph should be *your* original summary of that paragraph. In professional writing, unlike in law review articles, you do not need a citation for every sentence, so your opening sentence should represent your own thoughts and should not require a citation.

Fixate on Facts

Your job is not to show your broad knowledge of a topic—the issue spotting that professors look for on law exams—but to tailor your argument to fit your client's unique set of facts. A zealous advocate argues for a particular *client*, not for general principles of law. Therefore, build your argument around your client's facts, rather than vague legal rules. Arguing every issue that you stumble across in your research defeats your goals because it effectively increases your burden of proof. Review the facts of the precedent carefully to discern which cases help your client the most. Analyze your client's facts even more carefully so that you can distinguish your client's case from harmful precedent. Finally, argue the *facts* of the precedent, rather than general rules of law.

Write for Your Boss

The biggest difference between writing in law school and writing in the professional world is that you are now being *paid* to write. Think of who is paying you. Your first job as a writer is to meet your employer's expectations and give the supervising attorney what he or she expects. If your boss expects a certain style or form, you must write in that style or use that form—even if doing so violates everything you have ever learned about good writing and much of what I am suggesting here. Take heart. Someday you will be a boss and you can then inflict your neuroses on others.

Understanding the Big Picture 7

He can compress the most words into the smallest idea of any man I know.

> —Abraham Lincoln, commenting in the
> margin of a fellow attorney's writing

Know Your Client

What is the client's business? What is the client's purpose in this litigation? Will taking a certain position in a case or a transaction have long-term implications for the client? Is this a key piece of litigation where the client wants to take a public stance on an issue or does the client want to dispose of the matter as cost effectively as possible? The answers to these questions set the tone for your advocacy and negotiations.

Know Your Reader

You must also know your reader. What are the reader's implicit concerns? Answer those concerns even if it means going beyond the express purpose of the letter or memorandum. If a judge or colleague will be concerned about one case that actually has nothing to do with your research topic, you must still discuss that case in your memorandum or brief. Explain why the case has nothing to do with your topic.

Consider the Client's Relationship to Other Parties in the Case

For example, while the interests of co-defendants may be similar early in a case, at some point those interests usually diverge. A defendant may not want to join his or her co-defendants in a motion to transfer to a jurisdiction where the law is more favorable if that defendant has a personal-jurisdiction defense available in the jurisdiction where the action was originally filed. What are the consequences of one party settling out? How much information do you want to share with a co-defendant who might settle out of the case early? Remember that the joint-defense privilege is not recognized in all jurisdictions.

Understand the Procedural Context in Which an Issue Arises

What turns on the answer? Are you in discovery and just aiming to identify information? Or are you positioning for settlement, which might require a more aggressive presentation of your client's position? Are proposed motions dispositive or are you posturing for trial? Are you planning depositions later? If so, should you avoid serving dispositive motions until after depositions to avoid outlining your case for the opposition? Are there issues you want to save for trial? For example, do you simply want to lock the defendant into position at a deposition or through answers to interrogatories without revealing your hand? Are you aiming to trap the defendant in a lie so that you can use their answer to impeach them at trial? Again, the answers to these questions will set the tone for your advocacy and help you identify the most analogous precedent.

Understand the Rules of Procedure, Particularly in Summary Judgment Motions

The Rules of Civil Procedure are like the rules of chess. You can't play the game unless you know them. Many dispositive motions—particularly summary judgment motions—turn entirely on the standards established in the Rules. For example, under Rule 56, summary judgment is only appropriate if there is no genuine, material issue of fact. Therefore, if you are defending against a motion for summary judgment, you need only create a genuine, material issue of fact or credibility to win the motion. Alternatively, if you are moving for summary judgment, avoid long complicated statements of the facts. A ten-page factual statement may leave the court convinced that there is an issue of fact hiding somewhere and give the court an easy way to deny your motion.

Understand the Importance of Your Paper

A routine procedural memorandum merits less time and paper than a substantive dispositive memorandum. Indeed, the brevity of your presentation may go a long way towards convincing the court that every other court that has decided this issue has granted a similar motion.

Know the Goal of Your Particular Assignment

If your goal is to have the client dismissed from the case, you may not want to spend 50 hours researching a motion to dismiss for lack of personal jurisdiction if you discover that the statute of limitations has not expired and that the plaintiff may simply file again in another jurisdiction. Keep the supervising attorney informed of any unexpected discoveries in your research.

Research: Finding and Understanding the Cases

8

So the writer who breeds more words than he needs is making a chore for the reader who reads.

—Dr. Seuss

Begin by Reviewing Briefs or Memorada on Similar Issues

Don't reinvent the wheel. Begin every research assignment by finding out what learning already exists on the topic. Search your firm's document management system. Ask your colleagues for memoranda or briefs involving similar issues. Start and nurture your own research file.

Use Briefs Filed in Other Cases As Research Tools

If a recently reported case involved a similar issue, review the actual briefs filed in that case. Even if the court did not address the issue in its reported opinion, the parties likely briefed the issue and you may find that the brief is a good starting point for your research.

Briefs are easily available now. WestlawNext and LexisNexis include briefs in their databases, although those databases may not automatically capture all filed briefs. (But be very careful about searching databases that are not included in your subscription or you may incur an unexpected charge.) The availability of briefs filed in state courts varies widely by state. Various free portals, such as Findlaw.com, also include briefs, although their databases may be limited.

But—as we will discuss in more detail in Chapter 13, *Honesty and Authorship*—you should use these briefs simply as starting points or skeletons for your own papers. Several courts have recently held that flagrant copying may violate ethical rules. Your work must be your own.

Work Case to Case

Although newer search tools make finding the cases remarkably easy, you must still *read* the cases. Work case to case: read the relevant cases and identify the cases they rely on—and then read those cases. Follow seminal cases and their progeny to identify trends. Check the subsequent history and read those later cases. Your research is complete once your research circle returns to its start and the cases are referring only to cases you have already seen.

Know the Results of the Cases and Understand How Your Client Fits into the Fact Pattern

A case may contain great law, but if the party in the most analogous position to your client lost, you may not want to cite it as your leading authority.

Read the Whole Case

A seemingly helpful case may harbor contradictory authority or pronouncements that cut against you. Beware these land mines. They are likely to explode at the most unfortunate times—such as oral argument.

Remember That Federal Courts Do Not Make Common Law

State courts make common law, not federal courts. Federal court pronouncements on common law issues are not binding, although they may be persuasive.

Consider Choice-of-Law Issues

The law of the forum is not necessarily controlling. Remember that the forum will apply its own choice-of-law doctrine to determine whether another state's law applies. In cases involving contacts with more than one jurisdiction, determine which jurisdiction has the most favorable law and whether the parties have sufficient contacts with that jurisdiction to justify application of its law. (Always begin with your firm's Intranet to research choice-of-law issues. The issue is briefed regularly.)

Understand the Procedural History of the Cases, Particularly the Standard of Review

Was a case at the summary judgment stage, where the court looked only at undisputed facts to decide whether the party was entitled to judgment as matter of law? Or was the case an appeal in which the reviewing court deferred to the trial court and could reverse only for abuse of discretion? Did the court make its ruling after hearing evidence or did it grant a motion to dismiss on the pleadings? Decisions often turn entirely on the standard of review, so you must understand the procedural context of the cases you are citing. If you know that the court dismissed a claim, then you know not only the substantive arguments your client should make but also the first procedural move to recommend to the partner, to the client, or to the court.

Know Your Opponent's Authority

Read the cases your opponent cites. Distinguish those cases. Did a case arise in a different procedural context? What was the result? Did the party in the most analogous position win or lose? In particular, read the cases in your opponent's footnotes—the official burial ground for awful authority. Chances are you'll like those cases a lot.

Double-Check Internet Sources

Although the Internet has made research exponentially faster, the Internet is also the single best source for getting it wrong. If an Internet source is unknown, be cautious. Always check the date. An original posting of scientific or technical information can quickly become obsolete. Prefer sites that have gone through some review, such as sites that bear the endorsement of a reputable publisher or are maintained by educational or governmental institutions. (Look for the *.edu* or the *.gov.*)

Check the Subsequent History

Citing an overruled case will not help your client or your career. Many of us attribute our most embarrassing professional moments to this minor oversight. Always check the "negative history" on your cases.

Organizing Your Research for Efficient Writing

9

Writing is like driving at night in the fog. You can only see as far as your headlights but you can make the whole trip that way.

—E. L. Doctorow

Use Your Research Files As Your Outline

If you organize your research files carefully, those files can serve as the outline for your paper and spare you the need to create the dreaded traditional outline. Create files for your cases, either on your computer or in hard copy, and use these files as a substitute for a linear outline. The filing method suggested in this chapter generates an outline as you research and assures that all your cases are easy to find when you are ready to begin writing.

Create Subfiles for Each Major Topic in Your Paper

Before you begin researching, create files for obvious issues about your topic. For example, an assignment about misrepresentation should have at least five files: *intent, representation, reliance, harm* and *damages*. (Newer research tools, such as WestlawNext, allow you to file cases in files and subfolders as you research.) Create new files as new issues emerge. For complex topics, your files should correspond to each Roman-numeral or primary heading and to your subheadings, as well.

Consider Making Your Files Fact Specific

Even better, organize your cases based on fact pattern or by result. For example, if you are researching piercing the corporate veil, create files for *under-capitalization, misrepresentation of ownership, commingling of assets* and *palming off*. Create a file for opposing authority. You should also have files for your opponent's cases or other authority you need to distinguish.

Don't Be Afraid to Print Your Cases

The green quest for a paperless office had led many new lawyers to avoid printing their cases for fear of committing an environmental crime. But printing at least a few pages of your cases can make your writing more efficient, particularly if you have a small screen. Working from a printed copy of your case is like having a second window open on your screen. If you print your case, you can have the case in front of you while you are writing on the screen. Working from a printed copy is often easier than working in small side-by-side windows or clicking between the separate windows for your paper and your case.

Printing the case also makes it easy to make notes directly on the case. Yes, newer search engines, such as WestlawNext, allow you to highlight and notate cases directly on the screen so that you can save your notes electronically. But I often find my notes are more workable if I scrawl them in dark marker on a printed page.

But if you do print, print selectively. Print the first page, so that you have a quick summary of the case, and selective pages that contain key language or important background information. Print now. Recycle later.

Mark Up Your Cases

Do *not* take extensive notes. You will save time and be less likely to lose information if you write directly from marked-up cases. So make notes either on your electronic copy or on your printed pages. (If you are working from older software, you can trick the program to let you make notes on the electronic copy by inserting a text box where you want to make a comment and typing your comment in the text box.) Highlight key language. Label the facts with an *F* or *Facts* in the margin so that the facts are easy to find. Label the holding with an *H* and the reasoning with an *R*. Label other relevant language that you might want to cite as *see*, *contra* or *but see*.

Sound Bite Your Cases

Most important, jot down a sound bite that summarizes the facts or result at the top of each case. For example, jot down *zero capitalization* and *allowing pierce*. Even complicated cases can usually be summarized in a few well-chosen words. For example, a First Amendment case allowing some restrictions on religious practice can be summarized as *routine restriction* on free exercise.

Write Sentences As You Research

As you read a case, you may want to jot down the actual sentences that you will include in your paper. Circle or highlight key language and reference it with an arrow in your margin notes. Then jot down your sentence describing that thought. Think of these sentences as the "pods" or the middle of the paragraphs in your paper.

File Each Case As You Research

As you research, file each marked-up case in the appropriate file so that you are building your outline as you research.

Arrange the Files in the Order in Which You Will Address Each Topic

Arrange your files—in other words, your topics—in their order of importance or relevance. Your file names will eventually become the headings to your argument.

Order Cases Within Files and Subfiles

Arrange the cases within files in the order in which you will address them. For example, put the most analogous or the most recent case first. Continue with less important cases, cases from other jurisdictions and so on.

Write Directly from These Files

Because these files are now your outline. It's magic!

Consider Providing an Appendix Summarizing Key Cases

In complicated internal research memoranda, you may want to include an appendix listing relevant cases with a brief factual parenthetical for each case. Consider grouping the cases by topic, such as *intent* or *representation*, or result, such as *cases granting TRO* or *cases denying TRO*. Think of an appendix as a crib sheet for oral argument, and fit it on one page and only one page. But never let your appendix substitute for a plain-English discussion of your research. A research memorandum must do far more than simply list the cases.

If you create an appendix, keep it on a separate sheet and clearly title it as an appendix. You never want a later reader to think that you considered your one-page summary of cases to be a substitute for a full-blown research memoranda.

Beyond Research: Seeing the Big Picture in the Cases

10

Piglet: "Pooh?"
Pooh: "Yes, Piglet."
Piglet: "I've been thinking."
Pooh: "That's a very good habit to get into, Piglet."
                        —A. A. Milne, *Winnie the Pooh*

Divide Your Cases into Two Categories: *For You* and *Against You*

Real understanding of the case law requires that you think outside narrow legal categories, such as *intent, misrepresentation* or *reliance*, and that you look at your cases comprehensively. Your key cases will generally fall into two categories: those in which the court ruled *for* the analogous party and those in which the court ruled *against*. Therefore, before you begin writing, arrange your cases into two groups: *cases which help* and *cases which hurt* or *yes* and *no*. Within your *yes* and *no* files, arrange your cases in order of importance. Think about your *yes* cases and later, your *no* cases, as a group. What case have you put first? Why? Is it the most analogous case? The leading case? The most recent case?

Review Your *Yes* and *No* Cases to Identify Factual Trends

Now look for the factual distinctions between your *yes* and your *no* cases. For example, how egregious must palming off be before it justifies piercing the corporate veil? Is a court more likely to find reliance where a buyer was unsophisticated? If so, just how unsophisticated must the buyer be?

By considering your *yes* and your *no* cases as a group, you will see factual patterns that are not apparent from reading any single case but go to the core of the court's reasoning. If you know these factual patterns, you can comment authoritatively on the reasons behind the law, rather than simply parroting back citations with vague statements of law.

For example, Thurgood Marshall and his colleagues relied on factual distinctions to make history in *Brown v. Board of Education of Topeka*, 347 U.S. 483 (1954). There, Marshall and his colleagues had little precedent going their way. If they had organized their research into *yes* and *no* cases, their *no* pile would have been huge and their *yes* pile would have been empty. Since they had little law on their side, they did what brilliant advocates do. They argued the facts.

In their oft-cited brief (also cited in Steven Stark's, *Writing to Win*), Marshall and his colleagues effectively dismissed the Board's many equal protection cases by categorizing them as simple "nuisance cases, sewage cases and cases of overhanging cornices"—a "cautious calculation of conveniences" that could not compare to the rights of children "to be treated as entire citizens of the society into which they have been born."

Never prepare for oral argument without performing this *yes* and *no* review of the facts.

Group Your Cases by Fact Pattern

Obviously, you must identify factual analogies between your case and the precedent. However, you must also identify factual trends in the precedent. For example, if you are asking the court to pierce the corporate veil, review all cases in which the court did pierce the veil to identify any facts that will support a pierce. Then give the court concrete reasons to accept your argument by focusing on facts. For example, say *A court may pierce the corporate veil whenever a company's capitalization falls below a certain ratio.* Avoid generic statements of law, such as *A court will pierce the corporate veil to prevent fraud.*

Brainstorming 11

And will you succeed? Yes indeed, yes indeed!
Ninety-eight and three-quarters percent guaranteed.
                                                    —Dr. Seuss

Think with Your Hands

Once you have finished researching, wean yourself from your computer monitor and brainstorm your issue, by hand, on old-fashioned unlined paper (or on its modern equivalent, the iPad). Working with your hands, rather than on your computer, will force you to think on the right side of your brain. You'll step outside a linear mode of thinking and see new connections between ideas.

Get Your Project on One Page

Your job is to get your project on one page—your "work page." If you can't get your thoughts down to one page, you have not yet identified your major themes and arguments and you don't understand your project.

Think of your work page as a loose master plan for your paper or the top layer of your writing. It should be an overview of your big ideas and a catalyst for the writing process, rather than a linear outline of your paper.

Mind Map

In his 1991 book, *Use Both Sides of Your Brain*, Tony Buzan suggests a highly creative note-making technique called "mind mapping." To create a mind map, jot your central topic in a circle in the center of the page. Jot down other ideas on lines that branch off that central topic. Use words or phrases, not sentences. Print, rather than write in cursive. Use color, pictures, symbols, arrows, squiggles and highlighting. Be messy. A mind map is a tool to help you discover your own ideas. You can organize those ideas later.

Don't Outline Yet

By the end of the writing process, your linear outline should fall into place—but it's not yet time for a linear outline. Outlining at this stage would stifle your thinking. Why? Because outlining requires you to force a structure on your thoughts before you have even unearthed those thoughts. You can't force ideas into a rigid structure if you don't yet know what those ideas are.

Let Your Work Page or Mind Map Evolve As You Write

You do not need to create the definitive work page for your paper *before* you begin to write. Your work page should evolve *as* you write. Creative people are open to change during the creative process. So listen to your own new ideas and be ready to change your approach as you write.

Tear up old work pages and create new ones as you refine your thoughts. Redoing your work page is an important part of learning and understanding because it requires you to review your thoughts. The goal is to have your paper on one page by the time you *finish* writing your paper. Redoing a work page also helps cement your topic in memory because it forces you to review your notes.

Make Notes, Rather Than Take Notes

Your task is to *make* notes rather than simply *take* notes. Identify themes. Create a decision tree. Plot results. Work with both fact and theory. Jot down buzzwords. Draw arrows to show connections. Colors cement memory so use colors to highlight ideas. Don't limit yourself to words. Make images. Circle key points. Mark the "good," the "bad" and the "ugly." Reference cases. Note questions with question marks. Squiggle points that you need to return to.

Work on Unlined Paper

Lined paper is too confining and far too linear to accommodate our multi-dimensional brain. Our brains love pattern, color and diagram—tools that don't adapt well to lined paper. So get off the grid and work on a blank sheet of unlined paper.

Limit Yourself to One Page

Only the big thoughts go on a work page, so it should never exceed one page.

Use Words and Phrases—Not Sentences

Avoid the urge to write full sentences. Limit yourself to words and phrases. Your work page is meant to inspire new ideas and connections, not to be a first draft of your project.

Be Linear, If You Must, but Not Too Linear

I can never entirely escape my linear training so my work pages tend to be organized in columns or boxes. Be linear if it helps, but don't be so linear that you slip into outlining. For now, you are surveying your thoughts, generating new ideas and deciding what points matter. Stay loose. Put your thoughts in order later.

Keep Your Work Page or Your Mind Map Next to You As You Write

Keep your work page or mind map beside your keyboard and use it to organize your ideas. Having a blank sheet of paper beside your keyboard is like having another window open on your screen. It is a tablet for managing your thoughts and your writing.

Look to your work page reverently for inspiration. Jot down thoughts as you write. Add to it. Throw darts at it. Even if your work page looks nothing like an outline to your paper, the physical activity of working by hand on real paper (or a real tablet) has fired your synapses and warmed your brain. You may now begin the serious, methodical work of digging into your cases.

Go Back to Your Work Page Once You Have *Finished* Writing

Review your work page after you have finished your paper. Pare it down again. Reorganize, if necessary. It will become the guide for your project and the resource you'll use for meetings or even oral argument. If your final work page makes sense, chances are your paper works well too.

Record New Thoughts As You Think Them

Your brightest ideas may come to you while you are jogging, or cooking or driving home. If you don't record those flashes of brilliance, you will forget them. So develop the habit of saving those ideas. Keep a small notebook nearby, send yourself an e-mail or use a digital recorder. Leonardo DaVinci recorded his observations on everything from a water-walking machine to human anatomy on paper. His habit of saving his thoughts is a good habit for all creative people to follow.

The Process of Writing and Overcoming Writer's Block

12

"And I know it seems easy," said Piglet to himself, "but it isn't everyone who could do it."

—A. A. Milne

WRITING IS A discipline so it requires that you have efficient, disciplined work habits. Since you are being paid to write, you do not have the luxury of waiting for inspiration to strike. Like any professional writer, you must produce on demand.

If you develop good writing habits, those habits will become ingrained. Over time, you will find that writing becomes easier and faster. You will become less bogged down in the process and will have more time to immerse yourself in the final product. So focus on building good habits now. You'll reap results immediately in improved papers. You live the results for years as your writing life evolves to entail less struggle and more reward.

Work on a Big Screen

One of the most effective techniques for improving productivity is the size of your computer screen—and the bigger the better. A 2005 *New York Times* article, "Meet the Life Hackers," discusses research by one of the world's leading experts in "interruption science," Mary Czerwinski. She found that people completed tasks from 10 percent to 44 percent more

61

quickly if they worked on a massive, 42-inch screen. While most of us probably do not have the luxury of 42-inch screens, you should opt for as large a monitor as you can justify.

Keep Your Screen Clear

And keep your screen as clear as possible while you are writing. Czerwinski's research also showed that a clean screen led to a calm mind and improved productivity.

Find a Good Model

Before you begin researching or writing, find a good form or model to work from. If you are writing for a colleague, find a similar paper written by that person. You know they will like the format because they used that format themselves.

Working from a form isn't cheating. It's efficient and smart. Within a firm or organization, existing works already belong to that organization. Your employer wants you to build on forms and models that have already been vetted and have an official seal of approval. Indeed, most law offices compile databases of models just for this purpose.

The issue of working from briefs filed by other lawyers outside your firm is more complex and we'll discuss that issue in Chapter 13, *Honesty and Authorship*. The bottom line is that your work must be your own, and you must give credit where credit is due. But you may still turn to other briefs as models for your own work.

Vary the Form As Needed to Suit Your Project

Never be enslaved to a model. Use the model as a starting point, but tailor it to suit the needs of your client and your project.

Get Ready to Write by Organizing Your Research

Don't begin writing until you have a strong handle on the research. Have your research organized and ready to use. Before you begin to write, you should label, highlight and file your research, as suggested in Chapter 9,

Organizing your Research for Efficient Writing, so that your research files are a workable resource.

Find the "Flow"

Writing is a solitary activity. Writers and other creative people are often most productive—and most happy—when all other distractions are shut out so that they become totally immersed in their work. In his ground-breaking work, *Flow: The Psychology of Optimal Experience,* the influential psychologist, Haly Csikszentmihalyi, describes the feeling of "flow" that ac-companies total absorption in work:

> Concentration is so intense that there is no attention left over to think about anything irrelevant, or to worry about problems. Self-con-sciousness disappears, and the sense of time becomes distorted. An activity that produces such experiences is so gratifying that people are willing to do it for its own sake, with little concern for what they will get out of it, even when it is difficult or dangerous.

Carve Out Time for Writing

Because writing is so demanding, you must set aside time to make it hap-pen. Shut out the world, if only briefly. The essence of writing is reflection and a single hour of uninterrupted time will make you productive and focused.

Avoid Multitasking—Particularly E-mailing—While You Write

Yes, your colleagues expect you to check your e-mail constantly unless you are asleep or in a tunnel and your employment contract prohibits sleeping anyway. But switching between tasks makes you less efficient, particularly with complicated tasks such as writing. A 2005 study, *No Task Left Behind? Examining the Nature of Fragmented Work,* found that office workers were in-terrupted an average of every 11 minutes and that, after each interruption, it took 25 minutes to return to the original task.

After being interrupted, you may not remember where you were in writing your paragraph or dissecting a case and it can take as long as a half hour to get back in your groove. Turn off the incoming sound on e-mail so that you feel less like you are "on call." Check e-mail if you must but check it less frequently. Try holding your phone calls and shutting the door, if only briefly.

Stop Surfing

The Internet is irresistible. Resist. Resist. Resist. Disconnect for at least an hour, better yet for an hour and a half. The world will still be there when you return.

Think First. Write Later

Word-processing software is irresistible. It seduces us to start writing before we have begun thinking. Practice safe writing. Put your major thoughts in place, by creating a work page or a mind map, before you give into the urge to puts words on paper. (Chapter 11 on *Brainstorming* discusses how to create work pages and mind maps.)

But Begin Writing Before You Have *Finished* Thinking

You will learn about your topic simply by writing about it. So, while you must have some plan in place before you begin writing, that plan will change as you write. Let it change. If you stay flexible and open to new ideas while you write, your paper will become deeper and more relevant. And if you wait to start writing until you have finished thinking, you may never start writing at all.

Have a Plan

But you must have some plan in place before you begin—whether it is a scribbled work page or a detailed, numbered outline. For example, before William Langiewische wrote his 70,000 word article, "American Ground: Unbuilding the World Trade Center," in *The Atlantic Monthly* (July and August, 2002)—the longest magazine article ever published—he created a handwritten flow chart taking up several feet of butcher paper. (Langiewische's butcher-paper outline is reproduced in a Columbia journalism article, cited in the bibliography.)

Outline As You Go

Outlining works. It is a flexible, efficient tool for organizing your thoughts. But many lawyers avoid outlining, believing it requires them to have a global vision of their paper *before* they write. Instead, outline in piecemeal fashion *while* you write. Begin with the most obvious themes: What is your most important case or line of cases? What headings summarize those cases? Then work through your research, case by case, creating new headings and plugging cases into existing headings.

If you approach outlining as a tool, rather than a rigid guideline, outlining will give you control over your writing because it will keep you focused on the big picture. Again, the goal is to have a perfected outline in place by the time you *finish* writing.

Once you have finished writing and your outline is complete, use that outline as the master key for proofing the structure of your paper. If the outline is perfect, then so is the structure of your paper. The craft of legal writing becomes art through masterful use of structure so your finished outline is your best resource for fine-tuning structure.

Outline from Memory

The mind is a wonderful sifting device. If you let your ideas ferment in your brain, the cream will rise to the top. So begin outlining from memory. Your best ideas are probably the ones that come to mind first.

Use Your Research Files As an Outline

If you have filed your research in files, as suggested in Chapter 9, *Organizing Your Research for Efficient Writing*, those files can also serve as your outline. As suggested in Chapter 9, arrange the files in a logical order and order the cases or statutes within each file. The resulting order will resemble the dreaded linear outline and involves only a fraction of the effort involved in creating a linear outline from scratch.

Create a Routine

You will write more easily if you have a consistent routine. Do you need morning sun to charge your brain? Set aside morning time for writing. Does a messy desk sap your focus? Clean your desk before you start. Can't function without caffeine? Pour that coffee. If you have a consistent routine that works for you, use that routine consistently to transition to writing mode quickly.

Head Off Writer's Block by Thinking with Your Hands

Stuck? Again, try thinking by hand on a blank unlined sheet of paper, as suggested in Chapter 11 on *Brainstorming*. Working in a different mode, such as by hand, activates the right side of the brain and may release writer's block. The process of creating a work page is like the "prewriting" taught in schools. It works because it gets the juices flowing.

Write in Layers by Working from the Middle Out

Writer's block often begins with a misguided effort to write in a linear fashion, beginning at Point A and proceeding in an unbroken line to Point Z. But the process of writing is different than the process of reading. Although we want our readers to zip seamlessly through a paper in an unbroken line, legal argument—like Rome—is built in layers. Therefore, you may want to build your writing in layers, as well.

The "lead" sections of your paper are where you add the most value, but they are also the most difficult sections to write. So take shortcuts by writing the easier middle sections first because they are often straightforward case discussions. Layer on your top layers of thought—your opening, your headings, and your topic sentences—*after* you have written the easier middle sections.

- ◆ **Write pods or cells first.** Every topic has a few easy and obvious arguments that require only two or three sentences. Capture those sentences in small pods or cells. These pods or cells are the middle of your paragraphs.

   Again, you can write these pods as you research. You may even want to jot down these pods directly on the case before you file it. But if you do paste in pods from cases, you must then edit your final paper carefully so that it reads like a deep, thoughtful analysis of the case law, rather than a cut-and-paste exercise.
- ◆ **Label each pod with a topic sentence.** Next, determine the purpose of each pod. Ask yourself why you grouped certain cases together. The answer to that question becomes the opening sentence to your paragraph. Simply "label" each pod—and turn it into a paragraph—by "wrapping" it with your topic sentence.

- **Organize the paragraphs.** Move and group paragraphs to find a coherent order. Work from general to specific, using successive paragraphs to narrow concepts down.
- **Layer on headings.** After you have turned your pods into paragraphs and grouped paragraphs together, "wrap" those paragraph groups with substantive headings that explain why you grouped those paragraphs in one section.
- **Wrap your paper with your opening.** Next, "wrap" the body of the paper with an opening that includes the factual background, the issue (if it's not clear from the facts), and your conclusion.
- **Finally, make recommendations.** Finally, step back and tell your reader what to do next.

Or Write the Ending First

Or write your *Recommendations* section first. It will give you something to work for.

Get Your First Draft on Paper Quickly

Type your first draft yourself to get it on paper as easily as possible. Don't fuss over details yet. Simply aim to create a working document.

Some writers try to write their first draft slowly, aiming for a more finished first product. Although slow drafting is not efficient for professional writing, in which speed and efficiency are so important, common techniques for "slow" writing include writing in longhand or writing with the less dominant hand. Frankly, I don't recommend either technique.

Talk to Yourself As You Write

As you write, write notes to yourself to save your ideas for revisions or additions. Use a different colored font or make your notes in highlighted text. I put closed brackets before each note so that I can then search for the brackets to find my notes. If you use comment boxes to keep your notes, be sure to scrub those comments before finalizing the draft.

Find the Gold

If you use your first draft as a tool to "get it all down" or if you find yourself editing windy writing from a colleague, your first job is to separate the good from the bad. Work quickly through the paper, starring only those "Aha!" concepts that strike you as pivotal. Mark extraneous sentences with an X in the margin. Mark salvageable material with a question mark. Then rework the paper around those few concepts that you have starred.

Write Directly from Your Research Files

An advocate's job is to persuade a court that there is precedent for an argument, so precedent is the best place to start. Review your research files as you write. Build on the arguments and language you have already highlighted and labeled in the copied cases. Review the cases for factual analogies and focus on those facts as you write.

Edit, Edit, Edit

Writing is editing. Polish or perish. (See Chapter 26 on *Deep Editing* for tips on how to edit yourself.)

Edit in *Full Screen Reading View* or on Hard Copy at Least Once

You need to see what the document looks like to decide what must change. In the final stages of your writing, edit at least once in *Full Screen Reading View* or on hard copy.

Do Not Handle Detailed Word Processing Yourself

Do not waste your time or the client's money typing detailed edits yourself. Once you have a fairly clean draft, edit on hard copy and have your staff process the edits.

Save Deleted Material

As you write, save deleted material to the clipboard and label it as deleted material. When you have finished writing, copy the deleted material into a separate document, rather than leaving it to clutter up your clipboard or deleting it from your clipboard. If you save it your deleted material, you can retrieve your brilliant sentences and discarded research if you later have a change of heart.

Honesty and Authorship | 13

About the most originality that any writer can hope to achieve honestly is to steal with good judgment.
—Josh Billings (U.S. Humorist), 1818–1885

AS STUDENTS IN grade school, most of us learned that it is not right to copy another person's work and pretend that it is your own. We were taught that we must put our names on our papers and that we should try to write in our own words. In the best classrooms, our teachers encouraged genuine originality and we began to find our voices.

Now, as lawyers, we may find that originality doesn't come quite as easily. After all, our justice system is based on the rule of stare decisis, so we must turn to precedent to support our arguments. We save our research, then cut and paste as we write our papers. And lawyers have always borrowed freely from each other's work. Indeed, we keep databases of form files just to make our job of writing easier. After all, most of us are not writing the modern-day version of the Magna Carta, so requiring a forced originality in our writing may not add much value to the world we live in. And it's just plain efficient if our system allows us to play nice and share. It cuts down on writing time so that our clients pay less. In this cherished realm of share and share alike, how original must we be?

The basic rules of honesty and fairness that we all learned long ago should still guide us as lawyers. Indeed, given our unique ethical obligations as lawyers, those rules should play a heightened role in our writing lives. Under the Rules of Civil Procedure, when a lawyer files a paper in court, that lawyer represents that he or she has made a reasonable inquiry that the claims and theories advanced in that paper are warranted under existing law. At the very least, reasonable inquiry means that we must examine each client's situation with fresh eyes and tailor our representation—and our writing—to fit that situation. A brief that is simply a cut-and-paste exercise compromises credibility because it suggests that the lawyer has not analyzed the issues unique to that case.

Recently, courts have sanctioned lawyers for flagrant plagiarism and chastised lawyers who have copied work on a smaller scale. The issue of whether filed briefs may be subject to copyright protection has also begun percolating, as commercial services have created databases of briefs and begun charging for access. These fees may indeed add a new wrinkle to our long-cherished system of turning to other lawyers' work for guidance.

Before hitting the panic button and deleting our form files, we should all remember that our legal system requires consistency in our writing. Our jurisprudence is based on precedent and the predictability and certainty that come from applying the same rules consistently to different situations. Since those rules can only be expressed in words, consistent use of those words serves the higher purpose of promoting the rule of law. Legal thought needs to float freely in memes if it is to have any real-world effect.

And even if filed briefs are subject to copyright protection, copyright law has never prohibited fair use or protected pure ideas. When a lawyer makes an argument in a brief or in court, the argument itself is an idea. It becomes part of our jurisprudence and belongs in the public domain, regardless of whether the expression of that idea in pages and pages of briefing is protected by copyright. And even if briefs might be protected by copyright, they would still be subject to fair use. (Briefs prepared by government lawyers, like any work of government, are in the public domain.)

Copying model pleadings from formbooks is certainly acceptable. Those formbooks are designed for use by practicing lawyers and the authors expect those forms to be copied. Indeed, the widespread adaptability of those forms is was makes formbooks so marketable. Similarly, working from model documents within your firm is also good practice. Corporate lawyers, in particular, rely on established forms for both quality control and cost-saving reasons.

But you should be more careful when you rely on the work of other attorneys from outside your firm, including briefs filed in other cases. Like any writer, you must decide where the line between plagiarism and originality falls and guard against crossing that line. The basic rules of fairness and decency that guide all writers apply to lawyers, as well, and following those rules will keep us honest and authentic.

Give Credit Where Credit Is Due

Be sure to credit sources when appropriate. Within a firm or organization, existing works already belong to that organization, so you should certainly work from existing forms and models. Again, your employer wants you to build on forms and models that have already received an official seal of approval and most law offices compile databases of approved forms just for that purpose.

But professionalism and decency may still require that you give credit where credit is due. If you based your jury instructions on a colleague's forms and that colleague's contribution might otherwise go unrecognized, simply mention your colleague's contribution in the cover e-mail or during your next meeting with the assigning attorney.

Credit All Outside Sources

Again, a few recent cases have held that flagrant copying in a brief violates ethical rules against dishonesty. Those courts have not hesitated to impose sanctions, particularly if the attorney billed the client for work the attorney did not do.

For example, in *Iowa Supreme Court Bd. of Professional Ethics & Conduct v. Lane*, 642 N. W. 2d 296 (2002), the Iowa Supreme Court suspended an attorney for six months where the attorney had asked the court to award fees for "writing" a brief that included 18 pages of material that the attorney had cherry picked from a treatise. The court explained that "Honesty is fundamental to the functioning of the legal profession, and Lane's conduct in this case has compromised that honesty." (*Board of Ethics* is also available at **http://www.ethicsandlawyering.com/Issues/files/Lane.pdf**.)

In a similar case, the United States Bankruptcy Court for the Southern District of Iowa sanctioned an attorney who filed a brief that contained 17 pages of verbatim excerpts from a scholarly article, without crediting the author of the article. The court explained that "parroting a scholarly article in this way is not an effective type of advocacy." The court also chastised the attorney for copying a string citation that listed dozens of cases with parentheticals from the same article. The court warned that "[b]y passing off these citations as his own, Mr. Cannon plagiarized . . . just as surely as if he had copied an equivalent amount of text." *In Re Burghoff*, 374, B.R. 681 (N.D. Iowa 2007) (also available at **http://www.ianb.uscourts .gov/content/sites/default/files/decisions/20070821-pk-THEODORE_ BLAIR_BURGHOFF.html**.)

Copying even smaller passages may also violate ethical obligations. *In Kingvision Pay Per View, Ltd. v. Wilson*, 83 F. Supp. 2d 914 (W. D. Tenn. 2000), an attorney copied three footnotes and at least part of seven paragraphs from a treatise, without citing the source. The *Kingvision* court noted the copying might violate the provisions of the Code of Professional Responsibility that prohibit a lawyer from engaging in dishonest conduct.

And it's not just copying from treatises that can be problematic. Some courts have admonished lawyers from quoting from judicial opinions without attribution. In *Pagan Belez v. Laboy Alvarado*, 145 F. Supp. 2d 146, 160-61 (D. P. R. 2001), a lawyer copied several pages from an opinion by another judge in the same court. The court scolded the lawyer and admonished, "In the future, we expect counsel to maintain the highest standards of integrity in all of his representations with this court." (*Pagan Belez* is also available at **http://scholar.google.com**.) Similarly, in *Alamo v. Puerto Rico*, 2006 WL 1716422 (D.P.R. 2006), *aff'd in part on other grounds sub nom Torres-Alamo v. Puerto Rico*, 502 F. 3d 20 (1st Cir. 2007), the court scolded a lawyer for copying seven pages of a Supreme Court opinion directly into a brief, without citing the case.

Play Fair

Borrowing pages and pages from another attorney's brief may also be unfair—especially if it lulls you into complacency and leads you to avoid tailoring your paper to fit your client's needs. In *USA Clio Biz, Inc. v. New York State Department of Labor*, 1998 WL 57176 (E. D. N. Y. 1998) (unreported), an attorney copied 12 paragraphs from a brief filed by another lawyer in a different case. The court explained that the copying indicated that the copycat lawyer had not done independent research, as required by Rule 11 (b) of the Federal Rules of Civil Procedure. The court ordered the attorney to show cause why he should not be sanctioned. In a similar case, *Dewilde v. Guy Gannett Pub. Co.*, 797 F. Supp. 55, 56 (D. Me. 1992), counsel for the plaintiff copied legal portions of the defendant's brief "virtually verbatim." There, the court chastised the attorney because the attorney "did no legal research and was content with defense counsel doing all the work." (Dewilde is also available at **www.scholar.google.com**.)

Thus, regardless of whether copyright law covers briefs, the ethical rules against dishonest or misleading conduct prohibit flagrant plagiarism and wholesale copying without attribution. We are advocates—not human word processors—so we must do more than simply cut and paste our papers. Although we may turn to the work of other lawyers for guidance, we must also tailor every paper to address the facts and law of each case. And when we rely on precedent or other authority, we must still be sure to credit sources.

But lawyers who turn to other briefs for guidance should not automatically be hanged for plagiarism or a copyright violation. Borrowing general concepts from a filed brief is fair use. You may also use other briefs as research tools and starting points for your own research or as the skeletal outline for your own argument.

And the bottom line really hasn't changed much. Cite your sources. Play fair. Make your work your own.

The Distinction Between a Memorandum and a Brief | 14

His majesty the King requires that the Royal Chancellery in all written documents endeavor to write in clean, plain Swedish.

—King Charles of Sweden (1682–1718)

Make Research Memoranda Impartial Surveys of the Law

In a research memorandum, your job is to present both sides of an issue impartially and educate the assigning attorneys. Make your readers aware of opposing authority and potential weaknesses in an argument. Although you must state your conclusion about the law, you should also provide enough information about adverse authority so that your readers can make the judgment calls themselves.

And although a research memorandum must survey both sides of the law, it should not discuss *every* case you reviewed. Research requires judgment calls. Cite relevant cases only.

Think Ahead

Although a research memorandum must be an impartial survey of the law, you should still think ahead to the brief you may eventually find yourself writing. Include the arguments you will eventually need to argue the case. The best research memoranda include sections that can be lifted into a brief with little revision.

Make Briefs Persuasive

By contrast, in a brief or memorandum in support of a motion or appeal, you are writing as an *advocate*. Your job is to persuade your reader to adopt your position. While you must honor your ethical obligation to fairly represent both law and fact, you should put your own slant on the story and emphasize the strengths of your case.

Present the Facts Persuasively in Works of Advocacy

Use the facts to argue your case. Your reader should be on your side by the time he or she finishes reading the facts. For example, a plaintiff who claims he was injured by the pesticides used in an aerial spraying program will want to humanize his story and portray his helplessness against the patrolling airplanes. The brief for that plaintiff might explain: *Mr. Maine was hunting bear in the deep woods of northern Maine. As he waited, camouflaged in a tree, an airplane circled overhead, drew lower and released a spray from its wings. A light mist covered the woods and Mr. Maine.*

By contrast, the chemical manufacturer should emphasize its role in the state's efforts to control a pestilence. The company might say: *In the early 1980's, a tiny but formidable enemy—the gypsy moth—devastated the vast forests of northern Maine. As tens of thousands of acres of northern forest turned brown and silent, the State of Maine chose to protect its greatest resource. After months of study, Maine began a systematic assault on the gypsy moth with a carefully controlled program of aerial spraying, using ChemCo's Agent Bugbegone.*

And yes, these facts are from a real case. I know because I represented the chemical company.

Phrase the Issue to Be Answered Affirmatively in a Work of Advocacy

Think positively. Phrase your issue to take a *yes* answer if you can do so without torturing the language.

Using Structure to Lead from the Top 15

When the words appeared, everyone said they were a miracle. But nobody pointed out that the web itself is a miracle.

—E. B. White, *Charlotte's Web*

Lead from the Top

Structure will elevate your paper from craft to art. While sentence-level editing is important, most of your editing efforts should focus on structure. And all decisions about how to structure a paper build on one essential rule: lead from the top.

Why is leading from the top the essential rule for structuring a paper? Again, leading from the top tells your reader what to look for in the rest of the paper. If your reader knows to look for a point as they read, that point will click immediately once it is presented.

Again, the title explains the purpose of your paper in a clean, succinct phrase. The opening paragraph or paragraphs lead for the whole paper by explaining the facts, the issue and your conclusion. Headings lead for each section. The first paragraph of each section explains your conclusion about the section topic. Within each paragraph, the first sentence summarizes your conclusion about the paragraph topic. Before each block quote, an introductory sentence summarizes the quoted material.

These leading sections and sentences add an essential layer to your writing—the layer that represents your original thought. They are a higher level of content than the middle sections of paragraphs and they deserve a prominent place at the beginning of your paper, at the top of an argument, or at the beginning of your paragraphs.

Leading from the top will also make your work of writing the middle of the paper much easier. If you use your opening to tell your reader what to look for in the body of the paper, your reader will not need meticulous transitions between topics. You have already given them the courtesy of the big-picture view and that big-picture view provides a ready-made bridge between thoughts.

Think of Your Paper in Three Major Sections: an Opening, a Middle and Recommendations

Every legal paper, no matter how complicated, boils down to three major parts:

- The opening (The three parts of the opening are discussed next.)
- The body of the paper
- Recommendations.

Use Your Opening to Prime Your Readers

The opening is the most important part because it primes your readers by telling them what to look for in the body of the paper. A strong opening explains at least three things:

- The background facts
- The issue
- Your conclusion.

Imagine a Dotted Line After the Opening

Imagine your reader drawing a dotted line after your conclusion and cutting at the dotted line. Your readers should understand your entire paper by the time they have finished reading the material before the dotted line.

Tell It All in the Lead Sentence

Consider Robert Kennedy Jr.'s introduction to an article arguing that his cousin, Michael Skakel, had been wrongly convicted of murdering his teenage neighbor decades earlier. There, Kennedy opens by summarizing his entire article in one punchy sentence: "The tragedy of Martha Moxley's death, twenty-seven years ago has been compounded by the conviction of an innocent man." Robert F. Kennedy, Jr., *A Miscarriage of Justice, The Atlantic*, Feb. 2009.

Answer Five Questions in Your Opening:

1. *Who* are the parties?
2. *What* is the problem?
3. *Where* do things stand now? (For example, what has already happened in the proceedings?)
4. *What* do you want to happen next?
5. *Why* are your recommendations a good idea?

If your opening answers each of these five questions, you will have summarized your paper completely.

Capture Your Reader in the First Page and a Half

You will win or lose your reader in the first page and a half of your paper—or in the first paragraph—so even a brilliant *Argument* or *Analysis* cannot undo the damage wrought by a sloppy opening. Whatever structure or format you choose, *all* effective papers state the background facts and the conclusion in the opening paragraphs. A confident writer provides this introductory information in the first page and a half. The strongest writers "open" in the first paragraph. Avoid a vague discussion of abstract legal principles and frame your opening around facts.

Open in Your Own Words

The opening should be your original writing with no footnotes or citations.

Let Substance Drive Structure

In legal writing, structure is substance. Therefore, the structure of every legal paper is unique because its substance is unique. Ultimately, the substance of your argument will define your structure and the structure of any paper is solid only if it is founded on substance.

What does it mean to let substance drive structure? It means that if your case turns on facts rather than law—and most cases do—your structure must be based on those facts. Write fact-based headings and organize any discussion of case law by fact patterns.

It means that you must let substance decide what stays and what goes. In particular, avoid arguing every point you stumbled over in your research. If you argue every point, you may effectively increase your burden of proof by arguing points that you don't need to prove to win your case. An advocate argues only what is necessary to win a case. Focus on your client's situation, rather than abstract legal theory.

It means that if you have three main points, the body of your paper must also have three—and only three—main points. (Set these points off with Roman-numeral headings or primary headings.) Think like a structural engineer and tinker with your headings the way an engineer might tinker with the beams on a building. If the structural supports are off, your entire paper will tumble.

Follow Through in the Middle of the Paper

After the opening, the middle or body of the paper—the *Analysis* or *Argument*—develops and supports the opening but generally does not introduce any major material that you have not already summarized in the opening. The body of the paper provides detail for the main thoughts you introduced in the opening.

Let Your Headings Tell the Story

In longer papers, such as a three-page letter or a five-page memorandum, every new topic should be set off with a heading. Use centered structural headings to highlight the structure of your memorandum or brief, as in *Introduction* and *Analysis* (or the more traditional *Facts, Issue, Conclusion, Analysis*). Within your *Analysis* or *Argument*, use substantive headings to explain your argument, as in *Widget company's representation was not material because. . . .* (See Chapter 20, *Substantive Headings in the Analysis or Argument*, for suggestions on how to write effective headings.) Your reader should be able to follow your argument by reading the headings alone.

Follow the Local Rules Carefully

In addition to the Federal Rules of Civil Procedure, local rules contain formatting requirements. These local rules set specific formats for filings such as summary judgment motions and appellate briefs. They may also set page limits and spacing requirements. Courts often reject nonconforming pleadings, particularly papers that exceed page limitations, so you must follow these rules to the letter. One federal judge in Massachusetts deals with briefs that exceed page limitations by refusing to read anything over the page limit. (In the old days, he tossed the extra pages in the wastebasket.)

Work in *Outlining View* Within the *Analysis* or *Argument*

Work in *Outlining View* periodically and review different levels of headings. *Outlining View* enables you to visualize the structure of your paper with one click and defaults to the correct numbering.

Finish by Telling the Reader What to Do Next

Virtually all legal writing should help the reader decide what to do next. So finish your paper by reminding the court what relief you are seeking or by telling the client or partner what steps they should take next. Business law memoranda, in particular, often conclude with a *to-do* section.

Consider putting your *to-do* list on a separate sheet so that your colleagues and clients can tear it off and check it off as they follow your instructions. Similarly, make it easy for the court to grant your requested relief by attaching a form of order to your brief.

Memorandum Structure

16

You got to be very careful if you don't know where you're going, because you might not get there.

—Yogi Berra

Use Standard Memorandum Format

Although no unwritten law requires you to use standard memorandum format, standard structure is effective because it leads from the top, by beginning with the facts and the conclusion. There are two standard structures: traditional and informal. In traditional format, the opening includes separate sections for the *Facts*, the *Issue* and the *Conclusion*. In an infor-

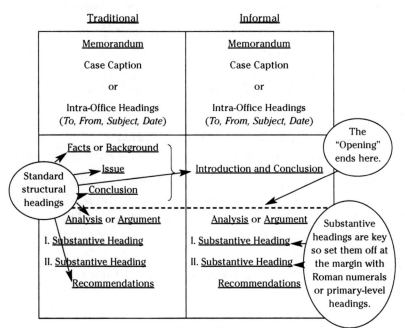

mal format, those three sections are condensed into a single section titled *Introduction* or *Introduction and Conclusion*.

Tell It All Before the Invisible Dotted Line

Again, in either format, your reader should be able to cut at the invisible dotted line and understand your paper. Indeed, most readers will mentally begin to fade away at the dotted line, so you must treat the real estate before that dotted line with reverence. In that opening space, you have the sacred gift of your reader's attention—even if you have not yet earned it. Your job is to show that you deserve their attention for the rest of the paper.

Do Not Use *IRAC*

Many law schools teach *IRAC (Issue, Rule of Law, Analysis,* and *Conclusion)* as the format for memoranda. (The acronym is not only wrong, it's also confusing because some schools teach the *C* in *IRAC* as *Cases.*) However, *IRAC* makes the reader wait until the end of the paper to learn the all-important conclusion. Avoid *IRAC* and put your conclusion in the opening of the paper.

Remember the Traditional Format by Its Acronym— FICA

FICA stands for *Facts, Issue, Conclusion,* and *Analysis* (or *Argument).* The informal format condenses the facts, issue and conclusion into one *Introduction* and is often more readable, particularly if the topic is not very complex. Business law memoranda usually use the informal format.

Write a Heading That Screams *Conclusion*

If you use the informal format, don't label the introductory section as just *Introduction.* Label it as *Introduction and Conclusion* so that the reader knows where to find your conclusion and so that you get credit for reaching one.

Include Case Law in Your Opening If You Need to

If your issue turns on the meaning of a key statute or case or on the procedural history of your client's case, consider outlining that law or procedure in the opening and before the *Analysis* or *Argument*. Including a section on law or procedure in the opening makes writing your *Issue* and *Analysis* or *Argument* easier because you have already put the law on the table.

You can include an introductory section on law or procedure in your *Background Facts* or set it off under its own heading titled, for example, *The Mango Case* or *Relevant Statutes* or *Procedural History*.

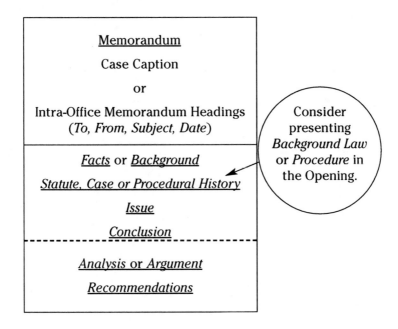

Center Structural Headings

Do not waste a precious Roman numeral or primary heading on a standard structural heading. Set off your structural headings (*Facts, Issue, Conclusion, Introduction, Analysis* or *Argument*, and *Recommendation*) by centering them on your paper. Save Roman numerals and other numbered headings for the more important substantive headings in your *Analysis* or *Argument*.

Love the Post-it

An emphasis on care in writing memoranda is not intended to mire your office in paperwork. Use post-its when you can. A simple post-it saying *To* and *From* is a marvel of tight writing!

The Story or Facts | 17

The universe is made up of stories, not of atoms.
—Muriel Rukeyser

EVERY CASE BEGINS with a story—the story of who the parties are, what brought them together and what went wrong. Stories win cases, not lists of facts or citations. Why? Because story is the context in which facts happen. Stories have emotional appeal. We remember stories but we forget facts. Therefore, you are missing an opportunity if you just list facts without telling the story first.

In legal writing, the story always turns on the parties. Who are the players? How do they know each other? What went wrong? Who did what to whom? Your job is to look beyond facts and data to find that bigger story. And while most legal issues may ultimately turn on narrow facts, those facts will be lifeless and forgettable if you have not wrapped them in the larger context of a story.

Put the Story First

Where do you tell your story in legal writing? It's all about the story so the story always goes first—ideally in the opening or the introduction. So begin every paper with a few short sentences that set the stage and tell the client's story. Again, your reader simply wants to know who the parties are, what brought them together and what went wrong. Save detailed facts for later. Even a colleague who admonishes you to "skip the facts" will not object to two or three sentences at the beginning of the paper explaining the context in which an issue arises.

If your paper opens with a detailed statement of facts, the first paragraph should focus on the background story. Tell the gory details in the later paragraphs. In a longer paper, where you may not cover detailed facts until later in the paper, the opening paragraphs should still tell the general story.

Keep the Story Short

The story or background facts rarely require more than three sentences.

Write for the *Next* Person to Pick Up the File

If your reader knows your topic, you need not restate every fact. However, your target reader is not just the attorney who asked you to write the paper. You must also write for the *next* person who might review the file—and who may not know the background of your case. Two or three sentences of factual background give your work context and perspective and make your work useful for other lawyers researching the same topic later. Therefore, always include enough background facts so that your paper is self-explanatory. A new reader should be able to understand your paper without needing to go back to the case file for basic background information. Similarly, you need not explain general legal principles or statutes if your reader already knows the relevant law, although you may want to paraphrase the law for later readers.

Make the Story Interesting

Again, lawyers should be storytellers. Consider the story Justice Roberts recounts in the well-known case involving a student who unfurled a banner proclaiming "BongHits4Jesus" at a school event:

> Respondent Joseph, a JDHS senior, was late to school that day. When he arrived, he joined his friends (all but one of whom were JDHS students) across the street from the school to watch the event. Not all the students waited patiently. Some became rambunctious, throwing plastic cola bottles and snowballs and scuffling with their classmates. As the torchbearers and camera crews passed by, Frederick and his friends unfurled a 14 foot banner bearing the phrase: "BONG HITS 4 JESUS." The large banner was easily readable by the students on the other side of the street.

Frederick v. Morse, 551 U.S. 393, Slip Op. at 2 (2007) (citations to record omitted) (also available at **http://www.supremecourt.gov**).

Use Interesting Words

Choose words you might find in a well-written magazine article or in a fine piece of children's literature. Imagine a story containing these words: *rambunctious, cola bottles, snowballs, scuffling, torchbearers, camera crews* and *14-foot banners*—the words Justice Roberts used to lure us into *Frederick v. Morse*. What reader can resist?

Write About People

Some details may not be central to the legal issues but are essential to telling a human story that the reader will remember. For example, consider a case filed by a man who was doused with pesticide during aerial spraying. The issue of whether an insecticide can cause harm to the immune system is not exactly a page turner. But the real story of a man hunting for bears while dressed in camouflage and hiding in a tree, when he was doused with pesticide, is both engaging and memorable. Although that story may not be relevant to the scientific issues, you should certainly tell it. Even if you represent the defendant (as I did), you sacrifice honesty and credibility if you fail to acknowledge a plaintiff's sympathetic story. Jurors and judges value compassion.

Tell the Story with the Issue in Mind

Putting the story first also enables you to follow with a short, colloquial statement of the issue, such as *Was the owner negligent?* That conversational statement of the issue is far better than *Was a storeowner negligent where he failed to shovel the sidewalk after a snowstorm and the plaintiff's injuries occurred at 5 A.M., before the store owner could reasonably have been expected to open his store?* If you have told an easy-to-remember story, you do not need to restate every condition in your issue.

Remind the Reader Which Party Is Your Client

The most important part of your story is whom you represent because it tells the reader whether you are going north or south on an issue. Your reader will flounder without this compass information.

Simply use the identifying term *our client* in your opening paragraph, as in *our client, Mrs. Right,* to remind the reader whom you represent. Identifying your client in the body of your paragraph spares the reader the need to look back to the top of the page to identify which party you represent. Although your colleagues on a case obviously know whom you represent, they will not object to the brief reference to *our client* and later readers will appreciate the information.

Introduce the Players

Start every statement of facts by explaining who the parties are, what their relationship is and what the dispute involves. This information tells your reader the context in which the legal issue arises and enables your reader to grasp that issue more quickly. With corporate players, always begin by identifying the corporations' business, as in *Both Stormy Corporation and High Seas Company sell marine engines.*

Find the Facts

Know the who, what, when, where and why. You are entitled to enough background information so that you can do your assignment properly. If the supervising attorney does not give you enough information, review the file. Often the facts have already been summarized in letters and pleadings and the file will provide a wealth of information you will not get from the supervising attorney's brief discussion of the assignment.

Research Your Client

In particular, learn everything you can about your client. The story is about them so you must understand your main characters.

Never Assume the Client Gives the Complete Story

Clients may not give you the full picture, either because they don't understand the nuances of the case or because they are putting their best face forward. Dig, dig, dig. Then dig some more.

Mine the Facts

You must dig deep into your facts if you are to understand them, particularly in complicated cases. One of the most important things you can do is create a chronology. Consider a case I once handled where a buyer purchased a company from a client and later sued that client for fraudulent misrepresentation after the company failed. The buyer had done very careful due diligence. Well into the case—after I had finally prepared a chronology—I realized that the buyer had not done its due diligence until several months *after* the sale closed. What a wonderful tidbit to discover—and shame on me for not discovering that information earlier. Good work habits, such as creating chronologies and summaries of witness interviews, lead to good results.

Create a "Master" Fact File

Organize the facts carefully, particularly in complicated matters. Create a "master" fact file that contains all helpful facts about each matter. Include background correspondence, statutes, notes from negotiations, contracts, key documents, chronologies, witness summaries, document indices, important memoranda. Maintain your normal filing system, but save a copy of key documents in this master file, as well.

Even in our computer age, you may still find yourself in settings where you need a hard copy of documents. At depositions, for example, you may need hard copy exhibits for questioning witnesses. If so, organize the documents in a notebook, with tabs, so that the documents are easy to locate.

Begin with a Lead Sentence or Paragraph That Gives an Overview of the Facts

Even fact paragraphs should begin with a lead sentence that boils the facts down to their essence. For example, in an equal protection case involving complicated student assignment plans, Justice Roberts introduced the plan by summarizing the plan in a few choice words: "The school districts in these cases voluntarily adopted student assignment plans that rely upon race to determine which public schools certain children may attend." *Parents Involved in Community Schools*, 551 U.S. at 701. In that same opinion, he also begins a later fact paragraph by summarizing the problem deftly: "Some schools are more popular than others." 551 U.S. at 711.

After Your Overview Sentence or Paragraph, Tell the Facts in Chronological Order

Once you have given the big-picture view of the facts in a lead sentence or paragraph, dig into the details and tell the facts in chronological order. A chronological presentation of the facts is usually easiest to write and understand. If your story jumps around chronologically, it will be difficult to follow.

Begin by Identifying Key Players

Again, the first facts are the identities of the parties, the nature of their relationship and the basis for their dispute. With corporate players, the first fact is the nature of their business. Then continue by asking, *What happened first? What happened next? What happened after that?*

Eliminate Unnecessary Facts

If a fact is unimportant to your story, take it out unless it adds human interest to the story.

Avoid Diluting the Facts by Repeating Them Unnecessarily

If you restate a key fact again and again, you risk diluting its impact. You will sound like you are selling something and your reader will dismiss the 99th repetition.

Avoid Meaningless Dates

Don't specify a date in your facts unless that date is important. By specifying a date in text, you are signaling that the date matters. Including unimportant dates signals incorrectly. Instead, convey the timeline with civilian words such as *first, next, after* or *then.* For example, explain that *After signing the contract, the defendant reneged on the agreement.*

Consider Presenting Negative Facts Yourself

Negative facts always come out eventually. Presenting them yourself may defuse their impact and will certainly add credibility to your advocacy.

Use Plain-English Identifiers to Name the Parties

Where many players are involved, use descriptive nicknames, such as *the Producing Companies,* to simplify your discussion. But choose a plain-English nickname that is easy to remember. Terms such as *Parent* and *Subsidiary* or *Landlord* and *Tenant* may be helpful for describing corporate players. Avoid the initial trap, as in *ABC Org. sued XYZ, Inc. under the ADA,* at all costs. Do not identify a term if you will not need to refer to it again. Consider boldfacing the identifiers the first time you use them to make them easy to find.

Again, Keep the Facts in a Summary Judgment Motion Simple

The prerequisite for summary judgment is that there is no genuine material issue of fact so, again, you must keep the facts in a memorandum for summary judgment short and simple. A long factual presentation may lead the court to conclude that some issue of fact remains.

So if you are moving for summary judgment on statute of limitations grounds in a complex products liability case where the plaintiff had an adverse reaction to a vaccination, then the *relevant* facts are simple—even though the case involves a roomful of documents generated over months of discovery. You should explain that the plaintiff was born in 1958 (to establish when she reached the age of majority) and vaccinated in 1959, that she had an immediate allergic reaction, that her parents admit that they immediately attributed her reaction to the vaccination and that she did not file her action until 30 years later. By boiling the facts down to a single paragraph, you show the court that the relevant facts are simple enough to be undisputed—and to warrant summary judgment.

Tell the Procedural History in Your Facts If It Helps

For example, if your issue is whether a court's dismissal of an earlier action bars a later, related action, explain the procedural history in your opening section: *A prior court in Nevada dismissed an action by the plaintiff against Company Z for lack of personal jurisdiction. Plaintiff has now brought this action against Company Z in New York, where the company does not have a personal jurisdiction defense.* This explanation allows you to move directly to a colloquial statement of the issue: *Is the New York action barred by the statute of limitations, even though the original action was filed on time?*

Use Facts to Limit Your Conclusions

Cover your tail. If you don't state your facts, you have not limited your conclusion.

The Issue 18

Sometimes the questions are complicated and the Answers are simple.

—Dr. Seuss

Don't Be Limited by the Supervising Attorney's Statement of the Issue

Your research may disclose additional issues that need to be addressed or suggest alternative approaches. A motion originally styled as a motion to strike may, in fact, need to be a motion to dismiss or you may discover other causes of action or defenses that the client should pursue. Your job is to answer the supervising attorney's initial question and identify the five other questions that need to be addressed.

Preface Your Issue with Facts

Again, before you state your issue, briefly explain the key facts in either a separate *Fact* section or in an *Introduction* section that combines facts and the issue. Stating facts first enables you to follow with a colloquial statement of the issue that flows from the facts, such as *Was the owner negligent?* or *Should our client bring an action against the company?*

Avoid Restating Every Condition in Your Issue

Again, if your facts set out the specifics of your case, you do not need to re-state those specifics in your issue. All-inclusive statements of the issue often lead to tortured questions.

Keep the Issue Short

Limit yourself to two lines, if you can.

Keep the Issue Simple

A civilian should be able to understand your issue.

Make the Issue a Question

End your issue with a question mark. Issues do not need to begin with *whether.*

Talk About the Client's Facts

Avoid an abstract statement of the issue and ask about the client's situation. Don't say *Should the court award a preliminary injunction where the plaintiff has shown irreparable harm?* Instead, talk in terms of the client's situation and say *Should the court award a preliminary injunction enjoining the sale of 639 Main Street?*

Make the Issue a Syllogism

Use syllogisms to snare your readers in your logic. The classic syllogism, *All men are mortal; Socrates is a man; therefore, Socrates is a mortal,* translates nicely into a legal context: *Widget Company promised bulk discounts on large orders. Mrs. Nice ordered one billion widgets and Widget Company never gave her the bulk discount. The cases establish that representations concerning price are presumed material. Was Widget Company's representation about giving bulk discounts material?*

Phrase Your Issue to Take a *Yes* Answer

Simplify your issue by stating it positively. Don't say *Did this Court reject the position that a consumer could appeal from a class action settlement even if the consumer had not intervened in the class action?* Instead, say *Must a consumer have intervened in the class action in order to appeal from the class action settlement?*

The Conclusion or Brief Answer

19

You're on your own and you know what you know. And you will be the guy who'll decide where to go.

—Dr. Seuss

Reach a Conclusion

Again, clients and assigning attorneys don't appreciate spending several thousand dollars to learn that the answer to their question is *maybe*. You must take a stand. If your research discloses a dispositive answer, conclude with *yes* or *no*. *Yes if* and *no if* are also acceptable provided that the *ifs* are fact specific, as in *The client may pursue his discrimination claim if he files his notice with the agency by February 1*. If the answer really is *maybe*, at least be definitive about being hesitant. Explain any split in the authority, state which view is the weight of the authority, and analogize and distinguish the facts that characterize each line of reasoning.

Assume Your *Conclusion* or *Brief Answer* Is the Only Thing Your Reader Will Read

Because it probably *is* the only thing your reader will read.

Again, Use Your *Conclusion* or *Brief Answer* to Prime Your Reader

Again, a *Conclusion* or *Brief Answer* in the opening primes your reader about what to look for in the body of the paper.

State Your Conclusion in Plain English

Imagine running into the partner who assigned you an issue as she is getting off the elevator and you are getting on. You have only a few seconds to answer her question, *How is the Widget research coming?* Your one-sentence answer is your conclusion.

Say the Conclusion Aloud

Saying the conclusion aloud will force you to use plain English and simplify. Again, imagine a quick conversation with a colleague on the elevator.

Do It Early

Put your conclusion at the beginning of your paper—usually on the first page, either in the *Introduction* or immediately after the *Issue* in a *Brief Answer*. Legal writing should not unfold like a mystery novel.

Explain Why

Your answer should not only state your conclusion. It should also explain *why* you reached that conclusion. Your readers cannot decide whether they agree with your conclusion unless you tell them how you reached it. Telling why in the *Answer* builds your credibility early.

Organize Your Conclusion to Correspond to Your Issue

For example, if you have presented your issue in two parts (*I* and *II*), you should also present your conclusion in two parts (also numbered *I* and *II*). Your *Analysis* or *Argument* should then use corresponding headings.

Make Your Conclusion Fact Specific

Avoid legal abstractions and explain what your conclusion means for *this* client. Don't say *the store owner will be found negligent for not maintaining his sidewalk with reasonable care if she reasonably should have known that pedestrians were likely to use that sidewalk by 7:00 a.m.* Be specific and say *Ms. Jones is negligent for not having shoveled the sidewalk because she knew that customers walked in front of her store early every morning.*

Write Your *Conclusion after* You Have Written Your *Analysis*

You will learn as you write, so draft your *Conclusion* last even though it will go at the beginning of your paper.

Do It Once

A second *Conclusion* at the end often leaves the reader wondering whether that second *Conclusion* is different than the earlier *Brief Answer*. The reader often ends up comparing the two—effectively undercutting the authority of the earlier *Brief Answer*. Except in a very long paper, once is enough. Instead of restating your conclusion at the end of your paper, conclude with your *Recommendations* about what the client should do next.

Substantive Headings in the Analysis *or* Argument

20

Be obscure clearly.

—E. B. White

Use Substantive Headings Liberally

Substantive headings are the roadmap to your paper. Even a 50-page paper becomes accessible if it is clearly divided into three substantive parts. Headings tell your reader that you are presenting the material in manageable bites and they force you to lay out your words systematically rather than just spilling those words randomly throughout your paper. Therefore, in addition to labeling the standard structural sections of your paper (such as *Facts*, *Issue* and *Conclusion),* use substantive headings within each section, and set those headings off with Roman numerals or a primary heading.

Identify the Big Themes

What are the key points you need to make? These points are your Roman-numeral headings or your primary headings. Again, if you outline from memory, these points will rise to the top.

Use a Standard Format for Numbering and Lettering Substantive Headings

Lawyers have long used a heading format based on Roman numerals. In that format, Roman numerals are the universal signal for a major shift in your argument. Think of your Roman numerals as gold. If you mix up the order and put capital letters before the Roman numerals, your headings will confuse rather than clarify. I'll also suggest a more modern format—a format that assures that your readers will always know where any heading falls in the hierarchy of your argument.

The traditional Roman-numeral format for numbering substantive headings in your *Analysis* or *Argument* looks like this:

<u>Traditional Format for Substantive Headings</u>

  I. <u>Initial Cap and Underscore</u>
 II.   "   "
    A. Initial Cap Only Without Underscore
    B.   "   "
       1. Initial cap first word only, no underscore
       2.   "   "
         a. Initial cap first word only, no underscore
         b.   "   "

Even though Roman-numeral headings are universally used in the legal profession today, there is a better way. Technical writers have long used sequentially numbered headings, in which each sublevel simply adds a decimal point, followed by a number. In sequentially numbered headings, each heading contains a complete reference to its position in the hierarchy, so your readers always know where they are in your analysis. (If you have ever designed a website, you are already familiar with this system.) This modern format is cleaner and kinder. It looks like this:

<u>A Modern Format for Headings</u>

 1. Primary heading
   1.1 Secondary heading
   1.2 Secondary heading
 2. Primary heading
   2.1 Secondary heading
   2.2 Secondary heading
      2.2.1 Tertiary heading
      2.2.2 Tertiary heading

Matthew Butterick—the guru for the design of legal papers—also endorses this modern format. In fact, he endorses it heartily so hope for change. (Both formats are available in modern word-processing programs.)

Organize Your Headings Around the Facts

Make your headings focus on the facts of your case or the facts of the cited cases. For example, if you are reviewing the different types of relief available for filing an inaccurate statement under the securities regulations, you should focus on the procedural results of the cases and organize your cases according to the type of relief they granted.

Your headings might look like this:

I. Forms of Relief Available
   A. Corrective Disclosure
   B. Sterilization of Shares
   C. "Cooling Off" Periods

Or focus on what happened in your case. In the "Bongs4Jesus" case, where a school superintendent had disciplined a student who unfurled a "Bongs4Jesus" banner at a school event, the lawyers wrote fact-based headings that effectively argued their case. For example, their headings argued:

- ◆ Discouraging the use of illegal substances is an undeniably important educational mission.
- ◆ Frederick's pro-drug banner interfered with decorum by radically changing the focus of a school activity.
- ◆ Principal Morse properly disassociated the school from Frederick's pro-drug banner.

Brief for School Board, *Morse v. Frederick*, United States Supreme Court 06-278, 2007, at ii. (available at **www.oyez.org**).

Put Similar Content at the Same Level of Heading

In writing headings, one of your most difficult tasks will be deciding what level a heading belongs at. Headings at each level should contain similar material. Indeed, mixing different types of content within a level is a fundamental structural defect and one of the most common mistakes poor writers make.

A Roman-numeral or primary heading will always represent a major part of the paper, much like a chapter heading. Subheadings are material that develops the Roman-numeral or primary heading. In the example above, the Roman-numeral heading, *Forms of Relief Available* represents one of the major points of the paper. (The other Roman-numeral headings in this paper covered *Existence of Private Cause of Action, Irreparable Harm Requirement, Availability of Money Damages as a Bar to Equitable Relief, Other Prerequisites for Injunctive Relief, Survey of Possible Grounds for Establishing Irreparable Harm,* and *Balancing of Harms*.) The subheadings—*Corrective Disclosure, Sterilization of Shares* and *"Cooling Off" Periods*—all represent examples of the forms of relief.

Proof your headings separately from the text. You cannot be sure that you have assigned a heading to the correct level unless you review all your headings together. Create a Table of Contents that shows all your headings or pull those headings onto a separate page, then study your headings carefully. If your headings are correctly leveled, then you have a strong foundation for your paper.

Do Not Let the First Paragraph Hang Loose Without a Subheading

If you do subheadings, *every* paragraph within that section should come under a subheading, including the first paragraph. Even a catchall subheading *A*, titled *Introduction* or *General Standards*, is preferable to letting the first paragraph hang loose without a subheading. Most new writers mistakenly let that first paragraph hang loose, without a heading, as shown in the box:

–pg. 2–

Therefore, this court should exclude the contents of the letter as privileged.

I. The Attorney Letter is Privileged

A communication is privileged if (1) it is a *communication* between a client and a lawyer; (2) the communication is intended to be *confidential*; and (3) the communication is to *obtain legal advice*. *United States v. United Shoe Machinery Corp.*, 89 F. Supp. 357, 358-359 (D. Mass. 1950). Here, the Attorney's Letters meets all three criteria.

A. Communication

The Attorney letter qualifies as a

The first subheading (Heading *A*) should go here, *before* the first introductory paragraph. Simply call it *Introduction* or *Overview*.

A catchall subheading labeled *Introduction* or *Overview* at least alerts the reader that more material follows on the major topic of the section—a helpful warning, especially if there is a page break before your next heading.

But Do Not Let Standard Numbering Throw Off a Logical Numbering System

For example, misrepresentation has five elements. Therefore, you must be sure that your discussion concerning the elements of misrepresentation is numbered *1* to *5* (or *A* to *E*). Although your section on misrepresentation may begin with an introductory paragraph *A* that sets out the elements of misrepresentation, you should not label your discussion of the first element of misrepresentation (*Intent*) as heading *B* because it will throw off your numbering. Instead, create an intervening heading *B* titled *Elements* and follow-up with the five elements of intent:

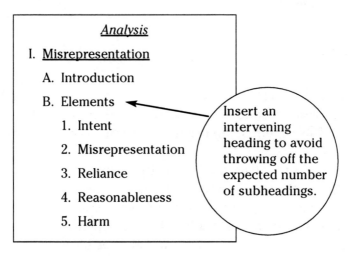

Similarly, if introductory paragraphs that explain case law or a statute interfere with a logical numbering system, break those introductory paragraphs into a separate structural section titled *Law* or *Relevant Statutes* and place that section in your opening, as suggested in Chapter 16 on *Memorandum Structure*. This technique will enable you to preserve that precious Roman-numeral *I* or primary heading *1* for the first true point in your *Analysis* or *Argument*.

Never Write Just One Subheading

If you write subheadings under a heading, there must be at least two subheadings. Since the purpose of subheadings is to subdivide the overarching material, you cannot have just one subheading.

Keep Headings and Text Together

Don't let your word-processing program insert an automatic page break between a heading and its text. (Again, select the headings and text that you
want to keep together. On the *Format* menu/drop down to the *Paragraph*
box/choose *Line and Page Breaks* and select *Keep lines together.*)

Consider Writing Your Major Headings As Sentences, Rather Than Phrases

For example, say *Irreparable harm requires continuing inaccurate disclosure*,
rather than *Irreparable harm requirement*. A sentence heading has muscle
and can often do the work of a whole paragraph or section. However, a
skeletal phrase heading may be more appropriate if sentence headings are
becoming too long to be easily digested.

Use Parallel Construction in the Same Level of Headings

If you write heading *I* as a sentence, headings *II, III* and *IV* must also be sentences. If you write heading *A* as a phrase, headings *B, C* and *D* must also
be phrases. (The same rule applies if you use the modern format for numbering your headings.)

However, you may vary the form between different levels of headings.
For example, all chapter headings in this book are written as phrases, but
the bold-faced headings to paragraphs are written as commands. In briefs
and memoranda, Roman-numeral headings are often written as sentences
and subheadings are written as single words or as phrases.

Write a Strong Title

The ultimate lead is the title of your paper. If you don't get the title right,
the court may not be able to find your paper or the client or supervising attorney may not see the need to read your paper.

The Analysis or Argument: General Thoughts | 21

"In my youth," said his father, "I took to the law,
And argued each case with my wife;
And the muscular strength it gave to my jaw,
Has lasted the rest of my life."
　　　　　—Lewis Carroll, *Alice's Adventures in Wonderland*

THE *ANALYSIS* OR *ARGUMENT* will be the bulk of your paper. Since most writers write the *Analysis* or *Argument* first, the *Analysis* or *Argument* becomes the foundation for the paper.

This chapter discusses general guidelines for writing an *Analysis* or *Argument*. The next chapters address more detailed issues, including how to talk about case law (Chapter 22), how to handle transitions (Chapter 23) and citation format (Chapter 25).

Argue Facts Over Law

Again, facts—not lists of authority—win cases. A fact-based analysis shows deep understanding of the issues. Therefore, organize your *Analysis* or *Argument* around the facts, rather than around vague rules of law. Rather than argue that *Information is material if an investor is reasonably likely to rely on that information*, argue that *Information is material whenever it concerns pricing.*

Structure the *Analysis* or *Argument* Based on the Facts of the Cited Cases

Analogize the case law to your facts and identify factual patterns in the case law. Then organize your *Analysis* or *Argument* based on the facts of those cases.

For example, if your cases involve piercing the corporate veil, talk about cases that allowed a pierce based on inadequate capitalization, cases that involved palming off, and cases that involved misrepresentation. If you are reviewing the relief available for violating disclosure requirements under the securities regulations, organize the cases by the types of relief they allowed. As discussed above, those headings might focus on corrective disclosure, sterilization of shares or "cooling-off" periods.

Organize Your *Analysis* or *Argument* to Correspond to Your *Conclusion* or *Issue*

If your *Conclusion* or *Issue* is divided into *I* and *II*, your *Analysis* or *Argument* should also be divided into *I* and *II*.

Assign Roman Numerals or Primary Headings to Your Most Important Arguments

Again, your key arguments will float to the top if you outline from memory. These Roman-numeral or primary headings become the bones of your *Analysis* or *Argument*. Lead from the top by putting your most important arguments first. Don't waste headline space on a subsidiary issue.

Conclude. Support. Apply.

Within each substantive section of your *Analysis* or A*rgument*, lead from the top by beginning with your conclusion and then follow up with more detail:

- ◆ **Conclude.** Just as you lead your entire paper with a *Brief Answer* or *Conclusion*, your opening paragraph or opening sentence should lead from the top by stating your conclusion about that topic.
- ◆ **Support.** The middle paragraphs or sentences of each section should explain the law that supports your conclusion.
- ◆ **Apply.** The final paragraphs or sentences should apply that law to your facts or give examples.

Use Pattern—Particularly Parallel Construction—to Move Your Reader Through Your *Analysis* or *Argument*

The human mind loves pattern. Poetry, for example, touches us through its rhythm, cadence and rhyme before it moves us with its meaning or symbolism. Although the patterns in legal writing may be extremely subtle, a strong writer exploits the human mind's inherent love of pattern by using pattern to make a work more readable.

The most common examples of pattern in legal writing are forms. Because we are so familiar with common legal forms, they make reading easier because we know where to look in the form for certain information. But don't be enslaved to a form. Use the form only if it works.

Within the *Analysis* or *Argument*, the most effective pattern is parallel construction. If you begin a paragraph with a strong introductory sentence stating your conclusion about the law, your reader will become conditioned to look for that introductory sentence in following paragraphs. If you begin each section by stating your conclusion and then supporting and applying that conclusion to the facts, your reader will easily absorb later sections following a similar pattern. A section in which you discuss a rule then distinguish exceptions to the rule leads your reader to expect a similar order in later sections. Once you have "conditioned" your reader by establishing a pattern, use that pattern consistently and your work will be more readable and accessible—even though your reader may not be consciously aware of the underlying pattern.

Work from General to Specific Within Each Section and Paragraph

Within a section, your first paragraph should be the most general and subsequent paragraphs should narrow the topic down. Similarly, within each paragraph, your first sentence should be a broad overview of the paragraph and each succeeding sentence should narrow the point down.

Brake for New Thoughts by Using Paragraph Breaks

Paragraphs are the most important tool a writer has because they are a visual cue showing where major thoughts begin and end. Every paragraph should represent a coherent chunk of information. Paragraph breaks also give your reader space to breath.

Deal with Only One Topic in Each Paragraph

Start a new paragraph whenever you move onto a new topic.

Make Every Paragraph Fit Under a Heading

Every paragraph in your analysis must relate to the heading above it. Review each paragraph to determine the point you are trying to make. If that point does not relate to the preceding heading, move the paragraph to another section or write a new heading.

Lead Each Paragraph from the Top by Beginning with an Original Sentence

You are being paid to think originally. Add value by beginning each paragraph with your original thought and then use the body of the paragraph to support that lead sentence. For example, every major paragraph in this book is headed by a bold-faced lead sentence written as a command. Unlike law review style, lead sentences in briefs and memoranda do not require slavish citation to authority and you should not simply parrot back case law in those lead sentences.

Make Your Lead Sentence Focus on the Facts or Results of Cases, Rather Than General Rules of Law

A paragraph discussing cases concerning the nature of the harm required to obtain an injunction under SEC Rule 13(d) might begin: *Anything short of continuing inaccurate disclosure will not be sufficient to support an injunction under 13d.* A paragraph discussing dispute settlement proceedings might say *The Healthcare Provider has a well-defined system for settling appeals by its members.* Better yet, use your introductory statement to argue your position or focus on the big picture, as in *Smith v. Jones represents an extreme departure from established authority.*

Write a Lead Sentence Even for Paragraphs That Deal Only with Facts

Even if a paragraph deals only with facts, summarize those facts in one plain-English sentence. Recall Justice Roberts' characterization of the factual problem in a school assignment case: "Some schools are more popular than others." *Parents Involved in Community Schools*, 551 U.S. at 711.

Within a Paragraph, Make Each Sentence Say Something New

Once you are in the body of your paper, as in the *Analysis* or *Argument*, each sentence must earn its weight on the page by saying something new. State your concept once and avoid repeating that exact concept. New sentences must add value by developing, refining or illustrating the concept.

Restating earlier sentences within the body of the paper is more than just a sloppy stylistic error. Repetition is a substantive failure because repetition interrupts the flow and pace of your paper and stalls your reader's line drive from point A to point Z. Culling repetitive sentences is one of the most difficult and most important jobs in editing your own work.

But the rule against repetition *within* the body of the paper does not prohibit repetition between the opening and the body of the paper. Since the purpose of an opening is to give an overview of the body of the paper, your opening and the body of the paper will necessarily restate concepts.

Use Signal Phrases to Tell the Reader Where You Are Going

Think of your argument or analysis as a line drive from point A to point B. Occasionally, you must detour to discuss an exception or a contradictory point and your reader will appreciate directional signals at those transitions. *Similarly, for example, in particular* and *in addition* let the reader know that you are developing the main point. *However, although* and *by contrast* signal a detour to discuss an exception to a rule or to distinguish opposing authority. *Therefore* signals a conclusion. *Again* tells your reader that, yes, you have already discussed this point. These directional signals are powerful tools that let your reader know the value of a sentence before they read that sentence.

Use these common signal or introductory phrases:

- *First, Second, Third*
- *For example*
- *Similarly*
- *In particular*
- *By contrast*
- *However* or *But*

- *Again* (which politely reminds the reader that they already know the point and can relax)
- *Also*
- *Therefore*
- *Finally* (every reader's favorite word).

But Do Not Begin Every Sentence with a Signal Phrase

Strive for variety. If you begin every sentence with a signal phrase, you will compromise the rhythm of your writing. Try varying the form of sentences in the middle of the paragraph to maintain flow. For example, instead of saying *Similarly, in Smith v. Jones, the court held that. . . .*, say *In Smith v. Jones, the court also held that. . . .*

Avoid Stuffy Introductory Phrases

Don't use pompous introductory phrases such as *that said, more plainly stated,* and *as such.* And choose the plain-English form for signal words. For example, use *but* instead of *however* and *also* instead of *additionally.*

Follow this Example to Create a Working Paragraph

If you follow my suggestions, an effective working paragraph might look something like this:

> *Rondeau*—the seminal case establishing that irreparable harm was necessary to obtain injunctive relief under Section 13(d)—involved a late-but-otherwise-accurate Schedule 13D. There, the Supreme Court held that the target company had not established irreparable harm, largely because the shareholder had now filed a proper Schedule 13D. 422 U.S. at 59. Similarly, in *General Aircraft*, 556 F. 2d at 95, the shareholder filed an inaccurate and misleading Schedule 13(d) three months after the statutory filing date. Although the *General Aircraft* Court found that irreparable harm would occur if the investors were allowed to *continue* their activities without correcting the schedule and issued an order enjoining further sales until the shareholder filed an accurate schedule, the court held that the late filing alone was not a basis for enjoining the tender offer. As the Second Circuit has explained, "the interests [that Section 13(d) seeks to protect] are fully satisfied when the shareholders receive the information re-

quired to be filed." *Treadway Cos. v. Care Corp.*, 638 F. 2d 357, 380 (2d Cir. 1980).

Or a strong paragraph might follow this example from a brief in the Martha Stewart insider-trading scandal:

> The proposed expert testimony from the law professor violated both prohibitions. Stewart sought to have the expert invade the province of the court to instruct the jury on the law. The proposed testimony would also have invaded the province of the jury. In order to opine that Stewart's trade did not violate the insider trading laws, he would have had to testify regarding his findings of fact, such as what information was in fact provided to Stewart; whether that information was material; whether Bacanovic directed that that the information be provided to Stewart; whether Bacanovic or Faneuil owed a duty to keep the information confidential; whether Bacanovic or Faneuil intentionally breached that duty; and whether Stewart understood that the information was obtained in breach of Bacanovic's or Faneuil's duties of trust and confidence. *See United States v. Falcone*, 257 F. 2d at 230-231 (describing elements of misappropriation theory). The District Court properly rejected this effort.

Brief for the Prosecution, *United States v. Stewart*, Second Circuit 04-3953(L) (2004) at 55 (available at **http://www.lawprofessorblogs.com/whitecollar/ linkdocs/martha_govbrief.pdf**).

Emphasize Theme Words

Use colorful words to emphasize themes and repeat those theme words throughout your argument. Although you should not repeat sentences in the body of your paper, you should certainly repeat theme words and phrases. Write about the *inequity and waste* of defendant's conduct, the victim's *fear* of a defendant, a plaintiff's *trivial* complaints, a defendant's *targeting* of minority applicants, a company's *knock-off product*, a defendant's *change of heart* or sudden *reversal of position*, a company's *orchestrated* efforts to conceal its conduct, a plaintiff's *history of conflict,* a plaintiff's *half-statements* or *fabrications* or an attorney's *mere presence* at a transaction.

Sound Bite Statutes or Legal Concepts

Similarly, use theme language to sound bite statutes or legal theory, as in *the purpose-and-character prong*, the *burden-shifting framework, the blackout period* or *preemptory eviction.*

Weave Fact and Law Together

While you may have some paragraphs that cover the law only, most of your paragraphs should weave fact and law together. A fact-and-law paragraph might look like this paragraph from a brief in the Ten Commandments case:

> Second, courts "not only can, but must, include an examination of the circumstances surrounding [the governmental] enactment." *Santa Fe Indep. Sch. Dist., 530 U.S. at 308.* Here, those circumstances reveal the innately sectarian backdrop to these displays. In 1999, local governments throughout Kentucky posted the Ten Commandments in courthouses, schools and other public buildings. The local governments invited legal challenges and these two received them amid wide publicity. They initially posted only the Ten Commandments and petitioner Greene candidly admitted his religious reasons for doing so. After being sued, petitioners cloaked their displays in textual excerpts celebrating religion and announced their purpose of "demonstrat[ing] America's Christian heritage." *McCreary County I,* 96 F. Supp. 2d at 674. And after the district court enjoined their second Ten Commandments displays, petitioners posted their third, purporting merely to display "historical documents." The district court was well within its discretion, as the appeals court concluded, in finding it no coincidence that the Ten Commandments was among the "historical documents" that petitioners opted to display. The petitioners "nevertheless[s] as[k the courts] to pretend that [they] do not recognize what every [one else] underst[ood] clearly—that this [display was] about prayer." *Santa Fe Indep. Sch. Dist.,* 530 U.S. at 319.

Brief of the American Civil Liberties Union in Opposition to Petition for Writ of Certiorari, *McCreary v. ACLU,* United States Supreme Court 03-1693, 2003, at 8 (available at **http://www.oyez.org**). Note the skillful use of language from the precedential cases to argue the ACLU's position.

Do Not Ask the Court to Overrule Established Precedent

A court never wants to overrule precedent so don't ask a court to do so. The answer will almost certainly be *no*.

Argue Statutes Over Case Law

A governing statute carries more weight than a relevant case, so argue statutes first.

Let the Cases Do the Writing

Again, once you have written your brilliant introductory sentence, you may cheat your way through the middle of your paragraph. Insert and borrow from the cases you have copied and highlighted. Reread the cases as you write, and quote or paraphrase from those cases.

Discuss Significant Cases Only

A memorandum should not be a summary of every case you reviewed. Research requires judgment and your job is to cull the cases.

Deal with Adverse Case Law in a Straightforward, Honest Fashion

Consider defusing your opponent's ammunition by introducing it yourself. Ignore adverse case law at your peril.

Avoid Restating the Other Side's Argument

Don't fall into the trap of restating the other side's argument as a prelude to attacking that argument. Opposing positions also rarely deserve dedicated sentences. For example, if your client has defrauded customers, don't dedicate a sentence to the other side's argument that *Courts will pierce the corporate veil where the corporation has defrauded its customers.* Instead, restate the argument from your client's angle: *Courts rarely allow a pierce where a corporation is adequately capitalized unless there are clear markers of fraud.* Or work opposing authority into an *although* clause to avoid dedicating a sentence to discussing that authority. For example, say *Although courts have pierced the veil where corporations have defrauded their customers, our clients never acted fraudulently.*

Use a Reply Brief to Do More Than Simply Reply

Avoid letting your opponent structure your argument. Use reply briefs to continue your offensive, rather than to simply defend against your opponent's points.

Do Not Comment About Your Opponents

Again, litigation is a battle between parties and about theories and facts. It should never deteriorate into a battle that is chiefly about the lawyers. Therefore, avoid disparaging comments about your opponents or their work. In particular, avoid language such as *For reasons that are not immediately apparent, plaintiff argues that.* . . . Even seemingly innocuous comments, such as *The defendants incorrectly cite Smith v. Jones for the proposition that* . . . . can shift the focus to the personalities involved and away from your point. Simply rephrase your challenge to the defendant's citation as *Smith v. Jones involves dramatically different facts.*

Break up Lists with Numbers or Bullets

For example, when listing the five elements of misrepresentation, number those elements *(1)* to *(5)*. (And remember that your reader will then expect you to follow through with a five-part structure.) Where all items in a list are of equal importance, you may use bullets. Because bullets enable you to leave out transitional words, they encourage spare writing.

However, be cautious about using bullets in formal documents, such as court filings. And never bullet case law. (See page 159 and the *Usage and Punctuation Guide* for answers to your burning questions about how to style, punctuate and capitalize bullets.)

Use Substantive Footnotes Sparingly but Artfully

Use substantive footnotes only for significant historical or background information, to respond to a minor point, or to bury opposing authority. Your reader won't bother with footnotes so be careful what you put there, or use your reader's reticence to your advantage by hiding adverse information in footnotes. But if you cite opposing authority in a footnote, be sure your paper also contains two or more "neutral" footnotes: a single footnote containing opposing authority highlights, rather than buries, the offending material.

Do Not Focus on Journals

Scholarly journals, such as law review articles and treatises, carry less weight outside the academic world. (Heartbreaking news, I know.) Focus on statutes and cases because they are the primary sources. Use scholarly works only where an issue has not been resolved in the courts.

Talking About Cases and Other Authority | **22**

Think left and think right and think low and think high.
Oh, the things you can think up if only you try.
—Dr. Seuss

YOU WILL PROBABLY spend most of your *Argument* or *Analysis* talking about the case law and handling case law is an art form. This chapter discusses how to deal with the substance of the case law. Chapter 25 on *Citations* addresses technical citation format.

Give a Global Picture of Your Research

Often the most important part of your research is what you did *not* find. If no court has ever ruled against your position, then you miss an opportunity if you simply cite the 1,001 cases that favor your position. Emphasize the absence of any opposing authority by stating, for example, that *No court has ever declined to find personal jurisdiction over a defendant who maintained an office within its jurisdiction.* If only two cases rule your way, a research memorandum must flatly disclose the paucity of authority, although you should not point out that lack of authority in a brief.

Discuss the Most Recent or Most Important Law First

Unlike in a *Fact* section—where we present the detailed facts in chronological order—you should not present your cases chronologically. Instead, give the reader a snapshot of *current* law by beginning with the most important or most recent cases. Provide historical context only if it helps explain current law.

Learn the Lingo for Talking About Cases

Discussing case law is an art form and shorthand phrases make your job easier, as long as you don't slip into legalese. A case can be *distinguishable, controlling, relevant, analogous, seminal* or *binding*.

Discussing patterns in the case law is even more challenging. Certain well-used phrases help:

- *In Smith v. Jones, this Court squarely addressed. . . .*
- *The First Circuit has long recognized. . . .*
- *No reported cases hold that. . . .*
- *Only one reported case holds that. . . .*
- *The most analogous cases hold that. . . .*
- *The Ninth Circuit has long expressed a strong preference for. . . .*
- *Although this Court has expressed a strong preference for . . . , it has frequently allowed . . . under similar circumstances.*
- *This Court has entertained. . . .*
- *This Court has considered. . . .*
- *This Court is poised. . . .*
- *The Supreme Court has not been sympathetic to. . . .*
- *This Court imposes. . . .*
- *This District follows a recent trend. . . .*
- *The court cautioned against. . . .*
- *No court has directly addressed. . . .*
- *As a general rule, the courts have. . . .*
- *That decision represents an extreme departure from. . . .*

Discuss Key Cases in Prose, Rather Than Parentheticals

Your most important cases should always be discussed in prose, rather than in a parenthetical. The decision to discuss a case in prose shows you assign a higher value to that case than to the cases that you discuss in parentheticals. But even if you discuss a case in prose, you might still need to write parentheticals to develop minor facts or the procedural history of the case.

Use Signal Phrases Every Time You Introduce a New Case

Readers want to know immediately whether a case is the leading or most analogous case or whether it narrows a concept, states a different position, simply provides an example or repeats earlier information. Therefore, always assign a value or weight to the case by using signal phrases that show why you are citing that case. Use phrases such as *in the leading case, in an analogous case, in particular, by contrast, however, for example, recently, also* or *again*. But, again, be careful not to begin every sentence in a paragraph with a signal phrase or you will compromise the rhythm of your writing.

Summarize Case Law Succinctly

In *Parents Involved in Community Schools*, Justice Roberts summarized the law before *Brown v. Board of Education of Topeka* with a gifted economy of words. He explained simply, "Before *Brown* children were told where they could and could not go to school based on the color of their skin." 551 U.S. at 747. If Justice Roberts can reduce decades of constitutional jurisprudence to a few pithy words, you should be able to discuss a statute-of-limitations case or the doctrine of piercing the corporate veil in a sentence or two.

Focus on the Factual Results of the Cases

Judges and senior attorneys already know the law cold. Your job is to explain how the law plays out in the real world of people and facts. Therefore, focus on the facts and results in the cases, rather than vague statements of law.

   For example, in its brief opposing certiorari in the Ten Commandments case, the ACLU summarized a huge body of First Amendment law in a masterful paragraph that focused on the results of the cases:

> Where "a governmental intention to promote religion is clear," *Edwards v. Aguillard*, 482 U.S. 578, 585 (1987), this Court has not hesitated to hold the challenged conduct unconstitutional. Thus, the Court has invalidated Louisiana's creationism statute, *Aguillard*; struck down a Kentucky law requiring the posting of the Ten Commandments in pub-

lic schools, *Stone*; struck down Alabama's moment of silence statute, *Wallace v. Jaffree*, 472 U.S. 38 (1985); and held unconstitutional the mandated daily reading of Bible verses and the Lord's Prayer in public schools, *Abington Township Sch. Dist. v. Schempp*, 374 U.S. (1963). Significantly, in each of these cases, this Court held that the challenged conduct was motivated by a religious purpose, and disregarded the government's assertion of a sincere non-religious purpose.

Brief of ACLU in Opposition to Petition for Writ of Certiorari, *McCreary v. ACLU*, United States Supreme Court 03-1693, 2003, at 7 (available at **http:// www.oyez.org**).

Explain the Facts of *Every* Significant Case You Cite— Even If You Must Use a Parenthetical to Do So

Never discuss a significant case without explaining its facts. In an ideal world, we would discuss all cases in prose and do away with cumbersome parentheticals. But parentheticals remain a useful, if imperfect, tool for preserving large bodies of research. They are the key to writing deep, substantive papers because they flesh out the factual and procedural context in which cases are decided and condense vast amounts of research into a small space.

So write a factual parenthetical *every time* you cite a case but don't discuss that case in prose. (But you do not need factual parentheticals for cases that discuss boilerplate propositions of law, such as the standard of review or the burden of proof.) Although parentheticals admittedly slow the flow of your paper, the trained eye knows to peruse them quickly and their substantive benefit far outweighs the stylistic hiccup they create. Parenthetical are not perfect but using a parenthetical is better than losing the information.

Make Your Parentheticals Factual

Again, judges and partners likely know the law cold. But they need you to explain what that law means by showing how the law plays out in the cases. The job of a parenthetical—like the job of sentences—is to add *new* substantive information. So write parentheticals that add value by explaining what happened in the cases.

So if you have discussed the holding of the case in text, your parenthetical must do more than simply restate the holding. The best parentheticals summarize key facts about a case or the result, as in:

Treadway Companies, 638 F. 2d at 380 (refusing to require cooling-off period where tender offer occurred four months after corrective disclosure).

If needed, use parentheticals to explain why you cite a case, as in:

W. A. Krueger Co. v. Kirkpatrick, Pettis, Etc., 466 F. Supp. 800, 803 (D.C. Neb. 1979) (action for damages is limited to actual sellers and purchasers).

If you are using a parenthetical for multiple purposes, such as explaining facts and reasoning, you can keep each part of the parenthetical distinct by separating the two parts of the parenthetical with a semicolon, as in:

General Aircraft v. Lampert, 556 F.2d 90 (1st. Cir. 1977) (action by target corporation under Section 13D; finding irreparable harm would occur only if investors were allowed to continue activities without correcting schedule 13D).

Parentheticals should also explain the procedural result of the case, not simply the rule of law, as in:

General Aircraft v. Lampert, 556 F.2d 90 (1st. Cir. 1977) (requiring shareholder to amend its Schedule 13D and enjoining further acquisitions until amendment was filed).

If a case summarizes a body of law, give an overview of the law and cite to the summary case with a parenthetical stating *(collecting cases)*. Citing to the case that gives the overview of authority saves you the need to cite the historical cases individually. A parenthetical simply stating *(same)* may be appropriate in a string citation.

Do Not Use Parentheticals to Simply Quote the Case Law That Supports Your Paraphrase

Don't waste a parenthetical simply quoting the part of the case that supports your previous prose sentence. The quote adds nothing new and suggests that you don't trust your own prose paraphrase.

Think of Your Cases As Places

Lawyers use shorthand to avoid cumbersome references to case law or procedural history. Think of your cases as places and use *here* to refer to your client's case and *there* and *where* to refer to the precedent, as in *There, the court held that . . . .* or *Here, by contrast. . . .* Avoid phrases such as *the instant* or *present* case. Simply say *this* case.

Quote Sparingly

Judges and senior attorneys want you to summarize the cases for them. Quote from cases only if the language is extremely significant.

Introduce Quotations with Substantive Sentences

The sentences that introduce your quotation should summarize the quoted language. For example, introduce a quotation with a sentence, such as *In Smith v. Jones, the First Circuit also outlined the factors that determine whether more than a corrective disclosure is required.* An effective introductory sentence spares the reader the agony of actually reading the quote. Avoid introducing quotations with bland phrases that tell nothing about the material to follow, such as *In Smith v. Jones, the court held that. . . .*

Avoid Long Quotations

Long quotations beg not to be read. Readers *love* block quotes because the block format highlights just what part of the page they may skip. If you must include a long quote, consider breaking it up into smaller parts so that you can keep it in your paragraph. Begin with *The court stated that. . . .* Continue with *The court explained. . . .* Finally, conclude with *The Court cautioned. . . .*

Block Long Quotes

If you must quote a long passage of fifty words or more, set off that quote in block format: double space before and after the quote, single space within the quote and indent five or ten spaces at the left and right margins.

Accept Cases As Law

Phrases such as *According to the 9th Circuit* suggest that you don't believe the court's conclusion. You may not like an opinion but it is still the law.

Point out inconsistencies, contradictions or conflicting authority but accept that a reported opinion is the law of the jurisdiction until it is expressly reversed or implicitly overturned by later authority. It is obnoxious and arrogant to criticize a decision with language such as *In a poorly worded decision.* . . .

Weave Adverse Case Law into Your *Argument* or *Analysis*

Adverse case law rarely deserves a dedicated introductory sentence that flatly states its holding. If you break adverse case law into a separate section or paragraph, you may find yourself arguing the other side's case, no matter how carefully you distinguish that law. Instead, weave opposing authority into *your* argument and present it offensively by using transitional words such as *however* and *although*.

For example, if you are arguing that the corporate veil should not be pierced, you should not begin your discussion of a case allowing a pierce by stating, *In Jones v. Nasty Corp., the court pierced the corporate veil where Nasty Corp. was undercapitalized*. Rather, explain that *Although Jones v. Nasty Corp. allows a court to pierce the corporate veil where a corporation is undercapitalized, our client—unlike Nasty Corporation—is adequately capitalized*. As explained earlier, couch any troublesome authority in an *although* clause to dilute its impact. For example, say *Although courts will pierce where the corporation has committed fraud, Client X never misrepresented its identity*.

Summarize Statutes in Your Own Words

When discussing statutes, summarize them briefly. If you are quoting a statute, use the sentence that introduces the block quote to explain what the statute does. Strong writers spare readers the need to wade through statutory language. For example, in *Federal Election Commission*, 551 U.S. at 457, Justice Roberts introduced the Bipartisan Reform Act by explaining that it "significantly cut back on corporations' ability to engage in political speech." But include the full text of the statute if your reader will need to see the full text eventually. If need be, you can include the full text in a footnote or in an attachment. (But if the statutory language will eventually be included in a brief, don't simply scan the statutory language into an attachment because your reader cannot copy and paste from a scan.)

Nickname Statutes

Identify a statute, as in the *Americans with Disabilities Act* (the "*Disabilities Act*"), to simplify your writing and remind the reader that you have discussed the statute earlier in the paper. If possible, use the popular name of the Act, as in the *Consumer Protection Act*.

The Truth About Transitions | 23

It is not the strongest of the species that survive, nor the most intelligent, but the ones most responsive to change.
—Charles Darwin

WRITING—LIKE LIFE and music—is hardest at the transitions, so many legal writers worry how to transition effectively. But transitioning between sections and thoughts is easier than you may think. If you follow the principle of leading from the top, your leading sections and sentences function as transitions. In other words, you already know how to transition. You just don't know that you know.

Don't Spend Too Much Time on Transitions

Lawyers often spend too much time transitioning, not realizing that the form of legal writing enables us to transition quickly between topics. Because our readers are trained to be familiar with the forms in which we write, transitions between topics can be more abrupt than in civilian prose.

Rely on Your "Leads" to Transition the Reader

An effective opening and strong leads make the work of transitioning later in the paper much easier. If you have opened your paper effectively, you have already primed your readers about what to look for and you need to spend less time easing them between sections because they already know where you are going. Headings and lead sentences also serve as transitions because they tell the reader what to look for in the section or paragraph.

Put the Transition *After* the Heading

Unlike in civilian writing—where the transition often goes before the next heading—the transition in legal writing goes *after* the heading because the heading itself is a form of transition. Thus, the first paragraph or the first sentence after the heading serves as the transition to the new topic. Many legal writers mistakenly put the transition before the heading—a mistake that leads to cumbersome transitions, such as *This memorandum will now address.* . . .

Transition by Leading Each Paragraph with a Strong Summary Sentence

Lead each paragraph with a transition sentence that simply states the writer's conclusion about the next topic. Consider these lead sentences from Justice Roberts' opinion overturning the school assignment system in *Parents Involved in Community Schools*:

- ◆ "The principle that racial balancing is not permitted is one of substance, not semantics."
- ◆ "Jefferson County phrases its interest as 'racial integration,' but integration certainly does not require the sort of racial proportionality reflected in its plan."
- ◆ "Similarly, Jefferson County's use of racial classifications has only a minimal effect on the assignment of students."
- ◆ "The districts have also failed to show that they considered methods other than explicit racial classifications to achieve their stated goals."
- ◆ "The reasons for rejecting a motives test for racial classifications are clear enough."

551 U.S. at 732-735, 742.

Justice Breyer also used strong declaratory statements to transition between thoughts in his dissent in that same case. Note his focus on facts:

- ◆ "The historical and factual context in which these cases arise is critical."
- ◆ "Overall these efforts brought about considerable racial integration. More recently, however, progress has stalled."

- ◆ "In fact, the defining feature of both plans is greater emphasis upon student choice."
- ◆ "Experience in Seattle and Louisville is consistent with experience elsewhere."
- ◆ "Indeed, the consequences of the approach the Court takes today are serious."

551 U.S. at 804, 805, 846, 849, 861, 865.

Use Your Lead Sentence to Lay the Groundwork for Later Paragraphs

A lead sentence that provides an overview of your argument serves as the transition to later paragraphs, as well. If the reader already knows where you will be going, you need not waste time on careful transitions as you move to new topics.

For example, consider Justice Breyer's transitions to his section discussing the interest in stake in school desegregation cases in *Parents Involved in Community Schools*. There, Justice Breyer used his opening sentence to summarize the three major elements behind that interest and then addressed each element individually. In this passage, his opening sentence establishes the bridge for transitions to later paragraphs. Here is how he begins four successive paragraphs:

- ◆ "Regardless of its name, however, the interest at stake possesses *three essential elements*."
- ◆ "*First, there is a historical and remedial element*: an interest in setting right the consequences of prior conditions of segregation."
- ◆ "*Second, there is an educational element*: an interest in overcoming the adverse educational effects produced by and associated with highly segregated schools."
- ◆ "*Third, there is a democratic element*: an interest in producing an educational environment that reflects the 'pluralistic society' in which our children will live."

551 U.S. at 838–840 (emphasis added).

Use Pattern or Repetition to Transition

You can also begin successive transitional sentences by using parallel construction or even repetition to draw the reader back into the rhythm of your argument. Parallel construction and repetition also add emphasis.

For example, in the preceding passage from *Parents Involved in Community Schools*, Justice Breyer begins his discussion of each of the three elements of the interest at stake in school desegregation cases with the same language: "there is an [historical or educational or democratic] interest: an interest in . . . . " The return to the familiar phrase reminds the reader that we are returning to the test laid out in the introductory sentence.

Later, Justice Breyer concludes his dissent and adds emphasis by using rhetorical repetition. He begins each of his final paragraphs by asking:

- "*And what of* respect for democratic local decision making by States and school boards?"
- "*And what of* law's concern to diminish and peacefully settle conflict among the Nation's people?"
- "*And what of* the long history and moral vision that the Fourteenth Amendment itself embodies?"
- "Finally, *what of* the hope and promise of Brown?"

551 U. S. at 866-867 (emphasis added). The repetition pulls the reader back to Breyer's core argument and through his final paragraphs because Justice Breyer has conditioned his readers to look for the signal phrase *what of.*

Transition by Transferring Words from One Sentence to the Next

You can also move your reader along by picking up and explaining words used in preceding sentences. For example, in describing the Massachusetts Consumer Protection Act, you might explain that *A plaintiff must be a "person."* The next sentence would explain that *The definition of "person" is extremely broad.* Continue by explaining that *A "person" must be engaged in "trade or commerce."* Conclude by explaining that *"Trade or commerce" includes any commercial activity.*

For example, in his dissent in from *Parents Involved in Community Schools*, Justice Breyer transitioned between paragraphs by transferring words or concepts between lead sentences to successive paragraphs:

- "First, the race-conscious criteria at issue only help set the *outer bounds of broad ranges.*"
- "Second, *broad-range limits* on voluntary school choice plans are less burdensome, and hence more *narrowly tailored*, than other race-conscious restrictions this Court has previously approved."
- "Third, the manner in which the school boards developed these plans itself reflects *narrow tailoring.*"

551 U. S. at 846-848 (internal citations omitted and emphasis added).

Do Not Transition—Or Waste a Sentence—
Simply Announcing What You Will Do Next

Never write a transition sentence that simply tells the reader what you are going to discuss next, as in *I will now turn my attention to, A question still remains, I might add, It is interesting to note that* or *This paper next addresses.* A sentence that simply tells the reader what you will do next wastes space because it does not say something new or add value. Simply leap into the next topic.

Tell Your Reader What to Do Next 24

Hard writing makes easy reading. Easy writing makes hard reading.

      —William Zinsser, author of *Writing Well*

Tell Your Reader What to Do Next

Again, your readers are not reading your paper for the joy of it. They are reading because they have a question or a problem that they are expecting you to solve. Answer that question and conclude by telling your reader what to do next.

Don't Simply Restate Your Conclusion

Most writers think that it seems rude to simply drop the reader cold at the end of the *Analysis* or *Argument*. As we all know, a well-written paper requires some sort of closure. So many writers finish by restating their original conclusion but varying the language slightly so that their paper does not contain two paragraphs that say exactly the same thing. But a final conclusion that simply restates the original conclusion in slightly different words undercuts the impact of the original conclusion. The reader recognizes that the language has changed slightly and ends up comparing the two conclusions to ask how the conclusion has changed.

Rather than finish with a conclusion that simply varies the language of the original answer, finish your paper by looking to the future. Tell your reader the next steps they should take.

Don't Be Afraid to Tell Your Reader What to Do Next

Even as a newly minted lawyer, you should be able to make recommendations. Although making recommendations on the ultimate issue would be presumptuous for a new lawyer, senior lawyers rarely ask the newly initiated to decide that ultimate issue. So don't be afraid to make recommendations on your narrow topic and within your newly acquired sphere of learning.

In a Pleading, Finish by Reminding the Court What Relief You Are Seeking

In a court pleading, finish by telling the court exactly what you are asking the court to do. Be specific. For example, ask the court to order that the defendant produce its witness for deposition on January 10, or that it grant summary judgment on Counts I and II, or that it issue sanctions of $500 against the plaintiff.

Attach a Form of Order to a Pleading

Make it easy for the court to grant your relief by attaching an exact form of the order you are asking the court to authorize. If you have done your job well, the court will use your form.

Consider Attaching a *To Do* List to Internal Memoranda

If your paper suggests a long list of steps to take next, consider attaching a one-page *To Do* list. Your colleague or client can simply tear the checklist off and keep it as a guide. They would likely be making a checklist anyway—if only in their head—so simplify their life by doing it for them.

Citations | **25**

The cite wasn't helpful either. It . . . sent the court . . . to another dead end.
—Wisconsin Court of Appeals in *Espitia v. Fouche*,
314 Wis. 2d 507, 758 N.W. 2d 224, Fn. 5 (2008)
(fining lawyer $100 for citing case incorrectly)
(unpublished disposition)

Recognize the Substantive Value of Citations

Everybody hates citations and rightly so. They are clunky, dense and technical. And the legal profession can work itself into a frenzy trying to decide whether to do away with case citations for good in an effort to clean up legal writing.

But the quest for clean writing should not lead us to sacrifice content for form. Our jurisprudence is based on the rule of law and the certainty and predictability that comes from respect for precedent. Therefore, citations are an essential and substantive part of legal writing. Used well, they are an indispensable writing tool. They show the weight and persuasiveness of the authority you are citing. They also show that you have done your homework and are a trustworthy advocate. Parentheticals, in particular, provide a shorthand way of condensing the facts, the procedure and the results of cases into a brief space—information that might be sacrificed if we were required to explain it in prose. Because I see citations as a substantive tool, I've put most of my suggestions on handling case law in the Chapter 22 on *Talking about Cases and Other Authority*.

But let's use this chapter to discuss technical citation issues—the scary part of any citation.

Expect Citation Format to Change for the Better

As we move to a paperless world and our readers grow accustomed to reading briefs and memoranda online, our method of citing cases should change. Traditional citations, with their unwieldy book and page numbers are a design defect—visual hiccups that make legal writing look archaic and unreadable:

> *San Francisco Real Estate Investment Trust v. Real Estate Investment Trust*, 701 F. 2d. 1000 (1st Cir. 1983).

Ideally, we would have a free, centralized database of cases so that we could simply hyperlink to the case itself. With a hyperlink to the case, the book and page reference would no longer be necessary because the brief or memorandum itself would be a complete research tool since it would link to all the cases. Thus, the simplified citation would contain the name of the case (so that we have a lingo for talking about the case) and the court and year (because they indicate the precedential value of the case)—but not the book and page reference. The pared-down citation would look like this:

> *San Francisco Real Estate Investment Trust v. Real Estate Investment Trust (1st Cir. 1983).*

Alternatively, we should able to preserve book and page information in comment boxes, leaving the substantive case information on the screen and preserving book and page information out of sight unless the reader needs it. Or, as we redesign legal documents in new mediums—mediums that have the functionality of web pages—book and page references could go in a side margin so that the reference information lines up with the case name in the sentence but no longer clutters the text itself.

For Now, Continue to Put Full Citations in the Body of the Paper—Not in Footnotes

But until we have a better alternative, the current convention of citing cases in text works well. Yes, some recent opinions follow a trend to move book and page references to footnotes. Yes, moving book and page information to footnotes makes the paragraph itself more readable. But dropping citation information to footnotes violates the essential design principle of proximity because it requires the reader to jump back and forth between footnote and text to piece together the complete citation. Thus, footnotes defeat the goal of keeping the reader's eyes moving seamlessly through the paper.

So if the case law is important to your paper—and the case law is essential in any research memorandum or any paper that will be filed in court—keep your full citation in prose. Although citations admittedly disrupt the flow of legal writing, it is more disruptive to require the reader to jump between text and footnote.

Unlike law review articles, litigation papers always cite cases in the body of the paper, rather than in footnotes, so judges and your colleagues expect to see citations in text. Therefore, you must follow established conventions until we have a better alternative and we don't have one yet.

In Business Law Papers, Put Cases in Footnotes If Your Colleagues Do So

Business law papers routinely drop citations to footnotes because transactional attorneys may be less concerned about the case law than about the structure of the deal. Follow the leader and use the format your colleagues use.

Never Use Endnotes

Citations should never go at the end of your paper. It's just too far for the reader to travel.

Put Your Citation in the Sentence If You Need to

Your citations will be less disruptive if you put them outside your sentence, rather than within a sentence. But although citations within a sentence are not ideal, they are often necessary. Again trained readers know to peruse them quickly so that they don't disrupt the flow of their reading. Put the citation at the beginning or end of the sentence, rather than the middle, as in: *In General Aircraft, 556 F. 2d at 95, the shareholder filed an inaccurate and misleading Schedule 13(d) three months after the statutory filing date.*

If You Do Cite in Footnotes, Keep the Name of the Court and the Year in the Prose Citation and Repeat *All* Citation Information in the Footnote

If you decide to ignore my advice and drop book and page references to footnotes, the prose reference within the paragraph should contain not only the name of the case, but the court and the year as well, because the court and the year both suggest the precedential value of a case. In turn, the footnote should contain *all* case information—the name, the book and page, the court and the year—to spare the reader the need to bounce from footnote back to text to piece together the complete citation. It is better to repeat information in the footnote than to ask the reader to go searching for that information in text. Remember your goal is to keep your readers' eyes moving.

Do Not Expect Anyone to Read Footnotes

And if you do drop your case citations to footnotes, understand that your reader will now ignore *all* your footnotes. The decision to use footnotes for citations has signaled the reader that your footnotes are unimportant. Therefore, if you drop your case citations to footnotes, don't put substantive material in footnotes. Footnotes are a place your reader should never need to go.

Don't Borrow Without Citing

Again, if you borrow another's work, you must cite the source. As discussed above, in Chapter 13 on *Honesty and Authorship*, several courts have recently held that unattributed borrowing—otherwise known as plagiarism—violates ethical obligations. While you may use briefs filed by other attorneys as research tools or as the skeleton for your own brief, you should never simply copy large sections of a brief or any other work.

Check Your Citations Carefully

In a rare display of almost-human concern for us mere mortals, the authors of *The Bluebook* concede that *"The Bluebook* can often be intimidating for new users." You don't say? But no matter how difficult cite checking may be, careful citation work will show attention to detail and lend credibility to your research. If you don't cite correctly, you will be labeled as sloppy—a label that is almost impossible to shake. Before you file any paper, use the cite-checking features on your search tools to finalize your citations. And take the time to double check any Internet citations so that you are sure the material is still available. Many lawyers insert a parenthetical after an Internet citation noting when the site was last checked, as in *(last accessed on December 2, 2010)*.

Use the Right Citation Manual

The local rules in many jurisdictions specify what guidebook you should use for citations. Some jurisdictions even specify a certain citation format. Many jurisdictions have their own guidebooks. California, for example, has the *California Style Manual* (although it also allows *The Bluebook*) and New York has the *Official Reports Style Manual* (better known as the *Tanbook*). Many local rules express a preference for vendor-neutral citations, recognizing that not all lawyers subscribe to services such as Westlaw or LexisNexis. So check your local rules before you begin drafting.

The most commonly used sources are the *ALWD Citation Manual* and *The Bluebook*. You must own one or the other and you must hope that you quickly become so proficient in citation formats that you rarely need to turn to either manual. The two manuals agree on most points.

Use the Common Introductory Signals Effectively

Effective use of citation format will enable you to condense vast amounts of research into brief passages. In particular, know the common introductory signals, such as *e.g.*, *contra, but see*, and *accord*. Used properly, these signals convey subtleties in your research. Remember that placing the *see* citation at the beginning of a citation does not turn that citation into a sentence.

Refer to Cases by the Name of a Party

Use the full case name the first time you introduce a case, as in *Arnold v. Jones*. In later references, refer to the case by the name of one party, as in *Arnold*. Don't say *the Arnold case*. The use of the word *case* will mark you as an amateur.

Italicize Case Names and Introductory Signals

The practice of underscoring case names and introductory signals developed because typewriters and early word-processing programs could not italicize. Although most style manuals provide that case names may be italicized or underscored, it makes sense to drop the older convention of underscoring now that word-processing programs can italicize. Educate your colleagues on this issue. Their innate fear of ever having to touch a style manual should make this argument a winner.

Again, Explain the Facts of Every Significant Case You Cite

Again, you must explain the facts of every case you cite, unless that case involves boilerplate law. If you don't discuss the facts of a case in prose, write a factual parenthetical to explain that case. Chapter 21, *The Analysis or Argument: General Thoughts*, explains how to write parentheticals so that they add substance to your paper.

Order Authorities Within String Citations Correctly

Cite the highest authority first—for example, the Supreme Court before Federal Courts of Appeals. Cite federal decisions before state decisions. Within each level of authority, put the most recent citations first. Arrange state decisions alphabetically by state and arrange citations within each state by rank, citing the highest authority first.

Set Off Citations Visually

Because parentheticals do interrupt the flow of your writing, use punctuation and placement to set them off visually. Group string citations at the end of the paragraph if you can. If you must cite within a sentence, put the citation at the beginning or end of the sentence. Putting the citation at either end of a sentence will also force you to keep your sentences short.

Use a Consistent Tense to Refer to Cases

Most lawyers prefer past tense, as in *In State v. Jackson, the defendant wore a white glove* or *There, the court held that . . . .* So use either past or present tense but don't switch between the two tenses.

Pinpoint Cite

Always include the precise page reference for cited material so that your reader doesn't end up jumping to find the page from which you pulled your quote. For example, say *Smith v. Jones, 400 F.2d 211, 222 (1st Cir. 1975)*.

Use a Book Reference, Rather Than *Supra*

Don't make your reader look back in your paper to piece together a citation. Again, your goal is to keep your readers' eyes moving and to make every citation as specific as possible. A *supra* citation—such *as Smith, supra at 222*—sends your reader scurrying back in your prose to find the book reference. Therefore, a *supra* citation violates the design principle that similar items should be near each other. Instead, repeat the book reference and say *Smith, 400 F.2d at 222*. If your reader will remember the name of the case, simply say *400 F.2d at 222*.

Use *Id.* Citations—But Not Too Many

Even though an *Id.* citation may also require your reader to look back in the paper, *Id.* citations are less troublesome than *supra* citations. Because an *Id.* citation refers to the immediately preceding citation, your reader would never have to wander far and an *Id.* citation is so short that it will rarely be disruptive. So, even though you should substitute the book reference for a *supra* citation, you do not need to substitute the book reference for an *Id.* citation.

But use your *Id.* citations as an editing signal. *Id.* citations at the end of two or more consecutive sentences usually mean the sentences can be combined.

Deep Editing 26

Rewriting ripens what you've written.
—Duane Alan Hahn

EDITING AND PROOFREADING are different skills. Deep editing is part of the art of writing. It is the kind of editing that a good writing coach might do for you and the kind that so many of us avoid. (Proofreading—the science of finding and correcting errors— is discussed in Chapter 27 on *Proofreading and Finalizing Your Work*.) Deep editing requires a systematic attack on your paper and an objective eye. While you must still keep your writing hat on, you must approach your writing as if you were a reader—or a plastic surgeon. Deep editing is precise, surgical work and it requires a well-tuned aesthetic sense.

Block Out Time for Self-Editing

Writing is editing. Leave time for rigorous self-editing because editing is the most important part of writing. Good writers are neurotic self-editors.

Edit with a Vengeance

Approach your paper as if you were a slightly deranged reader, with a knife in hand. Deep editing is driven by substance and requires you to review for structure, substance, sound, readability, appeal, clarity, and integrity.

Review Your Paper in *Print Preview*

You cannot edit effectively unless you can see what your work will look like to your reader. Edit at least once in hard copy. If you refuse to print for environmental reasons, then at least review your paper in *Print Preview* or the *Full Screen Reading View*.

Say Your Sentences Aloud

Writing is editing. Your first job is sentence-level editing to cure clutter and to check for plain English. Say each sentence aloud—if only in your head—to cure all sentence-level ills.

Edit for Structure

The craft of legal writing becomes an art through masterful use of structure and your structural edit may be your most challenging task. Again, use your outline—as captured in your headings—as the master document for proofing and fine-tuning the structure of your paper. If your outline is perfect, then the structural foundations of your paper are also sound.

First, focus on the *opening*:

- Does the paper "open" in the first page and a half?
- Does it begin by explaining the factual background or the "story" in two or three sentences?
- Is the issue obvious from the facts? If not, is the issue stated separately?
- Does the paper lead with a conclusion and is that conclusion stated in plain English? Is there a separate heading for your *Conclusion* so that the reader can find it easily?
- If the reader were to cut at the dotted line and read only the opening, would the reader understand the paper?

Second, pull your *headings* onto a single page and ask:

- Does the paper lead with the most important arguments?
- Are the main points highlighted with Roman numerals or primary headings?
- Are subsidiary points identified by indented subheadings?
- Does each heading lead logically into the next heading?
- Are headings correctly numbered?
- Do the headings run from general to specific?

Third, review the *body* of the paper (the *Analysis* or *Argument*):

◆ Does the *Analysis* or *Argument* support the conclusion?
◆ Does each section begin with an opening paragraph or sentence that summarizes the conclusion about that section in one sentence?
◆ Does each paragraph relate to its heading? (If not, create new headings.)
◆ Does each paragraph deal with only one topic? (If not, split the paragraphs.)
◆ Does each paragraph begin with a plain-English lead sentence that summarizes the paragraph?
◆ Does every sentence within that paragraph support that topic sentence?
◆ Does each sentence say something new? (Again, although the opening and the body of the paper repeat information, within the body of your paper, each sentence must say something new. Deleting repetitive sentences is one of your most important tasks as an editor because repetition slows the reader's movement through the paper.)
◆ Does the paper use signal phrases, such as *for example, by contrast, similarly* or *in particular* to tell the reader the function of a sentence? (But be careful to avoid beginning every sentence with a signal phrase or your sentences will sound formulaic.)
◆ Do the paragraphs and sentences flow from general to specific?
◆ Does the discussion of the case law clarify the "big picture" view of the research? Does it explain the weight of authority? The trends in the case law? The number of cases that address the issue?
◆ Does the paper discuss the facts and result of the cases?

Finally, have you made recommendations and told your reader what to do next?

Synthesize

You cannot appreciate a Monet or a Chuck Close with your nose two inches from the canvas. You must walk to the other side of the room and get some distance to appreciate the whole painting. So, too, you must get distance on your writing once you are through the more mechanical sentence-level and structural edits. Put your paper down. Think. What are your one, two or three key points? Do they sing through? Is the "big picture" view of the research clear? Is the paper balanced? Or are you spending too much time on minor points and, therefore, sounding defensive? What facts work? Are you playing to those strengths? Are you arguing points that are not essential to winning your case and effectively increasing your burden of proof? Are you arguing too many points so that the paper reads like an issue-spotting law-school exam rather than a piece of advocacy on behalf of a client?

If your paper is a research memorandum, have you culled the research down? If you include too much information, your reader may find that it is easier to read the research file itself, rather than wade through your paper.

Finally, are you being intellectually honest about the weaknesses of your case? Is the tone confident and integral?

Ask a Colleague for Comments

You have very smart friends. They are not only smart, they will also have a fresh perspective on your work. So ask a friend—preferably someone slightly senior—to review your paper. You'll be amazed at how insightful the comments will be. Friends don't let friends go unedited. And offer to return the favor. Editing other's work will make you a better writer.

Sleep on It

Take a long break—and get a night's sleep—before this final review. Writing ferments so the more time you leave between writing and editing, the better your editing will be. You'll be amazed at your insight if you approach your deep editing from a fresh perspective.

Proofreading and Finalizing Your Work **27**

I made a wrong mistake.

—Yogi Berra

So NOW YOU have you have mastered the art of written communication. You have self-edited your work to fine-tune structure, to nail down loose thoughts and to beat wordy constructions into plain English. Now you must turn your attention to the tedious, scientific task of proofreading.

Your work will live forever so it must be perfect. Sloppy proofreading errors detract from your credibility and will drive your colleagues to distraction. When senior attorneys complain to me about a young lawyer's work, they invariably focus on minor proofreading errors. This laser focus on perfection—justified, or not—means that you, too, must focus on proofreading. Senior lawyers and judges are crazy about the little things so you must aim for perfect. Yes, perfect is the enemy of done. But in the legal world, you are not done until it is perfect.

Failing to perfect your paper could damage your reputation permanently. In 2004, a federal district court judge in the Eastern District of Pennsylvania reduced the fees due to a lawyer by $30,000 where the court considered the lawyer's work "careless, to the point of disrespectful." In a scathing opinion, the court gleefully repeated some of its favorite typographical errors and characterized those errors as "epidemic." The court commented that "If these mistakes were purposeful, they would be brilliant. However, based on the history of the case and [the attorney's] recent filings, we know otherwise."

Devore v. City of Philadelphia, 2004 WL 414085 (E.D. Pa. Feb. 20, 2004). (Also available on **www.findacase.com**.)

The opinion has been widely discussed on the Internet—increasing its visibility on search engines. You never want to find yourself in the position where a Google search of your name delivers a scathing indictment of your abilities.

Go to the Zone

Again, proofreading is a different skill than writing or editing and it requires a different mindset. As you take this final pass at your paper, you must resist the urge to think the big thoughts. Ignore content. Get out your magnifying glass and drop down to the level of sentences and individual words.

Divide Tasks

Rather than reading your paper through from beginning to end, approach each proofreading task separately. First, read sentence by sentence for syntax errors. Next, check spelling. Next, check those troublesome end-of-line divisions to be sure that words are correctly divided. Next, check formatting and design issues. If you approach each proofreading task separately, you will assure that you complete each proofreading task and that you give each task the attention it needs.

Spellchck

Oops! I mean spell-check. *Spellcheck* is annoying—and annoyingly smart. It should be your front-line defense against embarrassing spelling errors. It won't catch misused words (such as *there* instead of *their* or *principal* instead of *principle*) but it will catch most of your spelling errors.

Many lawyers avoid spell-checking because *Spellcheck* highlights many legal terms as spelling errors. However, if you add these words to your custom dictionary, *Spellcheck* will stop chastising you every time you use these words. Simply right click on the squiggled word, and click the bold-faced word that appears at the top of the pop-up box to add it to your dictionary. Add common legal terms, client's names and technical terms that you use frequently.

Actually *Read* Your Work

Spellcheck will not reliably differentiate between common homonyms such as *there* and *their* or catch properly-spelled-but-misused words such as *complaint*, instead of *compliant*. (The *Usage and Punctuation Guide* lists commonly misused homonyms.) Read backward, sentence by sentence, to pick up errors.

Put a Check Beside Each Paragraph As You Read

Once you are satisfied with the overall structure of the paragraph, treat each paragraph as if it were an island. Work forward—or backward—paragraph by paragraph. Once you are satisfied with a paragraph, put a check beside it. For some reason, putting checks beside each paragraph will force you to slow down and read carefully.

And if you are really concerned about your errors, treat each sentence as an island. Work backward, sentence-by-sentence within each paragraph. Again, this technique will slow you down just enough to give you a laser-like eye for error.

Review Headings Separately from Text

Again, substantive headings are an editing tool because they verify a strong foundation. Therefore, even if your paper does not require a separate table of contents, pull your headings onto a single page and review separately. Are headings correctly numbered? (Again, confusing standard numbering will make your headings work against you, rather than for you.) Does each heading lead into the next? Are all headings written in parallel grammatical structure? Are subheadings correctly labeled?

Use Your Word-Processing Program to Help You Proofread

Use the *Autocorrect* function to correct proper nouns that you often misspell, to be sure you are using your chosen identifying terms throughout, or to assure consistent usage (such as % instead of *percentage* or *its* instead of *it's*). Set up *Grammar Check* to require periods inside quotations. (Click on the *File* tab/click *Options*/select *Proofing/*in the box for *When correcting grammar and spelling in Word*, click *Setting*/click *Punctuation required with quotes*/select *Inside*.)

Use the *Find* function to weed out pesky constructions and common punctuation errors. Search for *by* to weed out passive voice and for *ment* and *ion* to weed out nominalizations. Weed out pesky adverbs by searching for *ly*.

Edit in a View That Shows What the Printed Document Will Look Like

Again, as you get close to finishing your paper, work in a view that shows what your paper will look like when printed, such as *Print Layout* or—my favorite view—*Full Screen Reading View*. If you have been working with *Track Changes* turned on and are not ready to *accept all changes*, review the document in *Final* view, without markups showing. (Click the *Review* Tab/go to the *Tracking* box/keep *Track Changes* enabled/select *Final* (not *Final Show Markup*)). Editing in these views is similar to editing on hard copy—only better because you can make the actual corrections as you go.

The *Print Preview* view is particularly useful for catching formatting errors. (To get to *Print Preview* view, click on *File* and select *Print* or use *CTRL+F2*. The *Print Preview* view will show on the right of your screen.) Scroll through your paper quickly, using the *page up* and *page down* keys, to review for formatting and style. For example, scroll through to check that all Roman-numeral or primary-level headings are written in parallel construction, such as sentences or phrases. Now go back to the beginning and review each heading quickly for consistency in capitalization, such as the use of initial caps. Now scroll through even more quickly to be sure that those headings are sequentially numbered. Finally, page through at warp speed to check indents and line-spacing. Next, look for any tables to be sure that they are all aligned correctly. Now check page numbers. Next, drop down to your subheadings or secondary headings and run those headings through the same levels of review. If you page through very quickly, your eye will easily pick up on any problems with margins, indents or spacing. Indeed, as you proof some of these design elements, your eye can stay in the same place on the screen—making it easier to pick up things like a shift in indents or margins.

Yes, this is a multi-step process but each step goes quickly. And the errors show up in neon lights if you are focusing a laser eye on looking only for that type of error.

Scrub *Track Changes* and Any Other Editing History Before Filing or Sending Any Paper

Listen up because this is really important. Never send a paper that was edited in *Track Changes* to anyone outside your office without first scrubbing the document of editing history and comments. The editing history could embarrass you or your client or provide opposing counsel with free ammunition. Your opposing counsel does not need to see comments to a paragraph in your brief explaining that a certain case goes against your position, but that you have decided not to cite that case. Your opposing counsel does not even need to know when you created and edited the document or even how long you worked on the document.

The Lawyer's Guide to Microsoft Word 2007 contains an excellent discussion of this issue. The author, Ben Schorr, strongly suggests that you instruct *Word 07* to warn you before you save or send a file that has been edited with *Track Changes*. (Click on the *File* tab/select *Options*/go to the *Trust Center* box/click on *Trust Center Settings*/check *Warn before printing, saving or sending a file that contains track changes or comments*.) The author also suggests that you avoid the common practice of working from existing briefs, because existing documents may still contain metadata. He advises that you copy the text of those documents into templates instead.

Turning off *Track Changes* is not enough to scrub your paper. You must have the Document Inspector check your paper for any hidden metadata. (Click the *File* tab/In the *Prepare for Sharing* box, click *Check for Issues*/click the *Document Inspector*/Instruct *the Document Inspector* to *Remove All*: (1) *Comments, Revisions, Versions, and Annotations*; (2) *Document Properties and Personal Information*; (3) *Custom XML Data*; and (4) *Hidden Text*.

You should also be sure to turn off any highlighting. (Click the *File* tab/click *Options*/click *Display*/turn off *Show highlighter marks*.)

Using Design As a Writing Tool | **28**

Good prose should be transparent, like a windowpane.
—George Orwell, *Why I Write*

THE INTERNET HAS changed how the world reads and accesses information. Think about your expectations for your favorite news site. You expect pictures, video clips, links to sources, and the ability to comment and obtain news alerts that interest you.

Now think about that brief you are writing. Although we now file documents electronically, those documents are still formatted as if they were written on paper. Supporting information, such as cases or exhibits, is usually not accessible without going to another source, such as LexisNexis, Westlaw or an appendix.

As we move beyond electronic filing to widespread electronic *reading*, the options for designing briefs and legal documents should expand enormously. The ideal brief would be a complete research document, with links to cases, affidavits, deposition testimony and exhibits

In particular, our way of citing cases must change. We need a centralized database of cases so that we can simply hyperlink to cited cases. With a centralized database and hyperlinks in briefs, the judge could simply click through to a cited case and then skip from that case to other cases.

Once we can create hyperlinks to cases, we should finally be able to do away with the cumbersome book and page citations that have marred legal writing for eons. We should also have the option of designing call-out boxes for key cases—much like the commenting functionality that is now standard in word-processing programs. We could use those call-out boxes to explain the facts and law of cited cases in more detail, so that the reader has easy access to the information if they want it, but the information is not cluttering up the text itself.

The design of our papers should also change to take advantage of new technology. We can already include internal links to sections within a paper and do fancy formatting. But briefs may someday look more like web pages, with tabs to major sections and links to exhibits or deposition testimony. Imagine a home page for a brief that showed the headings to your argument, your proposed form of an order, and links to key cases. Imagine tabs or links to exhibits, affidavits and deposition testimony—even links to videotaped deposition testimony.

These types of changes would give our readers more control over their reading experience and provide for a deeper, more interactive exchange. Yes, that loss of control over our readers may frighten many lawyers who feel that we must require our readers to walk sequentially through our argument by flipping or scrolling through numbered pages. But, even with paper documents, we don't really control our readers. Our readers are already reading selectively and choosing where to focus and what to skip. We give them headings partly so they can make these choices intelligently. So we must concede that, even now, we cannot totally manage how our readers approach our writing.

If we can give our readers more control over their reading experience, we may find that they reward us by being more engaged. Reading on paper is a flat, two-dimensional experience. But reading a well-designed web page on a screen is a deep, multi-dimensional experience. It's simply more engaging. We live in an interactive world, and lawyers should take advantage of any design opportunity that makes our readers more likely to listen to us.

But, until then, we are still trapped in an 8.5-by-11-inch world. In the confines of that tiny space, certain design principles will make your paper easier on the eye. If your paper is easy on the eye, it is more likely to be read and it will certainly be easier to understand.

Your reader's first snap judgments about the quality of your paper are likely to be based on design, not substance. Those first impressions count enormously so design is an essential tool for presenting your ideas and telling your reader what type of advocate you are.

Use Modern Design Principles— Especially Alignment and Proximity— to Highlight the Structure of Your Paper

Use design to lay out your words carefully rather than just spreading the words haphazardly throughout the paper. Avoid visual clutter and aim to create sharp, professional-looking papers.

In an excellent survey of design principles, *The Non-Designer's Design Book*, Robin Williams highlights the four foundations of design: contrast, repetition, alignment and proximity. Of these four principles, alignment and proximity are essential tools in the design of legal documents.

Indents are structural tools because the alignment or indentation of headings is a visual clue suggesting how important a heading is. Headings at the left margin—Roman-numeral headings or primary headings—are the most important. The indent before a subheading or a secondary heading signals that an issue is subsidiary to the main point. The deeper the indent, the more subsidiary the issue. Scroll through your document to review each layer of headings as a group and to check that you have formatted and indented each layer of headings consistently.

Proximity is an equally vital guiding principle. Keep related items close together. For example, if your paper surveys the types of relief available for a violation of the securities laws, paragraphs discussing each type of relief should be grouped next to each other. Similarly, keep citation information near the case discussion—meaning in text. Again, putting citations in footnotes violates the design principle of proximity because it requires the reader to bounce around on the page to piece together the full citation.

My favorite reference on the design of legal papers is a jewel of a website, *Typography for Lawyers*, by Matthew Butterick. This careful, substantive site covers essential topics such as choosing a font and laying out text on the page. Butterick's recent book, titled *Typography for Lawyers*, covers design questions in more detail and also addresses many of the word-processing questions that bring great legal minds to their knees, such as how to keep headings and paragraphs from getting separated by a page break. Both the website and the book are listed in the bibliography.

Keep Your Design Conservative

While you should consider principles of modern design in laying out your paper, remember that the legal profession is not the advertising profession. Don't be too flashy or slick. Never let design overpower content.

Leave White Space

How big is your text footprint? Aim to walk lightly on the page. White space is polite because it gives the reader a rest. It's the reader's favorite part of any paper.

White space is also the best visual clue you can give your reader about the structure of your paper because it shows where you are shifting thoughts and it makes structure visual. In a shorter paper, such as a letter to a client, single spacing makes the structure of your work more apparent. In longer works, such as briefs or memoranda, double spacing (or 1.5-line spacing) is usually easier on the eye.

Here are some ways to add white space:

- Create wide margins.
- Double space between paragraphs.
- Double space before and after headings.
- Leave extra space before beginning a new Roman-numeral or primary heading.
- Increase the spacing between major sectional breaks, such as between the opening and the body of the paper.
- Insert a centered, light line between major sections. This line works especially well in letters and looks like this:

Focus on the Headings

Again, headings are the key to readability. Most readers skim headings before deciding whether to read more deeply. Headings, sub-headings and section breaks highlight structure and provide visual relief. Therefore, design your headings so that they command your readers' attention. Key headings, such as your Roman-numeral or primary headings, should be anchored at the left margin, rather than centered. (Subsidiary headings should be indented from the left margin.) Keep your heading with its text so that you don't end up with a lonely heading at the bottom of a page. (Work in an approved template to avoid widowed or orphaned lines. If you are still having a problem, select the heading and text that you want to keep together. On the *Page Layout* tab, go to the *Paragraph* box/click on the icon for more options/select *Line Spacing Options*/select *Line and Page Breaks*/ check *keep lines together*.)

Choose an Appealing Font

Choose an appealing, readable font. Use a serif font for body type. (Serifs are the horizontal lines at the top and bottom of letters.) Serif type is more readable than sans serif type because it gives the reader a horizontal line to follow. (Remember that cigarette manufacturers used to put health warnings in sans serif fonts.) Use sans serif fonts only in headings.

Century and Garamond are all good choices for body type. But standard operating fonts, such as Times New Roman, are so ubiquitous that they can never be compelling. And resist the urge to use trendy new fonts. Again, Matthew Butterick's website and his recent book, both titled *Typography for Lawyers,* are the ultimate resource for all font-related questions.

But always begin by checking court rules before getting too creative with your font choice. The Federal Rules of Appellate Procedure, for example, require "a proportionally spaced or a monospaced face" and even specify that proportionally spaced fonts must include serifs. *See* Fed. R. App. P. 32 (a) (5).

Choose a Standard Type Size

Be considerate of your readers and choose a readable-size type. Most local rules require size 12. Don't ever try to shrink wordy writing down by reducing the font size. Reducing the font size is cheating and it's mean to anyone over 40.

Put Your Firm's Brand on Any Paper That Goes to a Client

Since a firm's most important product is often its writing, most documents produced by a firm should show the firm's logo. Certainly any memoranda that goes to a client should show the firm's logo. However, briefs filed in court should not contain a logo because the logo smacks of advertising and is inappropriate in a judicial setting. A logo may also be too slick for the image you want to present to a judge or a jury.

Use Headers, Footers and Page Numbers

Don't forget to number pages. Use headers (or footers) where appropriate, such as in the second and subsequent pages of letters.

Don't Justify the Right Margins

Justifying the right margins will spread the words out within lines and create strange spacing. Lawyers are used to a jagged right edge.

Review Your Document in PDF

Before filing a pleading electronically in PDF, review it in PDF. Some fonts may lose their integrity on conversion to PDF. The local rules for many courts list which fonts transfer well to PDF and which fonts lose integrity. Keep in mind that font size may shrink slightly when it is converted to PDF.

Use Visuals

Charts, graphs and diagrams make information easier to process and make text appear less relentless. The outstanding resources on how to present qualitative information are Edward R. Tufte's, *The Visual Display of Quantitative Information*, 2nd Edition (Graphics Press, 2001) and its two companion books, *Envisioning Information*, 2nd Edition (Graphics Press 1990) and *Visual Explanations* (Graphics Press 1997).

Trust Your Charts to Tell the Story

Remember that charts should not repeat information in text. The purpose of a chart is to make information easier to digest. If you put the information in text as well, you are asking your readers to do twice the work and you are defeating the purpose of the chart.

Break Up Lists with Numbers

Even well-known lists—such as the five parts of misrepresentation—should be set off with numbers. The numbers make each item easier to identify and provide a numerical reference for later discussion of those items.

Use Bullets but Use Them Judiciously

Bullets allow you to write without transitional words and are invaluable for organizing simple material or lists. But be wary of simplifying complex material to fit in a bulleted format or you may find yourself sacrificing content for form—the fatal flaw of many a PowerPoint presentation.

Always know your audience. Bullets work well in letters and intra-office memoranda but may be too informal for documents filed in court.

Never Bullet Case Law

You should almost never bullet case law. If you bullet case law, your paper may end up looking like a simple transcription of your research notes—leading your reader to wonder if you understand the purpose of a research memorandum.

Be Careful of Grammar in Bullets

Many writers make grammatical errors when using bullets. In particular, they write bullets in which the front end of the sentence (the part before the colon) and the back end (the bulleted part) don't fit together. Mentally glue these two halves of the sentence together and read the glued version aloud to be sure it is grammatically correct. (The *Usage and Punctuation Guide* discusses parallel construction in bullets in more detail and provides examples.)

Punctuate Bullets Correctly

Bullets are a new style so many writers question how to format them. In a nutshell, you should:

- Put a colon at the end of the phrase of sentence that introduces the bullet.
- Capitalize the first word in the bullet.
- If the bullet is a word or a phrase, don't put any punctuation at the end (except the last bullet will take a period).
- If the bullet is a sentence, put a period at the end.
- Do not put *and* at the end of the penultimate bullet.
- Put a period at the end of the last bullet.

In other words, your bullets should look like my bullets above. (Again, the *Usage and Punctuation Guide* addresses your burning questions about bullets.)

Keep Bullets Simple and Clean

Bullets are not effective if spread over more than two facing pages because they become too visually complicated. Similarly, avoid bullets within bullets. The absence of any hierarchy will make the bulleted points hopelessly confusing.

Use Graphic Features Selectively

Use **boldface**, *Italics,* and <u>underscoring</u> to structure your work. *Italics* are particularly useful because they tell the reader just where to focus in a sentence and greatly reduce reading time.

But avoid overly complicated visuals, such as switching between fonts, overdoing the boldfaces, or using too many typefaces. Aim for a clean, uncluttered look. Be a minimalist.

Never Use ALL CAPS

All caps look ANGRY. If you want to add emphasis, use italics. The only place where you may use ALL CAPS is in your structural headings, such as the *Introduction*, the *Conclusion* or the *Analysis*, but I prefer to see even these structural headings in initial caps only.

Do Not Use Underscoring Except in Headings

Underscoring in text is not a modern style. Again, use italics instead.

Use *Print Preview* to Check Design Elements

Again, never print a document out without reviewing it first in *Print Preview.* (Again, to get to *Print Preview*, click on the *File* tab and select *Print*. The *Print Preview* view will show on the right of the screen.) Scroll through pages rapidly in *Print Preview*, using *the Page Up* and *Page Down* keys, to visually review design elements. Have you left enough white space? Have you spaced consistently before and after each heading and between paragraphs? Are the indents for each layer of heading consistent? Then check paragraphs and continue down the chain of design elements until you are sure you have a clean, appealing document.

Working with Junior Colleagues **29**

It is not often that someone comes along who is a true friend and a good writer. Charlotte was both.
—E. B. White, *Charlotte's Web*

ONE OF THE biggest challenges any lawyer faces is working with other lawyers—particularly junior colleagues who may still be getting their feet wet, or worse, drowning as they struggle to put words on paper. If a colleague is flailing, that colleague's problem is now your problem because a drowning person can take you down with them. Perhaps he should have mastered the art of legal writing earlier. Perhaps you have thrown her in over her head. But either way, your job is to throw your colleague a lifeline and to teach the skills that young lawyer needs to play on your team. Your job is to work with the *writer*, not just the writing.

Ranting at the moon won't solve the problem of the young lawyer who can't write and it certainly won't fix a disastrous paper. Instead, you should approach your work with junior colleagues as systematically as you would approach writing a major appellate brief. First, you must give out the assignment in a thoughtful, productive way. Second, you must edit your colleague's work efficiently and effectively. Finally—and this is the hard part—you must give your young friend constructive comments and you must do so in a way that promotes learning and collegiality. You are both on the same team and their success will ultimately reflect well on you.

Let's talk about each of these three steps in turn.

1. Giving Out the Assignment

Control the final product by how you give out the assignment

Control the quality of the work you will get back by explaining the project thoroughly when you assign it. Sharing information at the starting line promotes quality at the finish line.

Explain the facts

In particular, young lawyers are often handicapped in their research because senior attorneys have not explained the background facts to them. Don't simply explain the legal issue. Explain what the case is about. Otherwise, your colleagues will not be able to determine what cases are the most analogous.

Explain what has already been done

Be clear about where the case stands now. Your colleagues need to know what has already been accomplished in order to avoid duplication and to take advantage of available resources.

Explain what the assignment will be used for

Explain the result so that your colleagues can focus on that result as they research and write. For example, if you are planning to move for summary judgment, explain that goal early on so that your colleagues can focus their research on cases that were decided on summary judgment.

Explain what you know already about the law

You don't need to provide an introductory course on *Summary Judgment Standards 101*, but if you know that a key case addressed your issue, you should share that case when you assign the project. You are all on the same team. Every aspect of every assignment does not need to be a test.

Provide models

Most errors are formatting errors. Give models to show what you want the document to look like and as an example of your preferred style. Providing models is the best way to guarantee that you will like what you get back.

Be clear about expectations

How much time should your colleague spend on a project? How long should the paper be? Head off surprises early on.

Share the client's quirks

Does the client use specific terminology? Does the client want to avoid certain characterizations? Is the client unusually sensitive to certain issues? If so, do tell.

Ask your colleague to check back in

Avoid getting blindsided by problems late in the game. If the project is complicated or if you have concerns about whether the project will come back in a perfect form, insist that your colleagues touch base early in their research or writing.

Insist on self-editing

If you expect a perfect draft, be clear about your high expectations.

Set artificial deadlines

Leave yourself time to respond to last-minute surprises by setting artificial deadlines. Artificial deadlines are not artificial in a crisis.

Avoid writing by committee

If you parcel the sections of a brief among many lawyers, the final brief may not hang together as a whole because the style will be inconsistent. Sections may repeat and the flow will be lost. One brief deserves one author. If you must parcel out sections, assign one person to supervise the whole project and meld the brief together.

Assign research and writing to the same person

Legal writing is built on research, so try to have the same person do the research and the writing. If you assign the research and writing to different people, the final written product may lack the depth that comes from a deep understanding of the cases.

2. Editing Work from Junior Colleagues

Defend yourself against deep editing by appropriate staffing

Deep editing is time consuming—often more time consuming than it might have been to write the original draft yourself. If you consistently find yourself having to rework a junior colleague's writing, ask a mid-level colleague (or even an outside writing coach) to play editor and teacher.

Apply the key principles for effective writing as you edit

Most of your editing comments will boil down to the first two principles of strong writing—use plain English and lead from the top. (The third principle—tell the reader what to do next—is less important in the editing process.) Keep these two principles in mind as you edit.

Edit in two rounds

Read quickly through the paper once to assess the paper and make obvious plain-English edits. Use your second reading for deep editing. (Both levels of editing are discussed below.)

Aim to go beyond line-by-line comments

Effective teaching requires that you do more than simply correct the paper or make comments in *Track Changes*. Again, you must work with the writer, not just the writing. In addition to line-by-line comments, you will eventually need to explain your two or three most important concerns about the paper. (Pardon the cliché, but these are your "take away" points.) As you edit, keep a mental list prioritizing these concerns. Later, you will want to meet with your colleague for five minutes to explain your concerns.

Never use red pen

High school is over. Use purple or blue ink or work in *Track Changes*.

Round One—Assess and Edit for Plain English

- **Assess the paper.** On your first reading, aim to fix obvious plain-English issues and to identify strong points.
- **Use codes to assign a value to each sentence or paragraph.** As you read, make marks in the right hand column to identify the terrific, the good, the bad and the deeply mysterious. A good coding system will guide you as you rewrite the paper in the second round.

    I use these marks:

    ☆   Aha! (You will probably only have two or three *Aha!* moments in any paper.)
    √   Good. (Good point. Something you can work with.)
    ⸮   Huh? (Confusing, something you need to come back to. I squiggle about one third of most papers I read.)
    X   You've got to be kidding me. (Junk or repetitive material.)

- **Edit for obvious plain English.** On your first reading, you should also catch any obvious sentence-level clutter or awkwardness. At this point, most of your sentence-level edits will be deletions to remove clutter. Simply say the sentence aloud. If you would not use a word or phrase in conversation with a colleague, don't let it stay in the writing.

◆ **Take a deep breath.** If the paper needs deep editing, you are now ready to begin that challenging task.

Round Two—Deep Editing

◆ **Draw a line below the "opening."** Review the structural headings (the *Introduction* and the *Conclusion* or the *Facts*, the *Issue*, the *Conclusion* and the *Analysis* or *Argument*). Draw a heavy line before the *Analysis* or *Argument* begins. The section above your hand-drawn line is the "opening." Ideally, it is no more than a page and a half. That opening must explain three things: the story, the issue and the answer. The paragraphs before this line should summarize *everything* in the paper. If the opening is not working, ninety percent of your editing time will be spent above your hand-drawn line.

◆ **Look for the story.** Yes, *you* already know the facts but the judge or the next person in your firm who calls up the paper on your document management system will not. Every paper should begin with two or three sentences that tell the "story" and "set the stage." Who are the parties? Which one is your client? (In other words, which way do you want to come out on the issue?) How do they know each other? What is the problem?

◆ **Focus on the *Answer*.** Nothing else really matters. Aim for a few sentences summarizing the paper in plain English. Again, imagine a quick exchange as you are getting on the elevator and your colleague is getting off. The fingers-in-the-door answer to your question asking how the research is going is the *Answer*. If the *Answer* needs work, build on the *Aha!* moments you have already noted in the margins of the paper.

Or, even easier, wait until you can ask the writer about his or her conclusion. Even if your colleague has failed to present a clean answer in the paper, he or she will usually respond with a brief, plain-English conclusion. Once you have elicited this jewel, capture it in writing.

◆ **Jot down your two or three major headings.** You are the expert. If you drafted the paper yourself, what would the three major headings be?

◆ **Review headings separately from text.** Now review the substantive headings within the *Analysis* or *Argument*. Do these substantive headings highlight the major headings you have identified? If not, move paragraphs around to fit under your headings.

- **Read the introductory sentence to each paragraph.** Each paragraph must begin with one sentence summarizing the entire paragraph in the writer's own words. Indeed, you should be able to read only the first sentence to each paragraph and understand the entire paper. If the body of the paper is not effective, the problem likely stems from the writer's failure to write these summary sentences.

- **Look for lost lead sentences at the end of paragraphs.** If a paragraph is missing its lead sentence, look to the last sentence in the paragraph. New writers often bury the lead sentence at the end of the paragraph, rather than putting it at the beginning of the paragraph, where it belongs.

- **Make each sentence say something new.** Within the paragraph, each sentence must say something new—by developing the topic, however slightly, or by explaining new information about a case. Repetition within the body of the paper destroys momentum, so delete any repetitive sentences. If a sentence causes you to pause and wonder about its purpose, it is likely repetitive and should come out.

- **Use signal words.** Make sure that sentences use signal words to signal the purpose of a sentence. Look for words such as *first, second, third, for example, similarly, in particular, by contrast, again, also* and *finally.*

- **Edit for plain English.** As you work your way through your deep edit, continue editing for plain English. Simply say each sentence aloud, if only in your head, to cure all sentence-level ills.

- **Look for the "big picture" summary of the research.** The reader should not be required to determine which cases are the weight of the authority or which case is the most analogous. Similarly, the most important research result is often what the writer could *not* find. Make sure the paper summarizes the "big picture" view of the research. Look for phrases such as *No reported case has ever held that. . . . , The great weight of authority holds that. . . . , Only one case has ever held that. . . . ,* or *Courts routinely hold that. . . .*

- **Look for the facts of the precedent.** The law behind any case is a bore but the actual result will flesh out that law and push the paper deeper. Unless a case involves boilerplate propositions of law, insist that your colleague share the facts of every case discussed in the paper. Ask for at least a few words in a parenthetical that tell you what the case was about or what the court decided. Generally, the reader should never have to look at the cases themselves.

Step back

After completing any line-by-line edits, step outside the four corners of the document. What worked? What didn't? What is missing? Is the paper integral? Is the writer playing to strong points? Is the tone offensive, rather than defensive?

Identify your take-away points

Now step back again to assess your own edits. What are your two or three major comments on the writing? These are the teaching points you need to pass on to your colleague to turn them into a meaningful member of your writing team.

3. Giving Comments to Junior Colleagues

Give comments in person

You can couch concerns about a project in an appropriate tone if you take the time to deliver those comments in person so take five or ten minutes to talk with the writer. Lawyers must be mentors. Comments made in *Track Changes* fix the paper but may not change the writer. Your major teaching points will come across more clearly if you present them in person.

Sit next to your colleague and work from the paper itself

Ideally, sit next to each other at a table and keep the paper between you. The paper gives you something to look at other than each other.

Work with the writer, not the writing

Be thorough, professional—and kind. You are speaking to a colleague so you must be collegial. Your goal should be to mentor the person, not just perfect a piece of writing.

Give comments, not criticism

Biting criticism destroys morale and motivation. You can't build a team if your comments leave them wanting to play for someone else.

Keep advice neutral

In international negotiations, countries meet on neutral territory. So, too, you should meet with your young colleague in the neutral territory of ideas and thoughts and avoid personal attacks. Writing is already intensely personal, so personal comments can be devastating. Avoid comments directed at the person, such as *You are disorganized* or *You misunderstood the statute.* Instead, present paper-specific advice, such as *Reorder arguments A and B.*

Say something nice

Tell the writer at least one thing they are doing right and build on those strengths. For example, find the one time that the writer wrote an effective lead sentence to a paragraph and explain, "I like the way you opened this paragraph." Then suggest they use that technique again elsewhere.

And you can always find *one* nice thing to say. I once struggled to find that one good thing an unusually difficult paper. I finally settled on "nice choice of language to quote." If nothing else, young writers usually research effectively, even if they struggle in presenting that research. Acknowledge that contribution.

Limit your comments

A paper covered with ink leaves the writer confused about what changes are important and what changes are odd stylistic quirks. (Only writing coaches are allowed to comment in grand fashion.)

Focus on the opening of the paper

Again, ninety percent of your editing happens in the first page-and-a-half of the paper, otherwise known as the all-important opening. Focus your comments on the opening because that is the most valuable real estate in any paper.

Focus on two or three teaching points

What are the two or three major flaws in the paper? Does the paper fail to emphasize an important argument? Is the opening ineffective? Are lead sentences missing? By limiting your meeting comments to the most important points, you ensure that this writer will take away major teaching points that they can then to apply to the next paper.

Make advice specific

Be as specific as possible in your comments. For example, ask your colleague to put the *Brief Answer* on the first page, to reduce the *Answer* to two sentences, or to use headings. Point out what changes should be made. Comments such as *too long* or *too disorganized* are too vague to be effective.

Couch advice in terms of general rules

Try to phrase advice as a general teaching point that your colleague can apply to the next paper. For example, I frequently found myself deleting sentences within paragraphs because I felt that the offending sentences disrupted the flow of a topic. While I was always able to point to the specific breakdown in the flow, I had trouble articulating a general writing rule that might help the attorney on their next project—until I realized that sentences that did not say something new tended to stop the forward momentum of a paper. Now, when I delete those sentences, I can explain the rule: make each sentence say something new. (If you are at a loss for general rules, review Chapter 35, *The Nutshell Summary of This Book*. Chances are that you'll find the rule you need listed there.)

Use the word we

Use team language, such as *Can we improve this by. . . .? We* language diffuses tense situations.

Ask questions—and listen to the answers

The quality of the responses may leave you pleasantly surprised. Most of us speak more clearly than we write so asking your colleague to explain a proposition may yield the answer to your concerns.

Give an easy way out

Point out grammatical errors but acknowledge that they may simply be typographical mistakes—even if they are not. You'll make your point and spare the writer embarrassment.

Respect your colleague's voice

Avoid comments that aim to make your colleague's writing sound like *your* writing. Writing should never be reduced to an exercise in imitation.

Avoid passing on your own writing neuroses

In particular, young lawyers often obsess about partners' individual writing quirks, such as whether a partner insists that *however* come only in the middle of a sentence. (Newsflash: *However* can go at the beginning of a sentence.) Avoid being a nit-picky word maven. Try hard not to be weird.

Avoid labels

Labels such as *disorganized* or *poor writer* last forever and help no one. Don't stigmatize young talent by attaching labels.

Say thank you

People work for the recognition of their peers. Build on your writer's innate motivation by saying *thank you*. It's fast, it's easy, and it's motivational.

Give credit

If possible, acknowledge your colleague's contribution to a project by putting his or her name on the final product. Young lawyers need the chance to build their portfolio if they are to develop their career.

Share the final product

Make sure to copy your colleague on the final perfected paper. The final product is your greatest teaching tool.

Tips for Transactional Attorneys 30

by Ilissa K. Povich

This is not fine prose nor, by itself, terribly clear. It would appear to have been drafted by lawyers.
—Justice Cummings, *Bourke v. Dun & Bradstreet Corp.*,
159 F. 3d 1032, 1037 (7th Cir. 1998)

Understand the Deal

Even if you are drafting only a few of the documents in a transaction, you must understand the deal as a whole and how your documents fit into it. Without this knowledge, it will be difficult to draft a document that correctly references other aspects of the transaction and works with the other transaction documents.

Understand the Document

Understand the purpose of the document you are drafting in the transaction. What role does it play in the deal? Brainstorm the issues that should be covered in the document to protect your client's interests.

Understand Forms

Most transactional drafting begins with a form. Forms enable lawyers to avoid reinventing the wheel and include standard terms generally used in a particular type of document. Before changing or deleting a provision in the form, understand why it is included and the impact of the change. However, be wary of slavishly following the form and treating the drafting process as a fill-in-the-blanks exercise. Consider subtle ways in which your transaction may differ from the modeled transaction.

Choose Clear Language

Transactional documents create law—the private rules between the parties to a transaction. The documents must accurately reflect the deal, using language that is clear and internally consistent. After you have finished drafting, read through the document from beginning to end to make sure that one section does not conflict with another.

Use Defined Terms Effectively

Choose meaningful words to define the parties and significant concepts. For example, use terms that define the parties' role in the transaction, such as *Buyer, Seller, Landlord, or Tenant.* Define a term either the first time you use it or in a separate definitions section, always using initial capital letters in the defined term. In a lengthy document, a definitions section will help the reader find a particular definition when he is trying to interpret a provision in the agreement. Use the defined term every time you reference the concept in the document. Don't define a term if you use it only once.

Focus on the Details

Clients will notice if their names are misspelled. Inaccurate cross-references confuse rather than clarify. Although it's tedious, proofread, proofread, proofread. Small, nonsubstantive mistakes reflect poorly on you and the firm.

Make It Readable

Legal jargon does not make your writing more impressive. Clients often refer to transactional documents after the closing to determine the terms of their working relationship with the other parties. They need documents they can understand. Writing in plain English will make you look like you understand not only the transaction but your clients, as well.

Be Wordy If Necessary

However, your job is to address every reasonable contingency. While a plain-English explanation is always best, the need to cover the contingencies justifies sentences that an English teacher would describe as run-on.

Use Headings

In transactional documents, headings are the roadmap to the document. Break up each section with a separate heading. Transactional documents often place a heading before every paragraph.

Use the SEC's Plain English Handbook

The SEC's guide, *A Plain English Handbook* provides guidelines to ensure that disclosures about publicly traded companies are written in language civilians can understand. Follow these guidelines or you risk having your SEC filings rejected.

Letters | **31**

I never write "metropolis" when I can write "city" and get paid the same.

—Mark Twain

Know Why Lawyers' Letters Matter

In the legal profession, letters do more than simply convey information. Lawyers often use letters offensively—to create a record of an agreement or dispute, to memorialize conversations and to lock opposing counsel into a position. Letter-writing skills are an essential tool of our trade.

Know When to Write a Letter

You should write a letter to memorialize a conversation, to create a record of agreements with opposing counsel (particularly if opposing counsel has reneged on past agreements), to summarize demands, to explain the law to a client, to confirm administrative matters, to acknowledge good work or to say *thank you*.

Know When *Not* to Write a Letter

You should not write a letter to express anger if that is the only purpose of the letter, to address delicate matters that might be better handled in person or by phone, or before you have all the facts.

175

Know What Privileges Apply

Confidential communications between an attorney and client are protected by the attorney-client privilege. (The attorney-client privilege is discussed in more detail at page 188. Correspondence with opposing counsel is not protected by the attorney-client privilege, although other privileges—such as the privilege covering settlement negotiations—may apply. Correspondence with the court is never privileged, but may qualify as attorney work product. Correspondence with nonparties, such as expert witnesses, is arguably privileged work product and trial preparation material but the Rules of Civil Procedure allow for discovery of these letters in certain limited circumstances. (Fed. R. Civ. P. 26(b)(3)).

Protect Privileges

State what privileges apply in the letter. In particular, always label correspondence to clients as *Privileged and Confidential/Attorney Client Communication*. Although client correspondence is protected even without the label, the label will at least cause the client and the client's employees to pause before producing the letter in response to a discovery request. If a letter to opposing counsel is protected by a privilege, such as the privilege covering settlement negotiations, say so in the letter. Opposing counsel's failure to object may help you later.

Set Up Templates for Each Matter to Preserve the Privilege

A careless *cc* to opposing counsel may negate the privilege. Have your assistant set up letter templates for each client and review those templates to be sure that each template contains the privilege notation and the proper *cc* notations.

Do Not Use Firm Letterhead for Personal Matters

Personal matters belong on personal stationary. Your firm does not represent you and using firm letterhead for personal matters raises issues about conflicts, malpractice liability and insurance coverage.

Know the Purpose of Your Letter

Before you write any letter, ask yourself: Why am I writing? What is the recipient's position and role? What privileges apply? What topics do I need do cover? What am I asking the recipient to do?

Speak Human

Your letters should read as if they were written by a person, rather than by an institution. Clients are not impressed by our antiquated phrases, such as *per your request, pursuant to our conversation* and *enclosed please find*. Again, use modern English and say *as you requested, as we discussed* and *I have enclosed*. Avoid other pompous phrases such as *I might add, it is interesting to note* and *it should be pointed out that*. Instead of saying *The use of caution is advised,* say *Be careful.* Instead of saying *Further information will be provided to you shortly,* say *I'll keep you informed.*

Although you should be conversational, written language should be slightly more formal than conversation, so colloquialisms and slang are out. Humor is allowed.

Spell the Recipient's Name Correctly

Are you looking for a way to drive your recipient berserk? Try spelling his or her name incorrectly. It works every time.

Know Your Audience

Is the recipient a lawyer? If so, write as if you are writing to a colleague. If not, cover background material and law in more detail. Clients of big firms tend to be knowledgeable and sophisticated. Generally, you will not need to explain every point of background law.

Never Talk Down to a Client

Even if the client is not knowledgeable about the law, never assume a condescending tone. Laboring over obvious points may appear condescending. Similarly, a question and answer format—normally an effective writing technique—may suggest that you underestimate the client's knowledge. With a sophisticated client, stick with substantive headings.

Apply the Principles for Powerful Writing

The same principles that apply to briefs and memoranda apply to letters. Use plain English. Write short sentences. State your conclusion in one sentence and at the beginning. Use headings. Begin each paragraph with a topic sentence. Keep your paragraphs short. Put white space on a page. Read out loud to cure awkward constructions.

Lead Letters from the Top

Like briefs and memoranda, letters also have three parts—an opening, a middle and final recommendations or *to do* section. Like all legal writing, letters must lead from the top, so state your main point or the purpose of the letter in the first or second paragraph. Follow with supporting or explanatory information and conclude by telling the recipient what you are asking them to do.

Opening Paragraph:	Main Point
Middle Paragraphs:	Supporting Information
Final Paragraph:	Final Action/To Do List

If you need to bring your reader up to speed before you introduce your main point, insert an introductory paragraph before your main paragraph:

Introductory Paragraph:	Introductory Information
Main Paragraph:	Main Point
Middle Paragraphs:	Supporting Information
Final Paragraph:	Final Action/To Do List

Start Nicely

Even if your letter must cover a difficult topic, begin positively. Try saying *I appreciate.* . . . Remember your college rejection letters? Even they began by saying something nice, such as "Although we were impressed by your strengths in gym class . . . ."

Finish by Telling the Recipient What You Want Them to Do

Finish by reminding your client of a *To Do* list, concluding with a recommendation, or telling opposing counsel what you are asking them to do. The final paragraph of any letter to the court should explain what action you want the court to take, as in *Please mark the motion for hearing at the August 1st session.*

Know the Enemy

Litigation is not a play date. While your relationship with opposing counsel should be cordial and professional, you may want to document all dealings with opposing counsel by letter or e-mail.

Be Civil

Think big. Imagine you are testifying before Congress at a hearing to confirm your nomination to the federal bench. An angry senator produces a letter you wrote as a young lawyer. Does your correspondence suggest that you lack judicial temperament?

Avoid Fighting Words

Rather than referring to *your client's unjustified assertions,* explain that *The facts do not support these allegations.* Avoid phrases such as *bald conclusions, unsupported accusations* or *distorted interpretation.* Be firm but keep a calm, measured tone.

Attack the Idea Rather Than the Person

As with memoranda, avoid attacking the person and focus instead on their tactics. Instead of saying *Your suggestion that Mr. Bigwig should testify in person is ridiculous,* say *The law does not require Mr. Bigwig to testify in person.*

Take a Time Out

If you are boiling over at your keyboard, finish the letter—then wait overnight before sending it.

Discuss Bad News Early in the Letter

Presenting bad news early gives you time to recover and repair. Bad news in the last paragraph leaves a bad taste.

Be Careful What You Put in Writing and Expect to See Your Letter Again

When you send a letter or e-mail you are effectively publishing your material because you have no control over where the letter may land. Even a letter or message labeled *confidential* may wind up in unexpected hands, such as the hands of a disgruntled employee.

Remember That Everything You Say Can and Will Be Used Against You

In particular, letters to opposing counsel look lovely attached as an exhibit to a motion to compel or to a motion for sanctions. Scrutinize those letters for anything that may come back to haunt you, including your tone. You will never regret being civil.

Write for Whoever Might See Your Letter Next— Including the Court

If you know that opposing counsel is likely to attach your letter to a motion, use the letter to argue your case.

Show Copies to the Clients As Blind Copies

Opposing counsel should not see the name of your contact at a client company. Indeed, they should not see whether you have copied a client on a letter.

Stick to One Format

Most lawyers prefer modern block format, which aligns all text at the left, although some still use traditional semi-block format, with indented margins and a centered date and centered signatures. Either format is correct. Mixing the two formats is not.

Modern Block Format

Dewey, Billem & Howe, Main St., Anywhere, MA 01000

May 18, 2011

Jane Smith
Smith Corporation
Columbus Road
Nowhere, MA 09900

Re: *Smith v. Jones*

Dear Jane,

Xxxxxxxxxxxxxxxxxxxxxxxxxxxxxxxxxxxxxxxxxxxxx
xxxxxxxxxxxxxxxxxxxxxxxxxxxxxxxxxxxxxxx.

Xxxxxxxxxxxxxxxxxxxxxxxxxxxxxxxxxxxxxxxxxxxxx
xxxxxxxxxxxxxxxxxxxxxxxxxxxxxxxxxxxxxxxxx.

Very truly yours,

Adam Jones

Traditional Semi-Block Format

Dewey, Billem & Howe, Main St., Anywhere, MA 01000

May 18, 2011

Jane Smith
Smith Corporation
Columbus Road
Nowhere, MA 09900

Re: *Smith v. Jones*

Dear Jane,

   Xxxxxxxxxxxxxxxxxxxxxxxxxxxxxxxxxxxxxxxxxxxxx
xxxxxxxxxxxxxxxxxxxxxxxxxxxxxxxxxxxxxxx.

   Xxxxxxxxxxxxxxxxxxxxxxxxxxxxxxxxxxxxxxxxxxxxx
xxxxxx.

Very truly yours,

Adam Jones

Single Space

Single spacing forces you to create white space and highlights the structure of your letter. A single-spaced letter is much easier to digest visually than a double-spaced letter.

Include a Reference Line

Reference lines assure proper filing.

Copy Opposing Counsel on All Letters to the Court

Otherwise you are making a forbidden *ex parte* communication.

Be Thorough

Again, letters often form an agreement between parties and you may need to cover every contingency or memorialize every point you discussed. You will be forgiven for the extra paragraph. You may not be forgiven for a significant omission.

Do Not Incorporate Other Documents by Reference

Your recipient should not have to search for documents beyond the letter. If possible, summarize extraneous documents so that each letter reads as a whole.

Refer to Conversations by Content, As Well As Date

Again, summarize prior conversations, rather than simply referring to them by date. For example, say *In response to our conversation of January 1, during which we discussed the production of documents . . . .*

Be Specific About Dates

Don't simply state that *Responses to interrogatories are due within 30 days.* Explain that *Responses are due within thirty days on June 30, 2010.*

Justify the Bill

Every letter to a client should at least be worthy of the bill to follow. In fact, you may need to write letters simply to justify a bill. For example, after a conversation with the client summarizing research, you may want to send the client the relevant research memorandum or write a letter summarizing the scope of your research, as well as the results. What jurisdictions did you research? What alternative theories were considered? Even dead-end lines of research may deserve a brief mention if the client will eventually be billed for that research.

Use a Formal Closing

Most lawyers prefer *Very truly yours* or *Sincerely.*

P.S.

Use postscripts cautiously. Although the postscript is awkward and technically obsolete given the capabilities of modern word-processing programs, marketing research establishes that the postscript is the most read portion of any letter. Although postscripts are not appropriate in formal letters, understand their impact. You may occasionally want to use a *P.S.*

E-mail | **32**

Words are more treacherous and powerful than we think.
—Jean Paul Sartre

E-MAIL IS A perilous territory where people skills and writing skills collide. It is both the engine of business life and a bottomless time sink. Relationships are often built on e-mail exchanges. But e-mail is also the fountain of many a public relations disaster. It is powerful—and dangerous.

Each of us must set the terms of our relationship with e-mail. Will it rule your life and be your major mode of communication? Or will you impose strict limits on your life on-line? Are you casual and conversational or crisp and functional? How wide is your net? How accessible do you want to be?

Each of us also develops an e-mail personality, whether we plan to or not. You may be perceived as responsive or as inaccessible. Your tone may be chatty or terse. But you must recognize that each e-mail creates a perception of who you are as a professional. Whatever your individual style, you want people to value your e-mails so that they read and respond to those e-mails. Your e-mail reputation is one of your strongest assets.

As you cultivate your own style for e-mail, you must also be mindful of the unique ground rules that apply in our profession. E-mail is a minefield where the attorney-client privilege can easily explode and where confidential client information can be quickly sent astray. It is the place where disasters go to happen.

Let's review those ground rules and talk about the techniques that will guarantee that your e-mails break through the clutter and are worth reading.

1. The Perils and Pitfalls of E-mail

Send *less*

E-mail is relentless. A large firm may see 500,000 e-mails each day and the average office worker spends a quarter of every day managing e-mail. Each e-mail interrupts someone's workday and forces that person off task. So think before you hit *Send*. Is your e-mail really necessary?

Do not handle delicate situations by e-mail

E-mail's speed discourages the measured, deliberate response that many situations require. Hastily written words can polarize. E-mail is the perfect medium for routine administrative matters or scheduling but it cannot capture nuances. Handle sensitive matters by phone or in person. Be the essence of delicacy in your e-mails.

Don't hide behind e-mail

If you are shy or insecure or intimidated by some colleagues or even just plain old lazy, it is all too easy to hide behind e-mail. Get out of your chair occasionally. Walk down the hall. Talk. Smile. Business relationships are still built on personal connections—not on long chains of messages.

Remember your inhibitions

In normal conversation, we get immediate feedback in the form of visual or tonal clues that prevent us from crossing lines we should not cross. Those inhibitions are missing in e-mail, so we tend to say things in e-mail that we would never say in person. Rediscover your inhibited inner self. Your inhibitions will keep you from offending. Again, if you are angry, do not pass *Go* or hit *Send*.

Be nice

The State Supreme Court of Florida recently sanctioned two lawyers who traded scathing e-mail insults. They began by calling each other a "jerk" and "an old hack" and their language eventually deteriorated to monikers such as "bottom feeding/scum sucking/loser lawyers like yourself." The court required one lawyer to take a class on professionalism and suspended the second lawyer for ten days and required that he take an anger management class. Even worse, the exchange landed both lawyers on the front page of the ABA Journal. You never want this kind of publicity.

Write letters occasionally

Some things just do not work well in e-mail—love letters, a letter your recipient might want to frame, a letter that you never want to see forwarded, some thank you letters. Letters just seem more important. So if your subject matter is important, you may want to put it in a letter. You may even want to write that letter by hand. But if you want a reply to your letter, using e-mail makes it more likely that you will get a reply. Send the letter as a word attachment to your e-mail message. Convert the letter to PDF if you have any concern that someone may change your words.

Imagine yourself on the home page of The New York Times

E-mail practically begs to be forwarded. Before hitting *Send* think how easy it is for your recipient to hit *Forward* and for the next recipient to continue the gleeful distribution. Pretend that each message you send will be published on the home page of *The New York Times*. Never put any information that might embarrass you, your client or your firm in e-mail because you have no control over its distribution.

Imagine you are writing to your human resources department

If the thought of being on the home page of *The New York Times* is not enough to make you quake, imagine your Director of Human Resources scrolling through your e-mail. Employers have the right to review their employees' e-mail correspondence on office computers. Many employers routinely monitor their employees' e-mail. Be afraid. Be very afraid.

Avoid sending sensitive information to clients by e-mail

Sensitive client information may not belong in e-mail. While sending sensitive information by e-mail does not technically destroy the attorney-client privilege, the information becomes harder to protect in e-mail form because it is so easily forwarded.

Be the voice of your firm

Your e-mail correspondence may come back to haunt not only you but your employer as well. E-mails are often the smoking guns in litigation or the embarrassing source of public relations disasters. Keep your firm's anti-discrimination and harassment guidelines in mind as you message. You never ever want to become famous for an e-mail.

Think about the future

E-mail creates a searchable record. Remember that your words can be easily found and that you can be held responsible for them.

Treat faxes like e-mail

Faxes to large companies are usually distributed as PDFs. Therefore, even your fax may wind up as an e-mail attachment that can be easily forwarded.

2. To *E* or Not to *E*

Make yourself worth reading

If you frequently send unnecessary e-mails, your recipients will learn to ignore *all* your messages. Preserve your brand name by e-mailing judiciously.

Stop if you are angry

If your temperature is rising, ice off before sending that e-mail. If you are questioning whether you should send the message, you should not send it. Come back to it in an hour, or even a day. Ask a trusted colleague for his or her thoughts.

Spare the spam

Similarly, spam dilutes the value of your name. Your readers will learn to ignore *all* your e-mails if *most* of your e-mails are spam. Never spam from your office e-mail address.

3. Privilege and Work Product Issues

Understand how the privilege works

The law considers client confidences privileged and protected. Therefore, a client's communication to a lawyer is privileged even if that communication is by e-mail. As a corollary, attorneys' communications with clients are usually considered protected because they embody the client's confidential communication.

A communication is privileged if:

(a) It is a *communication* between a client and a lawyer;
(b) The communication is intended to be *confidential*; and
(c) The communication is *to obtain legal advice.*

U.S. v. United Shoe Machinery Corp., 89 F. Supp. 357, 358-359 (D. Mass. 1950) (emphasis added) (also available on **http://www.leagle.com**).

Be careful what you put in writing

Think long and hard before putting privileged material in writing. Even if you claim the privilege, a court will need to review the document privately to determine whether the privilege actually exists.

Understand how the privilege is waived

E-mail and the attorney-client privilege are dangerous bedmates. Generally, disclosing privileged communications to a third party waives the privilege.

Therefore, a simple click on *Forward* risks waiving the privilege entirely. Even more worrisome, disclosing privileged information to a wide circle within a client company can also waive the privilege.

Understand how much can be lost

A waiver of the privilege may apply not only to that e-mail but also to *all* communications involving the subject of that e-mail. There is much to be lost by a carelessly directed e-mail.

Create a need-to-know List

Decide who really needs to know the information in the e-mail and stay within that list. Determine who is in the inner circle and e-mail to that group only.

Educate your clients about the privilege

Make sure your clients understand that they will jeopardize the privilege if they forward your e-mails beyond the inner circle. Remind them that the privilege is theirs to protect.

Use Privileged and Confidential *notations on privileged e-mail*

But only use the notation if the e-mail really does contain privileged information. If you routinely affix a *Privileged* notation to *all* outgoing e-mail you will have a hard time convincing a court that your *Privileged* notation has meaning.

Be wary of putting work product in e-mail

Similarly, if you e-mail work product to a client, you create the risk that the client will forward the e-mail beyond the inner circle and destroy the work-product privilege. Again, advise your clients not to forward except to the privileged few.

If you are in-house counsel, consider separating business advice and legal advice into separate e-mails

In an excellent article on *The Risks of E-Mail Communication: A Guide to Protecting Privileged Electronic Communications*, Brenda Sharton and Gregory Lyons suggest that in-house counsel consider segregating business advice and legal advice into separate e-mails. Because the privilege only applies to legal advice, a plaintiff may argue that in-house counsel was only providing business advice in an e-mail and that the privilege does not apply. However, separating business and legal advice into different e-mails strengthens the argument that the privilege applies to the e-mails concerning legal advice.

Phrase e-mails to clients as responses

In the same article, Sharton and Levy also suggest that you phrase e-mails to clients as responses. Since the source of the privilege is the client's original communication to the lawyer, an e-mail phrased as a response should embody the privilege that attaches to the original communication. Begin with language such as *In response to your question concerning. . . .*

4. The Terrible *To* Line: An Accident Waiting to Happen

Think carefully about whom to send to

Most e-mail disasters occur not because the content is poorly drafted but because the e-mail is sent to the wrong person or to too many people. On messages to more than one person, triple check your distribution list.

Fill in the To line last

Make it impossible to send an e-mail until you have finalized the message. Type the text first, and don't fill in the *To* line until you have finished the message. If you are *Replying to All*, draft the text of your message in a blank message or a separate document, then copy the text into your reply once you are satisfied. This trick is especially prudent on e-mails to large groups or that concern sensitive matters.

Create distribution lists

Set up distribution lists for matters where you will frequently send messages to the same group of people.

Remove problematic e-mail addresses from your address book

Recently, an unfortunate attorney at a high-profile firm wanted to send an e-mail message about her client's $1 billion settlement negotiations to her co-counsel at another firm. Unfortunately, she didn't send her message to her co-counsel. She mistakenly sent it to a reporter at *The New York Times* with the same last name. *The New York Times* published a story on its website and followed up the next day with a story on its front page. The blogosphere lit up with claims that the misdirected e-mail was the source for the article, even though *The New York Times* reporter claimed the e-mail had been innocuous.

Protect yourself against the possibility of such a mistake by removing any problematic e-mail addresses, such as the addresses for reporters, from the e-mail field in your address book. Instead, paste the address in the notes section of your contact box so that you can retrieve the address if you need it, but so that your computer won't automatically fill in that address.

Guard the privacy of e-mail addresses

When you send an e-mail to several recipients, you are sharing their e-mail addresses with everyone on your distribution list. Think about the people behind those e-mail addresses before you send. Would any recipient mind if you shared their addresses with the other recipients? If so, make them a *bcc* or send them separately.

Acknowledge dropouts

Similarly, if you are dropping someone from an e-mail chain, acknowledge the deletion so that the next person replying knows that you have dropped that recipient. Simply say *I have not copied Adam on this e-mail.*

Put names in order in the To line

Respect the pecking order in the *To* line. List people in order of seniority or importance.

5. The *Subject* Line: High-Voltage Real Estate

Tell all in the subject line

Your title should be descriptive enough that your readers can determine whether they need to even open the e-mail simply by reading the title. A descriptive title also makes the e-mail easier to find. Think about the key words that you might use to search for the e-mail later and use those key words in the title. Catchall titles, such as *Question* or *Important Information*, often mean your message won't be read.

Never leave the subject line blank

Even if you are simply sending an attachment, fill in the subject line.

Capitalize on connections in the title line

If you are e-mailing someone for the first time, your message is more likely to be read if you explain your common connection in the title. Simply say *Marie Buckley suggested I contact you.*

Change the title as the topic changes

As the topic changes over a chain of e-mails, change the subject reference. Again, most people use e-mail to store information. The title should create a searchable record.

6. The Message

Relax about routine e-mails

E-mail's strength is that it moves information quickly. Therefore, don't think twice about a message to a colleague confirming a lunch date. Fire off routine administrative e-mail. You do not need to write in full sentences or even include a greeting or signature. But be aware that this casual approach applies only to routine e-mails going to one or very few people.

Otherwise, write your messages carefully

Every e-mail you send puts a demand on someone's time and you should use that time well.

Revise according to the rank of the recipient or the sensitivity of the subject matter

Know your audience. A message to a friend confirming lunch never needs editing. But you should carefully review messages to clients, senior colleagues, and large distribution lists and messages concerning important or sensitive topics.

If a message will be widely distributed, use proper English

If an e-mail will be widely distributed, if it is going to a more senior person or if it is likely to be forwarded to the powers that be, be especially careful to use proper English. E-mail should be conversational but it is not an excuse for sloppy, rambling writing. A carelessly worded e-mail will not promote your career and may waste your recipients' time. The dangers of carelessly worded e-mails are amplified when you send to a distribution list or *Reply to All*.

Greet your recipient by name

Simply begin with *Hi Chris* or just *Chris*. The name shows the message is not a mass mailing. If you are mailing to several people, name them in the greeting so that your reader knows who else is receiving the message. Don't assume your reader will check the *To* line.

Lead from the top—meaning the opening screen

Once you have persuaded your reader to read beyond the subject line, you need to convey the key part of your message on the opening screen or it may never be read.

Keep e-mail short

E-mail should generally fit on the opening screen. A busy reader doesn't want to read beyond that screen.

Limit your topics

Try to deal with only one topic in each e-mail so that your reader can answer your question quickly. If you send complicated messages, your message is likely to be skipped, which means it may never be viewed again.

Move the conversation along

For example, if you are trying to arrange a meeting, suggest three times that work.

Explain why you are writing

Begin your message with phrases such as *as you asked, following up on our meeting, as we discussed,* or *in response to your question.*

Explain what you want the recipient to do

Just as formal legal writing includes a *Recommendations* section, you should also finish e-mail messages by reminding your recipient what you are asking them to do. One of the reasons that people delay responding to a message is because they do not understand what they are being asked to do. Put your request in a separate paragraph and put that paragraph first in the message.

Limit options

When you tell your recipient what you want them to do, be specific. If you are asking them to choose options, limit those options to two or three choices.

Keep it friendly

E-mail is essentially just casual conversation transcribed to writing, so keep your messages friendly and conversational.

Say please *and* thank you

Remember what your mother told you. Say *please* and *thank you.* Politeness greases the wheels of communication.

Be aware of your position

If you are in a position of seniority, your e-mail can easily be misinterpreted as overreaching. A request to look at an issue can lead a junior lawyer to spend a lonely night with LexisNexis. Be aware of how junior people may interpret your request.

Think about time and time zones

If your reader will feel that your e-mail message requires an immediate response, either because they are junior to you or because they are extremely conscientious, think hard before sending that 2 a.m. e-mail. Write it at 2 a.m.

but queue it up to be delivered at 8 a.m. in the recipient's time zone. Similarly, be considerate when dealing with recipients in other time zones.

Keep it professional

Save cutesy representational abbreviations, such as ☺ (now available in automated format!), for civilian life.

PDF to prevent your words from being changed

If your message involves a sensitive topic and you have any concern that someone in the chain might change your words, send your message as a PDF document.

Keep your voice

In spite of my many cautions about e-mail, you should still think of e-mail as a medium to speak in your own voice. Keep your sense of humor, your choice of words, your unique tone. Use e-mail to build relationships.

7. Replying, Forwarding and Other Hazardous Activities

Reply only if necessary

Resist the temptation to reply to every e-mail. Most e-mail does not require a reply.

Reply to All *rarely*

Consider who really needs to see your response. *Replies to All* account for a large portion of unnecessary e-mail.

Treat Reply to All *with fear*

Reply to All is the most dangerous thing you will ever do from an office chair—I hope! One innocuous click may catapult you into office lore, so click *Reply to All* with caution. Again, you may want to consider drafting the text to important *Reply to All* messages in a separate document—either a new message, without filling in the recipients, or in a text document—and then copying the final text into your *Reply to All* message.

Know when to end the chain

Know when enough is enough. Get the information you need. Respond, if necessary. But do have the courage to end the chain. Often, there is no need to say *thanks*. Generally, three e-mails on a topic should be sufficient. If you are going into a fourth e-mail, you should probably change the *subject* line.

Do not forward if the writer might object

If there is even the slightest chance that the sender might object to your forwarding the e-mail, get permission first. Assume permission to forward routine administrative e-mail.

Be wary of forwarding e-mail threads or adding recipients to threads

Review e-mail threads carefully before forwarding to another person or adding a new recipient. Again, many e-mail disasters arise because someone unwittingly forwarded the most recent e-mail in a long thread—and buried deep within that thread were comments that should not have been passed on to the new recipient. Scroll through the chain to be sure that you are comfortable with the recipient seeing the entire chain. Adding recipients to long chains is an easy way to get in big trouble.

Name new recipients

If you do add a new recipient, alert others to that addition by including a note that "I have added Adam to the distribution."

Restate the question

Save your reader the need to reread the thread to determine what topic you are addressing. Restate the subject matter in the opening line. Simply say *I'm getting back to you to schedule the deposition* or *I looked into your question about delivery dates.*

Follow your firm's policy about archiving

If your firm has a policy about archiving (and it should), follow that policy for deleting e-mails. If your firm does not have a policy about archiving, be consistent about what you save and delete and when you do so. No one will question the reason you deleted an e-mail if you follow your standard procedure.

8. Window-dressing: Greetings, Signatures, Logos, and Design

Follow the leader

If you are having difficulty deciphering your firm's e-mail culture, do what others do. If your colleagues begin their e-mails with a formal greeting, consider beginning with a greeting also.

Sign off

Although the heading contains a line showing who the message is from, signing off with a closing adds a personal touch. Keep closings casual. Simply say *Thanks, Best, Best Wishes,* or *Regards,* followed by your name. Sign-offs are not necessary on quick e-mails within the firm but they are a warm touch on e-mails outside the firm.

Set up an automatic signature block for all out-of-office e-mail

A recipient who needs to call should not have to look up your number or other contact information. Therefore, include an automatic signature on all out-going e-mails. Your signature block should follow firm format and should contain your name, title, firm name, address, phone number, fax, e-mail address and web page.

Avoid embedded logos

Embedded logos gobble up bandwidth so avoid them.

Think carefully before attaching a scanned signature

Attaching a scan of your signature may give your e-mail legal effect and will certainly lead your recipient to assume that you have carefully reviewed the message and that the message reliably represents your word.

Avoid flags on outgoing e-mail

Avoid flagging your outgoing e-mail as urgent. Use your subject line to let the reader know if your message is urgent.

Be polite about requesting read receipts

It may not be polite to request a read receipt—particularly on messages to clients—because the recipient may feel you are checking up on them.

Avoid ALL CAPS

Again, stay calm. NO SHOUTING ALLOWED! Use *italics* if you want to add emphasis. If the urge to write in ALL CAPS is irresistible, the message is a missive—or a missile—that should not be sent.

But don't skip the capitalization altogether

In the haste to respond to e-mail quickly, many writers ignore capitalization entirely and use no capital letters. Upper-case letters still serve a purpose. They show that you passed third-grade grammar and that you are a careful writer.

Avoid fancy fonts and colors

E-mail is not the place to let your artistic inner self shine through. Again, choose an appealing, readable serif font and avoid sans serif. Times New

Roman, Garamond and Century are clean, readable fonts. (E-mail programs often default to sans serif fonts so be sure to change the default settings.)

Spell-check all e-mail

Set up automatic *Spellcheck* on all outgoing e-mail, and remember that using *Spellcheck* does not mean that you do not need to read the message yourself.

Consider sending hard copy if the information eventually needs to be printed

If the information needs to be printed in hard copy, save your recipients (particularly senior attorneys) the trouble of printing and send hard copy. Note in the e-mail that you will be following up with a hard copy.

9. E-mails to Opposing Counsel

Be cautious in e-mails to opposing counsel

Like letters, e-mail messages look lovely dressed up as exhibits to motions to compel or motions for sanctions. Plan accordingly. You may not want to see a careless e-mail attached as an exhibit to a pleading. You certainly do not want to see compromising or sensitive information presented to the court. Again, tone matters.

Request a "read receipt" on e-mails to opposing counsel

If opposing counsel is cantankerous, request a "read receipt." Why give opposing counsel the option of claiming they never read your message?

Use your message to argue your case

As with letters, if opposing counsel is likely to attach your message as an exhibit to a pleading, use your message to argue your case. Why miss an opportunity?

10. Managing E-mail

Manage your e-mail, rather than letting it manage you

You have been hired to do much more than respond to e-mails all day so do not let e-mail rule your life. Preserve time for work by managing the time you spend answering e-mail. Set aside regular time to manage e-mail but leave most of your day for real work. Otherwise, e-mail will suck you dry, destroy your neurons and take over your life.

Develop a system for managing e-mail

Aim to keep your inbox as empty as possible so that only action items live there. Handle items once and once only, if possible. The key is to deal with e-mail promptly:

- Immediately delete or file messages that do not require a response.
- Respond immediately to messages that can be dealt with quickly.
- Forward messages that can be delegated.
- Flag messages that require time to respond and set aside time every day for dealing with flagged messages.
- Periodically sort by sender and flag to be sure that you are staying current on important items.
- Create reminders as deadlines approach.
- At the beginning or end of every week, review your inbox or your "urgent" file to remove any straggling e-mail.

Do not ignore e-mail

E-mail is the engine of business life so you must respond to your e-mails. People expect a response. In particular, clients and senior colleagues deserve a quick response.

11. E-mail Mishaps

Expect mistakes to happen

The volume and warp speed of e-mail guarantee that the occasional misstep will happen. Remember that everything that can go wrong will go wrong.

Apologize in person

If you made a mistake by e-mail (and all of us do), don't blame it on e-mail. After all, you should have checked the *To* line before clicking *Send*. And you may want to apologize in person. Apologizing by e-mail can seem cowardly. If a public apology is also required, follow up with a *mea culpa* e-mail to everyone involved.

Forgive the mistakes of others

Be gracious and ignore the minor mistakes of others. If someone mistakenly *replied to all*, they do not need 800 responses pointing out their error.

12. Attachments

Do not send attachments needlessly

The primary goal of e-mail is to move information quickly. Sending a document as an attachment requires much more bandwidth than posting that same document into the body of your e-mail. Attaching the document also requires the reader to wait for the word-processing program to launch before the reader can read the document. Attachments are particularly frustrating for recipients who are using a handheld so most hand-held users don't bother to open attachments.

Give your reader the option of choosing how to read the content. If the attached document is not too long, paste its content into the e-mail and attach it as well. Simply note in the introduction that you have also pasted the content below and attached it separately. Pasting the content in the message is courteous and efficient, especially if your recipient will be reading your message on a hand-held device.

Avoid graphics

Similarly, avoid embedded graphics, stationery, borders and clip art because they require more processing time.

Scrub the editing history before attaching a document

Before you send any document by e-mail, scrub it of any metadata. The editing history is nobody's business and it may cause you great embarrassment. (See page 151 for information on how to delete metadata.)

Convert attachments to PDF format

Once you have scrubbed the editing history, you should also convert sensitive documents to PDF before sending those documents by e-mail. It only takes a moment to convert the document to PDF and converting prevents anyone else from making changes. Important documents, such as final contracts, should always be sent in PDF format. (To convert a document to PDF format, click on the *File* tab/click *Save As*/in the box labeled *Save As Type*, scroll up on the right arrow and choose *PDF*.)

Encrypt sensitive or confidential attachments

If you are sending a sensitive or highly confidential document—for example, a document that discusses confidential personnel information—encrypt that document and make it password protected. Then send a separate e-mail informing the recipient of the password.

Attach documents in the proper order

When attaching multiple documents, attach them in the order in which you want them read or the order in which you list them in your e-mail.

Edit file titles before attaching

If you named your file with a witty title, such as *Time-Killing Memorandum on Ridiculous Research Topic*, you should change that title before sending.

13. Cloud Computing: Storm Warning Advisory

Cloud-computing services, such as *gmail* and *Yahoo! Mail,* store e-mail and documents on a host site, outside the user's firewall. So cloud computing offers easy access to e-mail and documents from any device with Internet access. However, cloud computing raises as-yet-unresolved questions about confidentiality. While most lawyers are rightfully cautious about using cloud-computing services as their primary e-mail address, lawyers should also be equally cautious about sending e-mail to clients with cloud-computing addresses.

Using cloud-computing services may raise concerns about a lawyer's ethical obligation to keep client information confidential. For example, a 2008 Opinion from the New York State Bar Association cautioned that a lawyer may violate the ethical obligation to guard client confidentiality if the provider of the service reserves the right to disclose e-mails to third parties without permission or without a court order. The association warned attorneys to choose an e-mail provider that ensures that client confidences are protected. (There, the terms of service also allowed the provider to electronically scan the content of its users' e-mail so that the service could target computer-generated advertising—a common provision in most terms of service. The bar association ruled that *computer*-generated scans do not compromise client confidentiality but cautioned that it would find a violation if the e-mails were reviewed by human beings.) New York State Bar Association, Committee On Professional Ethics, Opinion 820 (2008).

And cloud computing does pose real questions about security. Concerns about the risk of a provider losing e-mail or documents are often overblown because reputable providers have usually built enough redundancy into their systems to minimize this risk. But e-mail stored in the cloud is more vulnerable to prying eyes than e-mail stored behind your employer's firewall. Most e-mail providers do not require multiple layers of authentication, so a hacker does not need to hack into your computer to view e-mail stored on the cloud. That hacker simply needs to guess your password. Are you willing to live only one password away from a potential hacker? You should also worry about whether the provider's own network is secure against hacking. Does the provider require multiple layers of authentication to log in?

Information stored in the cloud may also be more vulnerable to government scrutiny. Will your e-mail provider cave easily to a subpoena of your e-mail or your client's e-mail? Do you trust your e-mail provider to protect your client's confidential information or to assert the attorney-client privilege on your client's behalf?

Cloud computing is the wave of the future. Indeed, it may someday be more secure than our current systems. But you should view the cloud with caution for now. Advise clients of the risks of cloud-computing services. Avoid storing confidential information or work product on a cloud service and think carefully before sending confidential information to a recipient with a cloud-computing address. And never send anything that can be used against your client to a cloud-computing address.

14. Hand-Held Devices and Other Excuses

Thumb pick with abandon

The thumb picking required by BlackBerries and other hand-held devices means that many formatting recommendations are tough to apply if you are working from a hand-held device. Since the whole point of hand-held devices is to assure that you are always reachable, respond to messages quickly and do the best you can. But you should still take the time to capitalize the first word in a sentence and to spell your words out. Abbreviations such as *I will send 2 u* do not *play 2 well* in the professional world.

On second thought, thumb pick cautiously

But don't let the urgency of your hand-held device lead you to fire off an inappropriate message. Hand-held devices are immediate and demanding— like a crying baby. They are also so casual that they can lull you into letting your guard down. You must still think before you send. There is no disclaimer for inappropriate content. Complacency may also lull you to compromise the privilege.

Hold the big thoughts for later

Some messages are just too important, too delicate or too sensitive to be handled through a hand-held device. Hold those messages until you are at your computer so you can present them more effectively.

Attach an **Auto-Text** *disclaimer*

Create an *Auto-Text* disclaimer line stating that your e-mail was sent from a teeny-weeny-thumb-picking machine. The disclaimer assures that any technical errors will be forgiven.

Use a disclaimer for voice-recognition technologies

If you are using voice-recognition technology to dictate your messages, add a disclaimer so that you can blame any translation gaffes on the technology.

Blogging 33

If the writing is honest it cannot be separated from the man who wrote it.

—Tennessee Williams

YOU'VE HEARD THE buzz about social media. Perhaps you've even seen "the movie." Facebook. Twitter. Blogs. In this casual world of tweets and posts, what is a simple lawyer—trained in the delicate art of legal argument—to do?

The question of whether to blog professionally is a personal decision, as well as a business decision. Blogging, like any conversation on the Internet, carries real risks because the Internet is a mausoleum where your words may be forever set in stone—or its modern equivalent, computer code. And by going public with a blog, you sacrifice some degree of privacy. How much of your self do you want to reveal online? Where does your zone of privacy fall?

You must also weigh the effort required for blogging against its potential benefits. Although those benefits may be substantial, they will almost certainly be hard to quantify in cold, monetary terms. While social media in the civilian world may deserve its buzz, social media in the legal realm may or may not live up to its hype.

But blogging is now part of the legal landscape. It's a medium for establishing your credibility and knowledge and, therefore, a genuine marketing tool. It's the village square where you can trumpet your wisdom or embarrass yourself in an exponential fashion. Perhaps you'll be the next rock star of the blogosphere or perhaps you'll go down in infamy. More likely, you'll toil away unnoticed. But you should not venture into the village square that is the blogosphere unless you understand the medium.

As Andrew Sullivan commented in a recent article in *The Atlantic*, blogging is "writing out loud." A blog is different than a website because a blog allows you to allow your readers to post comments and ask questions. Traditional websites are a static one-way mirror. Your readers can see you but you can't see them, except in vague analytics. Blogs change that dynamic. Because your readers can comment on your posts, a blog allows you to carry on a conversation with your readers. Indeed, comments often turn into a conversation *between* readers and trying to manage that conversation can be like trying to herd stray cats.

Because blogs are such a dynamic medium, they also create an expectation that you will keep your blog current. If you succeed in building up a following, your readers will expect you to keep them informed about new developments in your topic area. And you must meet those expectations by posting regularly and keeping your blog up-to-date. So blogging is a deceptive medium. The posts may be short and sweet, but the commitment is long-term.

Since this is a book about writing rather than technology, I want to stay close to my mission and use this chapter to discuss the writing issues that this new medium presents, as well as some of the larger goals and concerns that arise in the blogosphere. For questions about the technical aspects of blogging and an overview of social media in general, I highly recommend *Social Media for Lawyers: The Next Frontier*, by Carolyn Elefant and Nicole Black.

So let's venture into the village square of the blogosphere.

Guard Your Rank

The goal of blogging is to talk to others, not to yourself. You want people to be able to find your blog easily, so you'll need to understand search engine optimization or SEO—a topic that is well-covered in the book, *Social Media for Lawyers*.

But optimizing your rankings, so that your blog rises to the top in a search, requires more than just tagging your pages with the right key words. As a professional blogger, you may face a stiff competitor in your reach for the top of the rankings—yourself. If you live your personal life online so that you have a strong internet presence in your civilian life—say as a food blogger or a party animal or because you sell mittens on eBay—those traces of your civilian self may compete with your professional blog in the search rankings. (Google yourself to search for these traces.)

You want your professional blog to show up as the first or second result when someone searches your name, immediately after (or before) your contact page on your office's website. To preserve this sacred ranking for your professional self, you may need to stifle your personal self online. Your Facebook page should be private or, at most, show only your picture to the public. If you comment on other blogs or on news sites, those comments should be professional in nature and you may want to limit those comments so that they don't compete with your blog in the rankings. If you have a personal blog, you may need to keep that blog private or blog under a pen name. If you tweet, tweet only about professional matters (and link back to your blog, of course). In short, tread lightly online in your personal life, so that you guard that precious high search ranking for your professional self.

Know the Purpose of Your Blog

Many legal blogs are substantive blogs about legal topics, in which the blogger aims to establish credibility about a certain topic in the hopes of attracting business. Other legal blogs are online gathering spots, where followers who are interested in a topic gather to share information and ideas—often vociferously.

A substantive blog has different rules of engagement than a let's-meet-at-the-water-cooler blog. In a substantive blog, you may want to monitor the conversation and keep the comments civil and professional. In a water-cooler blog, all traffic may be good traffic and your job may simply be to create that gathering spot where that conversation can happen.

So know the purpose of your blog and post to and monitor your blog with that purpose in mind.

Pick a Niche

Choose a niche and then aim to own it. Since content is key, your blog should be about a topic in which you have genuine expertise or, at least, enough knowledge to add to the conversation. And you are more likely to own that topic if it is not already well-covered in a thousand other blogs. So do some research and find out what is already out there before settling on your topic.

Know Your Audience

Are you writing for other lawyers, for the business community, or for the public? You must know your target audience so that you can modify your style and tone to suit that audience. If you are writing for the business community or other lawyers, you can assume that your readers are already fairly knowledgeable and craft your posts to add to that knowledge base. If you are targeting a more general audience, you should keep your posts general and casual.

Give Away Something of Value for Free

Most lawyers use blogs as marketing tools to establish their credibility and usefulness, in the hope that their blog will draw new clients to their practice. But you cannot establish your credibility and earn your followers' trust unless your blog adds value to the conversation. In the blogosphere, content is key. Your blogs must be substantive, accurate and reliable. Yes, you are giving information away "for free." But the payoff may come down the road, as your professional reputation grows and your followers—also known as potential clients—begin to trust you and turn to you for information. Build trust to build business down the road.

But Don't Give Too Much Away

Beware of making your blog so useful that your followers don't need to hire you for advice. If your blog discusses a topic from soup to nuts, your followers may not need to hire you to structure their deal or negotiate their contract.

Long ago, in the dark ages of the Internet, newspapers made the near-fatal mistake of giving away their content for free and that industry has since teetered on life support. Information may want to be free, but you probably don't want to be the person who gives it away for free. For example, I really wanted you to buy this book. So my blog on legal writing, A Lawyer's Guide to Writing (**www.mariebuckley.com**), gives an overview of important principles and answers frequently asked questions, but I have avoided putting the entire book online so that you still have some incentive to buy the book.

In blogging, you want to showcase your knowledge, establish your credibility and be useful enough that people will subscribe to your blog. But you should be very cautious about giving away *all* your expertise for free. A blog should be part treatise and part tease.

Keep Your Content Fresh

If your blog is going to be useful and trustworthy, you must keep your content current. So keep yourself current on major trends in your topic area and update your content regularly. An outdated blog is so yesterday.

Make Your Blog the Center of Your Web Presence

Other social networking tools, such as LinkedIn, Facebook and Twitter, are useful tools for directing traffic to your blog, but they are not as substantive or enduring as a blog. So if your goal is to build your professional reputation online and cultivate trust, your blog should be the center of your online presence. Use social networking tools to lure people to your blog.

Keep It Conversational

In the blogosphere, tone matters even more than in traditional legal writing. If your blog is not casual and conversational, no one will read it. And if you don't write in plain English, you will come across as odd and odd does not sell well in the legal world.

As with traditional legal writing, say each sentence aloud to be sure that you are speaking a modern language. Avoid pompous words and phrases that suggest that you spent your youth buried in the law library. Your blog is not the place to showcase our profession's unique ability to torture the English language. And the audience for Latin on the Internet is extremely thin, so you should resist the urge to use Latin phrases, such as *i.e.* or *e.g.*

Keep It Casual

A blog is not a law review article. Even if your posts are deep and substantive, you should still aim for a casual and accessible style.

Write in Proper English

Blogging is such a casual medium that it is easy to be lulled into thinking that your usual standards of excellence don't apply when you blog. But your posts should be written in careful, correct English. Edit for grammatical mistakes and spelling errors. Otherwise, your readers will take great delight in pointing out your errors. Keep your writing a bit more formal than your spoken conversation, but far less formal than in traditional legal documents.

Assume That Everything You Write on Your Blog Will Live Forever

Yes, you can delete and edit your own posts. But once you have posted something, your followers can copy and paste that language. So even though you have the ability to delete and edit your words, you should assume that everything you write just might live forever. As she said in the movie, the Internet is written in ink.

Be Real

Let your personality shine through in your blog. Dare to be punchy or pithy or succinct. Be friendly or be a curmudgeon. If you can write in a unique voice, people are more likely to follow you.

Never Give Advice Online

Never give client-specific advice online. You don't want to find yourself in the position where a follower claims that your response to their question created an attorney-client relationship because the malpractice implications are frightening. Post a disclaimer stating that your posts and responses are not legal advice and that comments or inquiries by readers do not create an attorney-client relationship. If a reader is pushing for advice on a specific situation and that reader sounds like they could become a paying client, suggest that they e-mail you or call you privately. Then follow your usual procedures for dealing with inquiries from potential clients.

Stay Legal

Blogging may be a new medium, but you are still a lawyer, even though you have entered cyberspace. The same ground rules that govern your professional conduct on terra firma apply in cyberspace. Indeed, you should be even more careful to guard professional ethics in cyberspace, because the consequences of careless behavior are multiplied since the entire planet may be listening.

Keep Client Confidences

Don't post anything that might betray a client confidence. Even if you couch your posts in general language that redacts client names and other client-specific information, you never want a reader to be able to deduce client secrets from your post. Stay mum.

Respect Privacy

Many states allow a cause of action for the publication of private facts about a private person. If you violate a private person's right to privacy, you may be liable for damages. Again, mum's the word.

Avoid Deceptive and Misleading Claims

The rules that govern lawyer advertising apply to the blogosphere. Avoid all forms of deceptive advertising. Check your local ethics rules. Stay clear of prohibited monikers or unjustified claims of specialization. A blog should not be a blatant advertisement. It should be a subtle forum for establishing your credibility and knowledge.

Remember Your Geography

Because your blog can be viewed from anywhere in the world, your home page should include a link to a brief statement explaining the specific jurisdictions in which you are authorized to practice law. You never want your blog to give rise to a claim of unauthorized practice of law.

Don't Post Anything Defamatory

In the wild west of the Internet, many bloggers think that they can say anything without being responsible for their words. And because the blogosphere lacks the facial cues that inhibit us in face-to-face conversation, people tend to say things on the Internet that they would never say in person.

But the rules of defamation are not suspended on the Internet. If you make defamatory comments, you may be held responsible for them. (Even if you post anonymously or under a pseudonym on a news site or another blog, a defamed and inflamed plaintiff might be willing to do the discovery work required to learn your true identity.) So post and comment responsibly. And remember that defamation laws grant special protection to a person's professional reputation, so be particularly careful of maligning someone's professional competence online.

Don't Steal

Our copyright laws protect all original content, even if that content is posted on the Internet. Recently, *Cook's Source* magazine learned this lesson the hard way. The magazine printed an article written by someone else, without crediting or compensating the author. When the author learned that *Cook's Source* had posted her material, she e-mailed the editor to ask that she be compensated. In a response that would have benefited from some inhibitory mechanisms, the editor replied ". . . the web is considered 'public domain' and you should be happy we just didn't 'lift' your whole article and put someone else's name on it!" The editor's response went viral, the blogosphere ignited, and *Cook's Source* is now history.

The episode reminds us of two things. First, don't put anything in an e-mail that you would not want to see in headlines. (Google *Cook's Source* to see why.) Second, content posted on the Internet is indeed protected by copyright. It is not free for the taking.

Add a Copyright Statement to Your Own Content

Just as you should not copy from others, you should also do what you can to deter others from copying your work. Content is protected by copyright once it is fixed in a tangible medium of expression, so you do not *need* to add the copyright symbol to protect your content. But adding a copyright symbol, with a brief statement that all rights are reserved, will remind others that your work is protected. You do not need to post the copyright notice on every post. Simply add it to your home page or some other prominent page.

Consider a Creative Commons License

Many bloggers allow non-commercial forms of copying. Clarify the types of copying that you will allow by applying a Creative Commons license to your blog. Go to **www.creativecommons.org** for details and instructions.

Enable Comments

The reason you are blogging, rather than just posting to a website, is so that you can engage with your readers. To take full advantage of this medium, you should allow your readers to post comments.

Respond to Comments

Once you enable comments, you have implicitly agreed to join a conversation. This means you must occasionally respond to comments. You do not need to be on call to respond to every comment, but you should occasionally weigh in on issues as they surface in the comments. A blog is a dynamic medium so you want to create some impression of availability.

But Don't Be Too Available

You also don't want to create the impression that you have nothing better to do with your time than attend to your blog. If you respond to comments hourly, your followers may think that you don't have enough paying work to keep you busy. So be responsive, but not too responsive.

Monitor Comments

It's your blog, so you don't need to host negative comments. Monitor comments as they come in and delete any comments that are off tone, that don't reflect well on you or your abilities, or that might offend someone else. But be aware that you may build credibility with your followers and generate interest in your blog if you allow some critical posts to stand. Everybody likes to watch a good battle.

Listen

Indeed, you will learn from your follower's comments. Listen to what your followers are telling you, even if it is critical. Comments often evolve into a conversation between listeners, so listen in on that conversation as well. Your followers will likely lead you to a deeper knowledge of your topic. As a blogger, you should embrace your readers even if they seem to be on the attack. The blogosphere is not for the faint of heart.

Post Regularly

In *Social Media for Lawyers*, the authors suggest keeping "office hours" during which you are available to respond immediately to comments. Most blogs won't generate enough traffic to warrant "office hours," but if your blog becomes hot enough to justify the commitment, try keeping office hours. (And good luck persuading followers to show up at the appointed times.)

Link Wisely

The World Wide Web is what it says it is: a web. So you should allow yourself to be ensnared and you should ensnare others. While it's not nice for people to copy your work, it is nice for them to link to your blog. So link to other sites and encourage links to your site (if you are asked).

However, the number of links to and from your blog will not have a huge impact on your rank in searches, so don't link just for the purpose of optimizing your blog. In the rarified world of the law, the quality of visitors to your blog matters more than the number of visits. It is better to play a prominent role in your narrow area of expertise than to attract a larger audience in an unfiltered field. A link to the local youth sports blog may bring you a few more visitors, but those visitors are likely not your target audience. So seek links that serve your professional goals and reflect your professional image or that will be useful to your audience.

Search engines give greater weight to content on another site that links to your blog than they give to links in the sidebar of another blog. Why? Because these internal links within other pages suggest that your blog is being used as a reference or talked about on other sites. The way to generate these internal links is to craft useful content. Again, in the blogosphere, content is key.

Follow Others

Choose a few well-respected blogs to follow and learn from the style and manner of those blogs.

Do It Right

If you are not good at blogging, your blog may be detrimental to your professional goals. Imagine a potential client researching your credentials online. They view your credentials online and eventually link through to your blog. If your blog suggests that you are odd or overbearing or that you can't write well, your blog may be the detour that turns that client away.

Housekeeping

34

When you find an adjective, kill it.
—Mark Twain, *Letter to D. W. Bowser, March 20, 1880*

Keep a "Master" Subfile for Each Case or Matter

Again, create one master file that contains essential information for each matter—chronologies, key letters, contracts, summaries of the law. Maintain your normal filing system but save a copy of key documents in this master subfile, as well. You may occasionally need a hard-copy notebook to use as an exhibit or as a reference while you question a witness. If so, organize your key documents in a notebook, with tabs, so that the documents are easy to find.

Maintain a Thorough Form File

A good form file will be a lifeline throughout your practice. Whenever you finish a paper, save a copy in your form file. Consider any good writing a candidate for your form file, including briefs and letters filed by other lawyers and authors. While you should not copy another's work outright, you can use these papers as models.

Within your form file, rename your document and folder titles so that they include a brief reference to the topic covered by each paper. If your titles include a brief reference to the topic, you can find a relevant paper by searching the names of files, rather than the text of the documents.

Backup Your Form File

Backup your form file regularly. You never know when you may want to have everything you have ever written near you.

Guard Client Confidentiality in Your Form File

Be careful to protect client confidentiality in your form file, particularly if you are backing up to a flash drive or a laptop, since either can be easily lost. If you are backing up to a flash drive or laptop, considering redacting all client confidential information, including the names of clients.

The Nutshell Summary of This Book | 35

Either write something worth reading or do something worth writing.

—Benjamin Franklin

ON THE THEORY that I should practice what I preach, here are my recommendations—and your *To Do* list.

Write in Plain English

If you would not use a word or phrase when speaking with a colleague, don't use it in your writing.

Say Your Sentences Aloud

Say each sentence aloud to edit for plain English and to cure clutter and awkward constructions.

Prime Your Reader by Leading from the Top

Your opening must establish your command of your subject and prime your reader by telling them what to look for. The first paragraph or, at most, the first page and a half must do three things. It must explain the story, it must make the issue clear and it must state your answer.

Begin with the Story

Your target audience is not just the attorney who gave you the assignment, but also the *next* person who reviews the file and who may not know the background of your case. Always set the stage by beginning with two or three sentences that explain the background facts or the "story."

Lead with Your Conclusion

Lead from the top by putting your conclusion in the opening page and a half or—better yet—on the first paragraph.

Be Confident About Your Conclusion

A conclusion that simply says *maybe* is not worth the cost of the research. Reach a definitive answer.

Keep Your Conclusion Brief and Client Specific

Imagine running into the attorney who assigned you the project as she is getting on the elevator. You have only a few seconds to update her on your research. Your one-sentence plain-English summary is your conclusion. Avoid abstract legal concepts and explain what your conclusion means for *this* client.

Use Headings

Identify your two or three key points and make these your major headings, under Roman numerals or primary headings. A paper without headings is impenetrable.

Conclude, Support and Apply

Within each section, lead from the top with an opening paragraph that states your conclusion. The middle paragraphs should explain the law that supports that conclusion and the final paragraphs should apply your conclusion to the facts or give examples of your conclusion in action.

Lead Each Paragraph with an Original Topic Sentence

Similarly, within each paragraph, lead from the top with an opening sentence that summarizes the paragraph. Your opening sentence should always be your original writing. Your reader should be able to understand your paper just by reading the opening sentence of each paragraph.

Focus on Facts, Facts, Facts

Facts win cases, not lists of authority. Know the facts of your case and the facts of the precedent. Argue the facts. Compare the facts. Weave law and fact together.

Make Each Sentence Say Something New

Once you are in the body of your paper, each sentence must earn its space on the paper by developing your topic, refining your argument or introducing new material. Work from general to specific and delete any sentences that simply repeat information.

Assign a Weight to Each Case

Let your reader know whether a case narrows a concept, states a different position, provides an example or repeats information, by using signal phrases such as *in particular, by contrast, for example*, and *again*.

Discuss the Facts of Cases

Do more than simply explain the general rule of law that emerges from a case. Explain what the case was about and the procedural result. Did the analogous party win or lose? What did the court order? Use facts to flesh out theory. If you can't work the facts into prose, write a parenthetical.

Think Factually About the Body of Law

Don't be limited by narrow legal topics such as *intent* or *misrepresentation*. Divide your research into two groups: cases that help and cases that hurt or *Yes* and *No*. Look for the factual patterns or trends in your *Yes* cases and build your argument around these themes. Distinguish your case from the common facts of your *No* cases.

Focus on the Big Picture

Convey the big picture view of the research by using phrases such as *the great weight of authority holds that, no case has ever held that,* or *courts routinely hold that.*

Make Recommendations

Finish by telling the assigning attorney or the client what to do next.

Have Fun

Nineteen-plus years of schooling should lead to some joy. Have fun with your writing. Master your craft and make it your art. Words are wondrous—the gift of our common humanity and the window on our unique intelligence. If knowledge is power, then words harness and liberate that power. Use your words wisely and celebrate the gift of language in your writing. The power of the written word is yours to claim.

A Usage and Punctuation Guide

By Marie P. Buckley

Table of Contents

I. The School of Overwriting (Alternatives to Legalese and Other Stuffy Words)........................220

II. Worrisome Words...............................225

III. Horrible Homonyms (Things *Spellcheck* Will Never Tell You)..228

IV. Commonly Misused Words......................229

V. What the Grammar Police Get Wrong..............230

VI. Numbed by Numbers............................231

VII. The Court of Capitalization......................232

VIII. Petrified by Punctuation.........................232

IX. Subliminal Fear of Subparagraphs................239

X. Wounded by Bullets............................240

XI. Pronoun Panic.................................242

XII. Singularly Confused About Plural Problems.........242

XIII. Petrified by Possessives.........................243

I. The School of Overwriting (Alternatives to Legalese and Other Stuffy Words)

A. Delete legalese or rewrite it in plain English.

Legalese	Plain English Alternative
aforementioned	none (delete)
whereas	" "
hereinafter	" "
heretofore	" "
in connection with	about, concerning, for
with respect to	about, concerning
pursuant to	under
whereas	while
in the present case	here, in this case
in the instant case	here, in this case
said (as in said contract)	this (as in this contract)
same (as in paragraph 6 of the same)	this (as in paragraph 6 of this contract)
such (as in such paragraph provides)	this (as in this paragraph provides)
i.e.	that is
vis a vis	compared to
per our conversation	in our conversation
e.g.	for example
inter alia	among other things
on all fours	analogous
arguendo	for example
in point of fact	none (delete)
set forth	explain, list
notwithstanding the fact that	although

B. Use familiar, concrete words rather than stuffy, academic language.

Stuffy	Plain English Alternative
in all likelihood	likely, probably
Let me offer an explanation of the cause.	Let me explain why.
statement for professional services	bill
Enclosed please find. . . .	I have enclosed. . . .
presently	soon, now
Pursuant to our conversation. . . .	As we discussed. . . .
Per your request. . . .	As you asked. . . .
I am of the mind that. . . .	none (delete)

terminology	*term*
signage	*sign*
Of particular import to this issue	*In particular,*
He was aware that. . . .	*He knew that. . . .*
He shall have the ability to. . . .	*He can. . . .*
It has the effect of. . . .	*It effectively. . . .*
few in number	*few*
In the alternative	*Alternatively*
on a daily basis	*everyday*
a variety of	*many*
It is imperative that the defendant. . . .	*The defendant should. . . .*
It is incumbent upon the defendant. . . .	*The defendant should. . . .*
your own	*your*
does not appear to be	*is not*
insofar as	none (delete)
as such	none (delete)
out of an abundance of caution	none (delete)

C. *Avoid turning strong verbs into stuffy nouns or nominalizations.* Search for *ment* and *ion* to weed out nominalizations.

<u>Nominalizations</u>	<u>Plain English Verb</u>
give notice	*notify*
make a statement	*state*
interpose an objection	*object*
make a decision	*decide*
reach a conclusion	*conclude*
register a complaint	*complain*
have an altercation	*fight*
make an assumption	*assume*
raise a question	*ask*
is dependent on	*depends*
is the continuation of	*continues*
make an amendment	*amend, change*
take into consideration	*consider*
take into account	*consider*
make inquiry	*ask*
provide assistance	*help*
put the plaintiff on notice	*notify*
turns upon a determination of	*depends on*
set out a list	*lists*

file a motion	*move*
is in accordance with	*serves*
has the intention of	*intends*
provide a divergent explanation of	*differ*
has the effect of discouraging	*effectively discourages*
was under the impression	*believed, thought*

D. Choose action verbs over the verb to be.

Weak *to be* verbs	Action alternative
They are the owners of the spoon.	*They own the spoon.*
The rule is applicable.	*The rule applies.*
It is the tenant's responsibility to. . . .	*The tenant must. . . .*
The statute is distinguishable from. . . .	*The statute differs from. . . .*

E. Avoid adding unnecessary prepositions to verbs.

Prepped-out verbs	Plainly dressed alternatives
I offered up my thoughts.	*I offered my thoughts.*
I faced up to the situation.	*I faced the situation.*

F. Avoid overkill. Don't overkill a concept by repeating it over and over and over and over and over:

null and void
free and clear
good and sufficient
convey and assign
last will and testament
full and complete
if and when
if and only if
including but not limited to
first and foremost

G. Avoid and/or. *And/or* fails the test for plain English because it is not even pronounceable. If you need to keep both the conjunctive and the alternative concepts, say *the apples and the oranges or both.* If you have more than two things in your list, say *the apples, the oranges, the pears or all of these things.*

H. *Don't overwrite prepositions or phrases involving time.*
Prepositions should be simple and clean so don't use many words if one preposition will do. Lawyers also tend to overwrite phrases that involve time.

Compound	Plain English Pronoun
at that point in time	*when*
at the present time	*now*
at this time	*now*
for the period of	*during, for*
during the time that	*while*
until such time as	*until*
during such time as	*when*
prior to the time	*before*
insofar as	*assuming that, if*
assuming for the sake of argument that	*if*
in connection with	*about, concerning*
with respect to	*about, concerning*
in the event that	*if*
despite the fact that	*although*
due to the fact that	*because*
at sometime before	*before*
in the process of	*during, while*
in order to	*to*
insofar as	*because, as*
assuming that	*if*
together with	*with*
for the purpose of	*for*
assuming that	*if*
for the reason that	*because*
at the conclusion of	*after*
as there are	*because*
with regard to	*for*
so long as	*if*
relative to	*about*
as a result	*therefore*
by virtue of its	*by its*
as of yet	*yet*

to the extent that	*if*
the question of whether	*whether*
whether or not	*whether*
as to whether	*whether*
on or about (as in *on or about Jan 1,*)	*on*
it is not uncommon for	*may*
upon	*on*

I. Avoid marrying verbs that are happy enough alone. In particular, the verb *to be* is a red light for wordiness.

Unhappily married verbs	Plain English verb
is going to provide	*will provide*
proceeded to consider	*considered*
went on to state	*stated*
has the power to avoid	*can avoid*
is bound to	*will*

J. Kill the verbosity, particularly phrases that begin with it is. Avoid phrases such as *It seems clear that* or *It is possible that*. Delete the phrase entirely or rewrite it with an adverb, such as *apparently* or *likely*. For example, *It is apparent that the company lost the documents* should be rewritten as *The company apparently lost the documents*.

Delete these:

It is clear that
It is logical that
It may be that
It is apparent that
It is likely that
It is probable that
It follows that
It is imperative to note that
It goes without saying that
It is axiomatic that
The fact that

The only *it is* phrases that are permissible are phrases that convey the weight of authority, such as *It is well established that* and *It is black letter law that*. These phrases add substance to the sentence and earn their weight on the page.

K. Steer clear of the school of redundancy school.

Redundant phrases	Plain English Alternative
the *end result*	All *results* are *end results.*
the *general public*	The *public* means the *general public.*
interrelationships	All relations are *inter.*
personal friends	All friends are *personal.*
return back	There is no place to *return* to but *back.*
individual person	Each *person* is an *individual.*
the *upcoming future*	The *future* is always *upcoming.*

II. Worrisome Words

Pay particular attention to the following words, which are often confused with each other or used incorrectly:

Worrisome Words	Meaning	Example
assure/ensure/ insure	*Assure* applies to people.	I *assured* my children that I would protect them.
	Ensure applies to events or things.	The escrow fund *ensured* that the builder would complete the project.
	Insure applies to money or guarantees.	I *insured* the debt.
affect/effect	Generally, *affect* is the verb and *effect* is the noun. Think of *affect* and *effect* in alphabetical order. You must *affect* something in order to cause an *effect.* Try putting *the* in front of the word. If it takes the article, use *effect.* If adding the article doesn't work, use *affect.*	The new paint job *affected* the plane's appearance but, unfortunately, had an unexpected *effect* on the plane's performance. He liked *the effect.*
	However, *effect* can also be used as a verb, meaning *achieve* or *bring about.*	He *effected* a change.

between/among	Generally, use *between* when two are involved and *among* when three or more are involved. But the rule requiring *among* when three items are involved is not absolute. For example, you can be *between* three cities but not *among* them.	Carrie and Scott kept the secret *between* themselves. We don't mind because we are *among* friends. I got lost *between* Boston, New York and San Francisco.
disperse/disburse	*Disperse* means to scatter or break up. *Disburse* means to pay out.	The police *dispersed* the crowd. I *disbursed* the funds.
each other or *one other*	Use *each other* for two and *one another* for two or more.	Carrie and Scott love *each other* but the neighborhood children hate *one another*.
farther/further	*Farther* refers to physical distance. Remember that *far* implies distance. *Further* refers to an abstract idea or extent.	I won't carry this luggage any *farther*. I won't discuss it any *further*.
fewer/less	*Less* means a smaller quantity of something. *Fewer* means a smaller number of individual things.	He owes *less* money than I do and has *fewer* worries.
Induce/deduce	*Induce* means *to persuade*. *Deduce* means *to infer* or *decide by reasoning*.	I *induced* them to buy my book. They *deduced* the answer to my question.
imply/infer	*Imply* means *suggest*. *Infer* means *conclude* or *consider a suggestion*. *Imply* and *infer* occur in alphabetical order: a speaker must *imply* something before than listener can *infer* it.	"You *imply* that I am illiterate," said Scott. "You *infer* correctly," said Carrie.
lie/lay	*Lie* means *to recline* or *occupy a space*.	Please *lie* down if you are tired. The boat *lies* on the shore.

	Confusion arises because the past form of *lie* is *lay*.	Last night, I *lay* down for a long rest.
		The boat *lay* on the beach last summer.
	The past perfect form is *had lain*.	I *had lain* down earlier in the day.
	Lay, as a present tense verb, means *to place*. *Lay* always requires a direct object, as in *Go lay an egg*.	*Lay* your luggage here.
	The past form of *lay* is *laid*.	I *laid* my luggage in the storage compartment.
	(The past perfect form of *lay* is *had laid*.)	(I *had laid* it on the ground earlier.)
		The boat had laid on the beach last summer, as well.
	In sum: *Lie-lay-lain* *Lay-laid-laid.*	
like/as	Use *like* to precede a noun.	The plane looks *like* a pink flamingo.
	Use *as* to precede a clause.	It flies *as* a pink flamingo does.
parameter/ perimeter	A *parameter* is a mathematical term, not a boundary. A *perimeter* is a boundary.	We walked the *perimeters* of the property.
disinterested/ uninterested	Disinterested means impartial.	The judge was *disinterested*.
	Uninterested means bored.	My students are *uninterested* in the finer points of grammar.
which/that	*Which* is not restrictive. *That* is restrictive. If you can drop the clause and not loose the point of the sentence, use *which*.	The corporate jet, *which* I ordered in light pink, is very expensive. But the plane *that* carries the president costs even more.
	Otherwise, use *that*.	The jet *that* looks pink is mine.

	Set off *which* clauses with commas. (Remember this rule as *comma which*.) *That* clauses are not set off with comas because they are an integral part of the sentence.	
strategy/tactics	*Strategy* refers to large-scale goals. *Tactics* are the smaller steps you take to implement those goals. Think of them in alphabetical order. You establish your strategy first (particularly, if you lead from the top) and you then determine your tactics for implementing your strategy.	Her *strategy* is to make partner. Her chief *tactic* is to master the art of legal writing.
who/whom	*Who* does something. *Whom* has something done to him or her.	The pilot *whom* I discussed has been assigned to my jet. *Who* is going to tell the pilot to be careful?

III. Horrible Homonyms (Things *Spellcheck* Will Never Tell You)

Homonym	Explanation	Example
their/they're/there	*Their* is the possessive of *they*.	I love *their* pilot.
	They're means *they are*.	*They're* not going to fly on my jet.
	There means *in* or *at that place*.	*There* is my plane.
who's/whose	*Who's* means *who is* or *who has*.	*Who's* coming on the plane with me?
	Whose is the possessive of *who*.	*Whose* plane is this?
you're/your	*You're* means *you are*. *Your* is the possessive of *you*.	*You're* not coming on the jet with me unless you leave *your* tarantula at home.

it's/its	*It's* means *it is*.	*It's* a beautiful day.
	Its is the possessive of *it*.	The plane is easy to spot because of *its* color.
	Its' is not a word.	
stationery/ stationary	*Stationery* is the paper you write on. (Remember that *stationery* and paper both contain *er*.)	I will write a letter on this *stationery* once the plane is *stationary*.
	Stationary means *in one place* or *standing still.*	
moot/mute	*Moot* means *not ripe for decision.*	The issue has already been resolved so the case is *moot*.
	Mute (pronounced *myoot*) means unable to speak.	The witness suddenly turned *mute*.

IV. Commonly Misused Words

Beware the most commonly misused words—some of which are not words at all.

Beware	Because	Example
irregardless	The correct term is *regardless*.	I'll spell it correctly, *regardless* of how he spells it.
preventative	The correct term is *preventive*.	Let's take some *preventive* measures to avoid these mistakes.
hopefully	In modern usage, *hopefully* is commonly used to mean *I hope* or *with luck*. Strict grammarians insist that *hopefully* be used only to mean *in a hopeful manner,* as in *He approached them hopefully*. The newest edition of *The Chicago Manual of Style* accepts the modern usage,	

> *The New York Times Manual of Style and Usage* avoids taking a position—just as I am avoiding taking a position here!

could care less	The correct phrase is *could not care less.*	My client's customers *could not care less* about the mistake.

V. What the Grammar Police Get Wrong

The grammar police are out there—self-appointed and determined to enforce ancient edicts they learned in 6th grade. Ignore archaic "rules" that are no longer modern usage. (These grammar police issues are discussed in more detail in Chapter 4 at page 30.)

However at the beginning of a sentence	*However* may go at the beginning of a sentence. The edict that *however* should be placed in the middle of a sentence originated in Strunk and White's *The Elements of Style*. But Strunk emulated high Victorian English and you should speak in modern English. Remember that *but* is the modern way of saying *however*.
But at the beginning of a sentence.	You may also begin sentences with *but*.
And at the beginning of a sentence.	And you may begin a sentence with *and*, although beginning a sentence with *and* may be too colloquial or artsy for formal legal writing.
Because at the beginning of a sentence.	You may also begin a sentence with *because*. Starting a sentence with *because* adds emphasis.
Split infinitives	You may split your infinitives. Again, the edict against splitting infinitives arose because English is derived from Latin. In Latin, the infinitive is a single word (such as *amore* for *to love*) that could not be split. But the admonition against splitting infinitives has no relevance for English where the infinitive form is two words practically begging to be split.

VI. Numbed by Numbers

Any number that begins a sentence	Always spell out numbers at the beginning of a sentence.
one to *nine*	Spell out the numbers *one* to *nine*. Civilians and lawyers agree on this point.
11 to *99*	The convention in legal writing has always been to spell out *eleven* to *ninety-nine*, but the civilian world prefers the numerical form, *11* to *99*. Live bravely, defy convention, and use the number form.
Round numbers	Lawyers generally spell out round numbers, such as *one hundred*, *ten thousand*, or *one million*.
Second and *third*	Spell out *second* and *third* when they are used in text. However, you'll occasionally need the number form in the text of a sentence, as in *The 102nd Congress passed the legislation*. When using the number form in text, use the modern *2nd* and *3rd*, rather than *2d* and *3d*. In citations, use *2d* or *3d*, as in *100 F.2d 201*. In any case, do not superscript the numbers in text. Since the numbers in citations do not get superscripted, it looks inconsistent to occasionally use superscripted numbers. (Each time a number superscripts, go to the *Edit* tab and click on *Undo Autoformat* or disable *Superscript* entirely.)
Numbers with percentage signs or dollar signs	Use the number with no space between the number and the sign, as in *50%* or *$50*.
Fractions	Lawyers generally spell out fractions, as in *three-fourths*, unless the fraction is used with a whole number, as in $1^1/_2$. So if your fraction is a fraction with a friend, use the number form.
Numbers in a series	Format numbers in a series in the same fashion, even if you must break a rule in order to do so. Don't *say But nine out of 99 voters voted for Mr. Cool*. Be consistent and say *9 out of 99 voters voted for Mr. Cool* or *Nine out of ninety-nine voters voted for Mr. Cool*.

Plural Numbers   Great minds differ on whether or not to use an
                                  apostrophe before the *s* but most authorities
                                  prefer the apostrophe, as in *1980's.*

VII. The Court of Capitalization

Capitalize *court* if you are referring to the Supreme Court, the highest court in
a jurisdiction, or the court in which you are filing your paper. Otherwise
lower case *court.*

VIII. Petrified by Punctuation

Punctuation	Particular Situations	Explanation	Example
period	.	Put one space after the period, not two.	Putting two spaces after a period is old-fashioned. Be green and save a space.
serial comma	___, ___, *and* ____.	The serial comma is a topic of great debate among the grammar police. In general, the civilian American approach does not put a comma before *and*. (*The New York Times Manual of Style and Usage* does not endorse the serial comma.)	*My American students bring me apples, pears and cherries.*
		The British approach uses the comma.	*My British students bring me crumpets, tea, and sugar.*
		In legal writing—where precision is essential—the serial comma is more precise. Always use the serial comma when drafting contracts. (Google *million dollar*	*This provision applies to the Seller, the Buyer, and any Assignee.*

comma to find out why.) You will never offend anyone by including the serial comma—and you may trigger comma neuroses in your colleagues if you don't use it. (*The Chicago Manual of Style*, the U.S. Government Printing Office, and Bryan Garner all endorse the serial comma.)

But be aware that the serial comma often compromises the pacing of the sentence. Consider the famous line by Robert Frost: *The woods are lovely, dark and deep.* The stately and majestic pacing of this line changes once the serial comma is added: *The woods are lovely, dark, and deep.*

The bottom line: Always use the serial comma in transactional drafting. In traditional prose documents, the serial comma is optional. But it may be easier just to be consistent and use the serial comma in all your legal writing.

| ellipses | . . . | Three ellipses replace omitted words in the middle of a sentence. The *Bluebook* requires a space before and after the ellipse and between each period within the ellipse. | *The pink plane . . . brought her back to Boston.* |

	. . . .	Four ellipses replace omitted words at the end of a sentence. (The fourth dot represents the period at the end of a sentence.) Again, put a space before the ellipse and between each period within the ellipse. (Since the fourth dot is the final period, place one space after that dot, as you would after a period.)	*The instructor droned on and on and on . . . .*
	. . . ?	If the original sentence ended in question mark or an exclamation point, preserve that final punctuation mark as the fourth and last mark in the ellipse.	*Did the instructor ask whether . . . ?*
semicolons	;	You can use a semicolon, instead of a period, to join sentences that are not joined by a conjunction. In terms of degrees of separation, a semicolon suggests less separation than a period and more separation than a comma.	*I bored them to death; they yawned throughout my presentation.*
		Semicolons also separate items in a series. They are particularly useful when a series contains internal commas.	*I've brought several things today: my lecture notes, which I prepared yesterday; cookies; and a silly prop.*
colons	:	Colons introduce items in a series.	*We must order three things: tea, a corporate jet and biscuits.*
		Colons are also used to introduce ideas. The colon indicates that what follows the colon	*The tea is essential: it keeps me from falling asleep while I speak.*

explains or summarizes the material before the colon.

But never put a colon between a verb and its object.	Not: *We must order: mint tea, a corporate jet and biscuits.*
Colons also introduce quotations	*I live by my favorite saying: "Swallow one elephant at a time."*
Generally, lowercase the word immediately after the colon unless that word is a proper noun or a complete sentence that is essentially a quotation.	*She promised this: She would edit until her fingers dropped.*

long dash or em dash	—	The long dash (or em dash) sets off material that interrupts a sentence or marks "aside" thoughts.	*We went to the Tinker Theater—one of the most beautifully renovated theaters in the country—and saw Swan Lake.*

Em dashes add emphasis and isolate the material between the dashes.	*I love old theaters—especially at night.*
The em dash is standard modern English, even if some old school legal writers consider it too informal or colloquial for legal writing. The em dash is always followed by a phrase, not a sentence.	
If the clause occurs at the end of a sentence, rather than in the middle, use one em dash.	*We saw Swan Lake at the Tinker Theater—one of the most beautifully renovated theaters in the country.*
Em dashes can also be used to simplify complicated sentences with multiple commas. Where	*Correspondence with opposing counsel is not protected by the attorney-client privi-*

a clause itself contains commas, replace the outside or inside comma or commas with a dash or set of dashes to make the structure of the sentence visually clearer.

lege, although other privileges, such as the privilege covering settlement negotiations, may apply.

becomes:

Correspondence with opposing counsel is not protected by the attorney-client privilege, although other privileges—such as the privilege covering settlement negotiations— may apply.

| En dash | The smaller dash (also known as single dash or the en dash) indicates a range of values or contrast. | *2000–2010*
Exhibits 1–7
the rich–poor gap
the *east–west divide* |

spacing
em dashes

Bring your text right up to each side of the em dash, with no space between the words and the em dash. Although *The New York Times Manual of Style and Usage* requires a space before and after the em dash to accommodate newspaper columns, lawyers do not need that space since we do not write in columns.

How to
make dashes

Alt0150 (en dash)
Alt0151 (em dash)

or on the *insert* tab/click *symbols* on the far right/ choose *special characters* and select *em dash* or *en dash*. Then simplify your life by assigning a shortcut key to the each dash.

hyphens	-	Hyphens divide words at the end of a line.	*I am very fond of my corporate jet.*
		Hyphens are also used with some multipart words.	*cost-effective* *mother-in-law*
		Hyphens also combine two or more descriptive words before—but not after—a noun unless the words could be used separately and still make sense.	*My blue-eyed brother is pig headed.* *My pigheaded brother is blue eyed.* *My crazy younger brother is pigheaded.* *He always takes a heavy-handed approach.* *I deal with my brother on a day-by-day basis.* *The court focused on the cause-and-effect prong.*
		There is no limit to the number of hyphens you may use.	*My above-average-but-not-yet-ready-for-prime-time children are making progress.*
Hyphens with *ly*		But don't use a hyphen with any word ending in *ly* or any other adverb. (The rule for hyphens with *well* is next.)	*My exceptionally messy children.*
Hyphens with *well*		Use a hyphen if *well* precedes the noun, but not if *well* follows the noun.	*My well-chosen words* *My words were well chosen.*

Hyphens with *Mid* and *Non*	*Mid* and *non* are not followed by a hyphen unless the next word begins with a capital letter. *Spellcheck* will often insist on a hyphen when it is not appropriate.	*nonsectarian* *nonspecific* *non-American* *midsection* *midterm* *midpoint* *mid-Atlantic*
Hyphens with *self, quasi, ex*	Use a hyphen with *self, quasi* and *ex*.	*quasi-official* *self-regulating* *ex-husband*
Hyphens with Numbers	Use a hyphen with the numbers *twenty-one* to *ninety-nine* and with fractions.	*one-fourth* *ninety-nine*
Hyphens with *inter*	Don't use a hyphen with *inter*.	*interoffice*
Hyphens with *co*	Check the dictionary.	Some words beginning with *co* are not hyphenated, such as *coed*, while others, such as *co-defendant*, use the hyphen.
parentheses ( )	Parentheses also set off material that interrupts a sentence. Parentheses downplay the material.	*I take my favorite things (mint tea and corporate jets) whenever I travel.*
	They are rarely appropriate within a prose sentence. In legal writing, you should generally save parentheses for references to exhibits.	*The corpse was naked. (Photo, Exhibit A).*
[sic]	Don't use *[sic]*. *[Sic]* is scolding and uppity. Just replace the misspelled or misused word with the correctly spelled word in brackets, if you can do so without changing the meaning.	*The bana [sic] tree* sounds mean. Simply note the correct spelling in brackets and say *the [banana] tree.*

periods and quotations	In American usage, periods, commas and other terminal punctuation go *inside* the quote.	*She had warned me, "Always put the period inside the quotation." Then she asked me, "Do you understand?" I said, "Yes."*

IX. Subliminal Fear of Subparagraphs

When using subparagraph format:

(1) put a colon at the end of the sentence that introduces the subparagraphs;
(2) conclude each numbered subparagraph with a semicolon;
(3) put *and* or *or* after the semicolon in the penultimate paragraph; and
(4) conclude the final subparagraph with a period.

You may also use subparagraph format without indenting the subparagraphs: (1) use a colon to introduce the subparagraphs; (2) separate the subparagraphs with semicolons; (3) put *and* or *or* at the end of the penultimate paragraph; and (4) finish with a period.

In other words, your subparagraphs should look like the subparagraphs I just wrote.

Use parallel construction throughout the subparagraphs. Writers frequently make grammatical errors when writing subparagraphs because the front half of their sentence (the part before the colon) does not fit grammatically with the back half (the part after the colon). To avoid these grammatical errors "glue" the front and back of the sentence together: mentally copy the words in each subparagraph to the end of the introductory phrase before the colon. Does the glued-together sentence make grammatical sense? If not, make whatever edits are necessary to make the two halves of the sentence fit together grammatically. Continue by gluing each subparagraph onto the introductory front half to check for correct grammar.

Or simply obey the fundamental law requiring that each subparagraph be written in parallel construction. Even the most subparagraph-challenged writers usually write the first subparagraph correctly. So use the same construction in successive subparagraphs and your subparagraphs will glue together in the most grammatically wonderful way.

X. Wounded by Bullets

A. *When not to use bullets.*

Because bullets suggest that there is no hierarchy to the bulleted items, you should use bullets only if all entries in the list are of equal importance. If some entries are more important than others, use numbered subparagraphs and list the important items first.

B. *Consistency between Bullets.*

Don't mix different types of items in one bulleted list. For example, don't bullet a list about:

- Representation
- Reliance
- Intent
- Harm
- Giraffes.

C. *Bullets and case law.*

Never bullet case law. The medium simply doesn't fit the message. Bullets are so simplified and slick that they can rarely do justice to the nuances of case law. A bulleted list of cases looks like just that—a list. You must show your clients and the court that you have thought deeply about the cases and gone well beyond simply listing your research.

D. *Parallel construction between bullets.*

Use parallel construction between bullets. If the first item is a word or fragment, later items must also be a word or fragment. If the first item is a full sentence or question, later items must also be a sentence or question.

Failure to Use Parallel Construction

The client asked us to consider several issues:

- Choice-of-law
- Personal jurisdiction
- What is the standard of review?

Note: The first two bullets are phrases so the third bullet should be a phrase also.

Correct Parallel Construction

The client asked us to consider several issues:

- Choice-of-law
- Personal jurisdiction
- Standard of review

E. Grammatical continuity when using bullets.

Each bullet must also fit within the phrase or sentence before the colon. This is where most bullet-writers shoot themselves in the foot. They write a bullet where the front end of their sentence (the part before the colon) and the back end (the part in the bullet) just don't fit together. Mentally copy the words in each bullet to the end of the introductory phrase before the colon. Is the sentence grammatically correct or are words missing? Make whatever edits are necessary to make the two ends of the sentence fit together correctly. (This is the same technique discussed for proofing subparagraphs.)

Incorrect grammar within bullets	Correct Construction
The court will review:	The court will review:
♦ Choice-of-law issues ♦ Personal jurisdiction ♦ Did the trial court abuse its discretion?	♦ Choice-of-law ♦ Personal jurisdiction ♦ Abuse of discretion
Note: The third bullet does not match up with the sentence before the colon.	Putting the third bullet in parallel construction solves the problem—as it often does.

F. Punctuating and formatting bullets.

Bullets are standard modern usage, but they are so new to our arsenal that usage mavens often disagree on how to style them. Some people suggest punctuating bullets the way we punctuate subparagraphs, with semicolons and the word *and* before the penultimate item. However, I prefer a modern, clean style, as suggested in the box at right.

G. Keeping bulleted lists clean.

Bullets pack their power because they are an efficient, modern way of presenting information. Bullets lose their power if they become too com-

---

Punctuating and Formatting Bullets

To punctuate and format bullets:

♦ Put a colon at the end of the phrase that introduces the bullet.
♦ Capitalize the first word of the bullet.
♦ If the bullet is a word or a phrase, don't put any punctuation at the end of the bullet (except the final bullet always takes a period).
♦ If the bullet is a sentence, put a period at the end of each bullet.
♦ Skip the penultimate *and*.
♦ Always put a period at the end of the last bullet.

In other words, your bullet should look like the bullet in this box.

plicated, so they are not appropriate for complex material. Similarly, don't spread bullets over multiple pages because your reader will get lost visually. And avoid bullets within bullets. The absence of any hierarchy will make the bulleted points hopelessly confusing.

XI. Pronoun Panic

A. Me *or* I? *(Or* he *or* him? *Or* she *or* her?)

To choose between *me* or *I*, simply complete the implied sentence that goes with the preposition.	*He dislikes the pilot more than I* means that *He dislikes the pilot more than I dislike the pilot.*
	He dislikes the pilot more than me means that *He dislikes the pilot more than he dislikes me.*

B. Myself *(and other* selves).

People who are completely confused about the choice between *me* and *I* often use *myself* incorrectly.	*Let Jane and myself know your thoughts.* (Wrong!)
Again, simply eliminate the other person.	If you can *Tell me your thoughts*, you should feel free to *Tell Jane and me*—not *myself*—*your thoughts.*
The *selves* are best used to add emphasis or to refer back to the subject.	*I flew the plane myself. The pilot himself was afraid to fly. And he called himself a pilot!*

People frequently use *myself* incorrectly when speaking in public because they are trying too hard to avoid grammatical errors. For example, they may say *Give your evaluations to John and myself*, instead *of Give your evaluations to John and me*. Don't be afraid to say *me* in public.

XII. Singularly Confused About Plural Problems

Plural people:	Plural people terrify us. To make most people plural simply add *s*.	the *Smiths*
Names ending in *s, sh, ch, x* or *z*:	Add *es*	*Joneses* *Charleses*

Compound words:	To make compound words (with or without a hyphen) plural, make the key word plural.	*mothers-in-law* *attorneys general*
Plural numbers and plural acronyms	Most writers still use the apostrophe to make numbers and acronyms plural. But a modern trend abolishes the plural apostrophe so stay tuned on this issue.	*1980's* *REIT's*

XIII. Petrified by Possessives

Great minds quibble on this issue but there are only two ways to make a possessive under modern usage:

Singular Words:	Add *'s* even if the word ends in *s, z* or *x*.	*Degas's paintings have so many ballerinas! (Degas' paintings is no longer modern usage.)*
	However, use only the apostrophe if the word is a Biblical or mythological reference or if the next word begins in *s*. Remember this final rule as the rule against three consecutive *s's*.	*They are carrying Zeus' thunderbolt.* *Degas' sister loves Degas's paintings.*
Plural Words:	(1) add *'s* if the word does not end in *s*.	*I'll send those ballerinas to the men's room.*
	(2) add an apostrophe without the *s* if the word already ends in *s*.	*Shouldn't you send them to the ladies' room instead?* *They can borrow the girls' costumes.*
Except *it* and *who*:	*It* and *who* become *its* and *whose*.	*Whose business is it anyway?* *The men's room is known for its inclusiveness.*

Bibliography

Books of General Interest for Legal Writers (in order of preference)

Richard C. Wydick, *Plain English for Lawyers,* Carolina Academic Press, 2005 (the best source for sentence-level editing; contains excellent exercises for curing awkward constructions and wordiness within sentences).

Steven D. Stark, *Writing to Win*, Main Street Books, 1999 (a modern, clean approach to legal writing).

Bryan A. Garner, *The Elements of Legal Style*, 2nd ed., Oxford University Press, USA, 2002 (a very readable guide by the leading proponent of plain English and the legal profession's leading word maven).

Mathew Butterick, *Typography for Lawyers: Essential Tools for Polished and Persuasive Documents*, Jones McClure Publishing, 2010 (the best source on designing clean, crisp documents and for answering all your word-processing questions). Also check out Butterick's website at: *Typography for Lawyers*, **http://www.typographyforlawyers.com**.

William Zinsser, *On Writing Well*, 30th Anniv. Ed., Harper, 2006 (a classic reissued).

Peter E. Meltzer, *The Thinker's Thesaurus: Sophisticated Alternative to Common Words*, 2nd ed., Norton, 2010 (the ultimate tool for word mavens).

Edward R. Tufte, *The Visual Display of Quantitative Information*, 2nd ed., Graphic Press 2001; *Visual Explanation*, Graphics Press, 1997; and *Envisioning information*, 4th ed., Graphics Press, 1990 (beautifully produced commentaries on effective chart making by the DaVinci of quantitative information; Tufte's books are essential tools for anyone who works with data).

Securities Exchange Commission, *A Plain English Handbook: How to Create Clear SEC Disclosure Documents*, Montezuma Publishing, 2004 (also available at **http://www.sec.gov/pdf/handbook.pdf**) (the SEC's guidebook).

Frederick Bernays Wiener, *Briefing and Arguing Federal Appeals*, 4th printing, The Lawbook Exchange, 2001 (an authoritative and detailed source on this art form).

Bill Bryson, *The Mother Tongue*, Harper Perennial, 1991 (a humorous collection of trivia, tidbit and history, which will persuade you that our language is still evolving and leave you laughing at its mighty power to define, betray, and ennoble us).

William Strunk, E.B. White, *The Elements of Style*, 5th Anniv. Ed., Longman, 2008 (another classic, also recently reissued, but some sections are considered outdated).

Kevin Wilson, Jennifer Wauson, *The AMA Handbook of Business Writing: The Ultimate Guide to Style, Grammar, Punctuation, Usage, Construction and Formatting*, American Management Association, 2010 (yet another useful usage guide; easy-to-find alphabetized entries).

Usage Guides (also in order of preference)

Allan M. Siegal, William G. Connolly, *The New York Times Manual of Style and Usage,* 1999 ed., Three Rivers Press (clear, alphabetized answers to the nitty-gritty questions you'll face at the keyboard—an essential resource. Every writer should own this book).

The Associated Press Stylebook, 3rd ed., Basic Books, 2009 (same format as *The New York Times Manual*—choose one or the other. *The Associated Press Stylebook*, frequently cross references from one entry to another, so I prefer *The New York Times Manual*).

Patricia T. O'Connor, *Woe is I*, 2nd ed., Riverhead Trade, 2004 (a relaxed, funny and workable approach to usage issues).

Bryan A. Garner, *The Elements of Legal Style*, 2nd ed., Oxford University Press, USA, 2002 (a very readable guide by the leading proponent of plain English and the legal profession's leading word maven).

Zinsser, *On Writing Well*, 30th Anniv. Ed., Harper, 2006 (a classic reissued).

Strunk, White, *The Elements of Style*, 5th Anniv. Ed., Longman, 2008 (another classic, also recently reissued, but some sections are considered outdated).

Bill Bryson, *Bryson's Dictionary of Troublesome Words*, Broadway Books, 2004 (in Bryson's own words, "A Guide to Everything in English Usage that the Author Wasn't Entirely Clear About Until Recently").

Bill Walsh, *Lapsing Into A Comma*, McGraw Hill, 2000 (another grammar guide; the most thorough discussion of compound and hyphenated words; targeted to the newspaper industry).

Theodore Bernstein, *The Careful Writer*, Free Press, Atheneum, 1995 (a particularly helpful resource for ESL students because it shows which prepositions go with various verbs).

Diane Hacker, *A Writer's Reference*, Bedford St. Martin's, 6th ed., 2006 (excellent, practical handbook).

Lynn Truss, *Eats, Shoots and Leaves*, Gotham, 2006 (a best seller in Britain and the USA; more a commentary on the importance of punctuation than a how-to-punctuate book; some funny punctuation jokes but the book itself often differs from standard American usage).

Sources for Individual Chapters

Chapter 1: Welcome to the Publishing Business

Dave Barry, *Dave Barry is Not Making This Up,* Crown Publishers, Inc., 1994.

Report of the National Commission on Writing for America's Families, Schools and Colleges (available at **http://www.collegeboard.com/prod_down loads/writingcom/writing-ticket-to-work.pdf**).

Chapter 4: Plain English and Other Tricks to Help You Sound Human

Philip B. Kurland, Gerhard Casper, *Landmark Briefs and Arguments of the Supreme Court of the United States*, University Publications of America, 1975.

Siegal, Connolly, *The New York Times Manual of Style and Usage*, 1999 ed., Three Rivers Press.

Stark, *Writing to Win*, Main Street Books, 1999.

Strunk, White, *The Elements of Style*, 5th Anniv. Ed., Longman, 2008.

Maurice Sendak, *Where the Wild Things Are,* Harper and Row, 1963.

Lattman, Peter, *The Inimitable Judge Posner Strikes Again,* The Wall Street Journal, Jan. 17, 2008 (available at **http://blogs.wsj.com/law/2008/01/17/the-inimitable-judge-posner-strikes-again/**).

Chapter 10: Beyond Research: Seeing the Big Picture

Stark, *Writing to Win*, Main Street Books, 1999.

Kurland, Casper, *Landmark Briefs and Arguments of the Supreme Court of the United States: Constitutional Law, 49 and 49A*, University Publications of America, 1975.

Chapter 11: Brainstorming

Tony Buzan, *Use Both Sides of Your Brain*, 3rd ed., Penguin Group, 1991 (a readable guide to how our minds function, with excellent suggestions on organizing information, improving reading skills and memory, and mind mapping).

Michael J. Gelb, *How to Think Like Leonardo da Vinci*, Bantam Dell, 2004 (the chapter on Arte/Scienza contains an excellent discussion of mind mapping).

Chapter 12: The Process of Writing and Overcoming Writer's Block

Clive Thompson, *Meet the Life Hackers*, N.Y. Times, October 16, 2005.

Haly Csikszentmihaly, *Flow: The Psychology of Optimal Experience*, Harper Perennial, 1991, p. 71.

William Langiewische, *American Ground: Unbuilding the World Trade Center,* The Atlantic, July and August, 2002.

Gloria Mark, Victor M. Gonzalez Harris, *No Task Left Behind? Examining the Nature of Fragmented Work*, Proceedings of the SIGCHI Conference of Human Factors in Computing Systems, 2005, p. 113–120 (also available at **http://www.ics.uci.edu/~gmark/CHI2005.pdf**).

Scott Sherman, *Going Long, Going Deep*, Columbia Journalism Review, Nov.–Dec., 2002, pg. 48-57 (available at **http://research.uvu.edu/albrecht-crane/Comm2010/Sherman.pdf**).

Alina Tugend, *Multitasking Can Make You Lose . . . Um . . . Focus*, N.Y. Times, Oct. 24, 2008.

Chapter 15: Using Structure to Lead from the Top

Robert F. Kennedy, Jr., *A Miscarriage of Justice*, The Atlantic, Feb. 2009.

Chapter 17: The Story or Facts

Daniel H. Pink, *A Whole New Mind: Why Right-Brainers Will Rule the Future*, Riverhead Books, 2006 (an interesting book about creativity, with an excellent commentary on the importance of story at pages 100–115).

Chapter 20: Substantive Headings in the Argument or Analysis

Mathew Butterick, *Typography for Lawyers: Essential Tools for Polished and Persuasive Documents*, Jones McClure Publishing, 2010.

Typography for Lawyers, **http://www.typographyforlawyers.com**, by Matthew Butterick.

Chapter 25: Citations

The Bluebook: A Uniform System of Citation, 18th ed., Harvard Law Review, 2008.

Official Reports Style Manual (N.Y. St. Unified Ct. Sys. 2007) (available at **http://www.courts.state.ny.us/reporter/New_Styman.htm**).

California Style Manual: A Handbook of Legal Style for California Courts and Lawyers, 4th ed. (available at **http://www.sdap.org/downloads/Style-Manual.pdf**).

ALWD & Darby Dickerson, *ALWD Citation Manual,* 4th ed., Aspen Publishers 2010.

Williams, *The Non-Designer's Design Book*, 3rd ed., Peachpit Press, 2008.

Chapter 27: Proofreading and Finalizing Your Work

Ben M. Schorr, *The Lawyer's Guide to Microsoft Word 2007*, American Bar Association, 2009.

Chapter 28: Design As a Writing Tool

Robin Williams, *The Non-Designer's Design Book*, 3rd ed., Peachpit Press, 2008.

Tufte, *The Visual Display of Quantitative Information*, 2nd ed., Graphic Press 2001; *Visual Explanation*, Graphics Press, 1997; and *Envisioning information*, 4th ed., Graphics Press, 1990.

Typography for Lawyers, **http://www.typographyforlawyers.com**, by Matthew Butterick.

Mathew Butterick, *Typography for Lawyers: Essential Tools for Polished and Persuasive Documents*, Jones McClure Publishing, 2010.

Chapter 30: Tips for Transactional Attorneys

Securities Exchange Commission, *A Plain English Handbook: How to Create Clear SEC Disclosure Documents* (1998).

Chapter 32: E-mail

Debra Cassens Weiss, *Lawyers Sanctioned for E-Mail Insults, Including 'Scum Sucking Loser' Comment*, ABA Journal, January 3, 2011 (available at **http://www.abajournal.com/news/article/lawyers_sanctioned_for_ e-mail_insults_including_scum_sucking_loser_comment**).

Brenda R. Sharton, Gregory J. Lyons, *The Risk of E-Mail Communication: A Guide to Protecting Privileged Electronic Communications*, ABA Business Law Today, v. 17, Number 1, 2007 (available at **http://www.abanet.org/ buslaw/blt/2007-09-10/lyons.shtml**).

Jonathan Zitrain, *Lost in the Cloud*, N.Y. Times, July 19, 2009.

New York State Bar Association, Committee On Professional Ethics, Opinion 820, 2008.

Katherine Eban, *Lilly's $1 Billion E-Mail Mailstrom*, Portfolio.com, February 5, 2008 (available at **http://www.portfolio.com/news-markets/top-5/2008/02/05/Eli-Lilly-E-Mail-to-New-York-Times**).

Debra Cassens Weiss, ABA Journal, *Did Lawyer's E-Mail Goof Land $1B Settlement on NYT's Front Page?*, ABA Journal, February 6, 2008 (available at **http://www.abajournal.com/news/article/lawyers_e_mail_goof_lands_on_nyts_front_page/**).

Chapter 33: Blogging

Andrew Sullivan, The Atlantic, November 2008, *Why I Blog* (available at **http://www.theatlantic.com/magazine/archive/2008/11/why-i-blog/7060/**).

Carol Elefant, Nicole Black, *Social Media for Lawyers: The Next Frontier*, American Bar Association, 2010.

Index

a (article), keeping, 27
Academic writing, transitioning to professional writing from, 39–41
Acronyms, avoiding complicated, 28
Action verbs, 222
Adjectives, avoiding qualifying, 21
Adverbs, choosing strong verbs vs., 20
Advice, online, blogging and, 208
Advocacy, works of
  persuasiveness and, 76
  phrasing issues to be answered affirmatively in, 76
affect/effect, 225
Against you cases, thinking about, 55
Alamo v. Puerto Rico, 72
ALL CAPS
  design and, 160
  e-mail and, 196
Alliteration, 18–19
ALWD Citation Manual, 139
among/between, 226
Analysis/Argument
  adverse case law and, 117
  assigning Roman-numbers/primary headings for, 110
  avoiding restatement of other side's argument in, 117
  avoiding sentence repetition in paragraphs, 113
  avoiding use of journals in, 118
  breaking up lists in, 118
  commenting about opponents in, 118

conclude, support, apply for, 110
  facts for, 109
  fitting paragraphs in, 112
  lead sentences in paragraphs of, 112
  organizing, 110
  paragraph breaks in, 111
  paragraph for new topics in, 112
  parallel construction for, 111
  signal phrases in, 113–114
  structure for, 110
  substantive footnotes in, 118
  theme words in, 115
  using cases for, 117
  using reply briefs for, 117
  weaving adverse case law into, 125
  working from general to specific in sections of, 111
and, for beginning sentences, 30, 230
and/or, avoiding, 222
appears/apparently, avoiding hedging research with, 37
Archiving, e-mail and, 19
Argument. *See* Analysis/Argument
as/like, 227
assure/ensure/insure, 225
Attachments, e-mail, 199–200
Attorneys, writing skills and, 2. *See also* Transactional attorneys
Autocorrect function, 149
Auto-Text disclaimer, 202

Backups, and form files, 213
Bad news, presenting, in letters, 179

because, for beginning sentences, 30, 230

Berra, Yogi, 83, 147

between/among, 226

Big picture, focusing on, 218

Billings, Josh, 69

Black, Nicole, 204

Blind letters, 180

Blogs/blogging, 203–212
  assumptions for, 207–208
  availability for, 211
  casual style for, 207
  as center of online presence, 207
  client confidence and, 208
  conversation tone for, 207
  copyright statements for, 210
  Creative Commons license for, 210
  deception and, 209
  defamatory comments and, 209
  doing it right, 212
  enabling comments for, 210
  ethics and, 208
  following models for, 212
  free content and, 206
  fresh content and, 206
  giving online advice and, 208
  goal of, 204–205
  introduction, 203–204
  knowing audience for, 205–206
  links and, 212
  listening to comments, 211
  monitoring comments, 211
  personality and, 208
  picking niche for, 205
  privacy and, 209
  proper English for, 207
  purpose of, 205
  regular posting and, 211
  responding to comments, 210–211
  specifying jurisdictions and, 209
  stealing content and, 209–210

The Bluebook, 139

Boldface, design and, 160

Bourke v. Dun & Bradstreet Corp., 171

Brainstorming, 57–60

Breaks, paragraph, in analysis/
    argument, 111

Brevity, 14

Breyer, Stephen, 128, 129, 130

Briefs. *See also* Memorandums
  copyrights and, 70
  persuasiveness and, 76
  for research, 47–48

*Brown v. Board of Education of
    Topeka,* 56

Bullets
  consistency and, 240
  design and, 158–160
  grammatical continuity and, 241
  punctuating and formatting, 241
  simplicity and, 241–242
  usage guide, 240–242

Business law papers, citations in, 137

but, for beginning sentences, 30, 230

Butterick, Matthew, 105, 155, 157

Buzan, Tony, 57–58

California Style Manual, 139

Capitalization
  "court" and, 232
  e-mail and, 196

Carroll, Lewis, 109

Case law. *See also* Law
  bullets and, 240
  in openings of memorandums,
    84–85
  weaving adverse, into analysis/
    argument, 125

Cases
  accepting, as law, 124–125
  appendixes for key, 54
  arranging, within files and subfiles,
    53
  assigning weights to, 217
  checking Internet sources, 50–51
  checking negative history of, 50
  creating *for you* and *against you,* 55
  creating master files for, 213
  creating sound bite for, 53
  explaining facts of *every,* 122
  filing, in research files, 53
  finding and understanding, for
    research, 47–50
  grouping, by fact pattern, 56
  identifying factual trends in, 56
  knowing results of, 48
  lingo for talking about, 120
  marking up, 52–53

parentheticals and, 122–123
as places, 123–124
printing, 52
quotations and, 124
reading entire case, 48
reading opponent's, 49
signal phrases for introducing, 121
structure for talking about, 119–120
understanding procedural history
of, 49
using prose vs. parentheticals for,
120
working case to case, 48
writing sentences when research, 53
Cells, writing, 66
Century font, 157
Characterizing one's work, avoiding, 38
Charles (king of Sweden), 75
Charts, purpose of, 158
Choice-of-law issues, 49
Citation manuals, using correct, 139
Citations, 135–141
avoiding endnotes for, 137
book references for, 141
business law papers and, 137
explanation of facts and, 140
footnotes and, 138
Id., 141
introductory signals for, 139
italics for, 140
online, 136
ordering authorities within, 140
placement of, 136–137
plagiarism and, 138
recognizing substantive value of,
135–136
referring to, 139
in sentences, 137
tense and, 140
visually setting off, 140
Citizens United, 34
Civility, letters and, 179, 180
Clichés, avoiding, 21–22
Clients
avoiding referring to, as *We,* 28
knowing, 43
relationships of, to other parties in
case and, 44
writing for, 40–41

Closings
for e-mail, 196
for letters, 183
Cloud computing, 200–201
Clutter, removing, 17
co, hyphens with, 238
Coding systems, for assessing plain
English, 164
Colleagues. *See* Junior colleagues
Colloquialisms, avoiding, 22
Colons, 23, 234–235
Commas, 23
limiting use of, 24
serial, 232–233
Comments
enabling, blogs for, 210
giving, to junior colleagues, 167–170
listening to, blogs and, 211
monitoring, blogs and, 211
responding to, blogs and, 210
Common law, 48
Communication, privileged, 188
Computer monitors, working on big
screen, 61–62
Conclusions
assumptions for, 99
avoiding hedging language in, 40
avoiding repetition of, 101
brief and client specific, 216
confidence and, 216
drafting, 101
leading with, 216
organization of, 100
placement of, 100
plain English for, 100
for priming readers, 100
reaching, 99
saying aloud, 100
specific facts for, 101
stating reasons for reaching, 100
Confidence, phrases for, 37
Confidential communications, 176
Confidentiality, form files and, 214
Copyrights
blogging and, 210
briefs and, 70
Corporations, using *it* for, 29
could care less/could not care less, 230
Court, capitalizing, 232

Creative Commons license, 210
Crediting sources, 71–72
Csikszentmihalyi, Haly, 63
Cummings, Justice, 171
Czerwinski, Mary, 61–62

Darwin, Charles, 127
Dashes, using, 23, 235–237
Deception, blogging and, 209
Deduce/induce, 226
Deep editing, 143–145, 165–167. *See also* Editing
Defamatory comments, blogging and, 209
Defendant, identifying once for, 29
Deleted material, saving, 68
Dependent clauses, avoiding, in middle of sentences, 28
Design
    ALL CAPS and, 160
    boldface and, 160
    bullets and, 158–160
    charts and, 158
    conservatism and, 155
    fonts and, 156–157
    foundations of, 155
    headings and, 155
    indents and, 155
    introduction to, 153–154
    italics and, 160
    lists and, 158
    logos and, 157
    modern principles of, 154–155
    page numbers, 157
    Print Preview for checking, 160
    proximity and, 155
    reviewing PDFs for, 158
    right margins, 157
    selecting type size, 157
    <u>underscoring</u> and, 160
    visuals and, 158
    white space and, 155–156
Detail, avoiding excessive, 35–36
Devore v. City of Philadelphia, 148
Dewilde v. Guy Gannett Pub. Co., 72
disburse/disperse, 225
disinterested/uninterested, 227
Disparaging comments, avoiding, 37
disperse/disburse, 225
Doctorow, E. L., 51

each other/one other, 226
Editing. *See also* Proofreading; Writing
    comments, giving, to junior colleagues, 167–170
    deep, 143–145, 165–167
    for plain English, 164–165
    in *Print Preview* view, 150
    sentence-level, 14
    synthesis and, 145–146
    work from junior colleagues, 163–167
    writing and, 68
effect/affect, 225
Elefant, Carolyn, 204
Ellipses, 233–234
E-mail
    ALL CAPS and, 196
    archiving and, 195
    attachments, 199–200
    capitalization and, 196
    closings for, 196
    cloud computing and, 200–201
    encryption, 199–200
    flagging, 196
    fonts for, 196–197
    forwarding and, 194
    greetings, 195
    hand-held devices and, 201–202
    in-house counsel and, 189
    introduction, 185
    judicious use of, 188
    To line and, 190–191
    logos and, 196
    managing, 197–198
    message section, 192–194
    mishaps, 198
    to opposing counsel, 197
    perils and pitfalls of, 186–187
    privilege and, 188–190
    replying and, 194
    requesting read receipts for, 196
    sending hard copy of, 197
    signatures and, 196
    spellchecking, 197
    Subject line and, 191
    work product and, 189
Em dashes, using, 23, 235–237
Encryption, for e-mail, 199
En dashes, using, 236
Endings, writing, 67

Endnotes, citations and, 137
ensure/insure/assure, 225
Envisioning Information (Tufte), 158
Espita v. Fouche, 135
Ethics, blogging and, 208
Euphemisms, avoiding, 35
ex, hyphens with, 238
Excess detail, avoiding, 35–36
Exclamation points, avoiding, 23

Facts, 217. *See also* Stories
    for analysis/argument, 109
    arguing, vs. law, 109
    avoiding meaningless dates and, 92
    avoiding repetition of, 92
    chronological order for, 92
    creating "master file" for, 91
    eliminating unnecessary facts, 92
    fixating on, 40
    focusing on, for substantive
      headings, 105
    identifying key players and, 92
    lead sentence for, 91
    for limiting conclusions, 94
    mining for, 91
    plain-English identifiers for names
      of parties and, 93
    prefacing issues with, 95
    presenting negative, 93
    procedural history and, 94
    stories and, 90
    in summary judgments, 93
    weaving law and, 116
Fairness, 69–70, 72–73. *See also*
    Honesty; Plagiarism
farther/further, 226
Faxes, 187
Federal courts, common law and, 48
fewer/less, 226
FICA (Facts, Issue, Conclusion, and
    Analysis or *Argument)* format, 84
Files
    creating master, 213
    maintaining form, 213–214
First drafts, writing, 67
First person, avoiding, 37–38
"Flow," finding, for writing, 63
Fonts
    design and, 156–157
    for e-mail, 196–197

sans serif, 156–157
serif, 156
Footnotes, citations and, 138
Formbooks, copying from, 70
the former, avoiding, 27
Form files, maintaining, 213–214
Forwarding, e-mail and, 194
For you cases, creating, 55
Franklin, Benjamin, 215
Frederick v. Morse, 83–84
further/farther, 226

Garamond font, 157
Gender, plurals for, 29
Goals of assignment, knowing, 45
Grammar Check, 149–150
Grammar police issues, 230
Greetings, e-mail and, 195

Hahn, Duane Alan, 143
Hand-held devices, e-mail and, 201–
    202
Headings, 216. *See also* Substantive
    headings
    indents for, 155
    in longer papers, 80
    placement of transitions and, 128
    sans serif fonts and, 157
Hedging language, avoiding, in
    conclusions, 40
Homonyms, 228–229
Honesty, 34, 69–70. *See also* Plagiarism
hopefully, 229–230
Housekeeping, 213–214
however, for beginning sentences, 30,
    230
Hyperbole, avoiding, 35
Hyphens, 237–238
    with *co,* 238
    with *inter,* 238
    with *ly,* 237
    with *mid and non,* 238
    with numbers, 238
    with *self, quasi, ex,* 238
    with *well,* 237

Id. citations, 141
I/me, 242
imply/infer, 226
induce/deduce, 226

infer/imply, 226
Informal format, of memorandums, 83–84
   Introduction and Conclusion section, 84
In-house counsel, e-mails and, 189
in re Burghoff, 71
insure/assure/ensure, 225
inter, hyphens with, 238
Internet. *See also* E-mail
   avoiding surfing on, 64
   checking sources on, 50–51
Introductory phrases, avoiding stuffy, 114
Introductory signals, for citations, 139
Iowa Supreme Court Bd. of Profes-sional Ethics & Conduct v. Lane, 71
IRAC (Issue, Rule of Law, Analysis, and Conclusion) format, avoid-ing, 84
irregardless/regardless, 229
Issues
   avoiding abstract statements of, 96
   avoiding restating conditions in, 96
   length for, 95
   making questions from, 96
   phrasing, for *Yes* answers, 97
   prefacing, with facts, 95
   simplicity and, 96
   statement of, avoiding being limited by, 95
   syllogisms for, 96
it
   avoiding ambiguous uses of, 27
   beginning sentences with, 26
   for corporations, 29
Italics
   for citations, 140
   for clarifying, 29–30
   for design, 160
it is clear that, avoiding, 26
it's/its, 229

Jargon, avoiding, 17–18
Journals, avoiding use of, 118
Junior colleagues
   editing work from, 163–167
   giving comments to, 167–170

   giving out assignments and, 162–163
   working with, 161
Jurisdictions, specifying, blogging and, 209

Keller, Helen, 39
Kennedy, Robert, Jr., 78–79
Kingvision Pay Per View, Ltd. v. Wilson, 72

Langiewische, William, 64
Latin words/phrases, resisting, 18
the latter, avoiding, 27
Law. *See also* Case law
   accepting cases as, 124–125
   arguing statutes vs., 116
   weaving facts and, 116
Lawyers, writing skills and, 2. *See also* Transactional attorneys
lay/lie, 226–227
Leading from the top, 215, 216
   for analysis/argument, 110
   for letters, 178
   principle of, 9–11
   for structuring papers, 77–78
Lead sentences, 78–79. *See also* Sentences
   to lay groundwork for later paragraphs, 29
   for paragraphs in analysis/argument, 112–113
Legalese
   avoiding, 17
   examples of deleting, and rewriting with plain English, 220
Legal papers
   body section of, 78
   headings in longer, 80
   local rules for, 80–81
   opening section of, 78–79
   recommendation section of, 78
   substance driving structure in, 79–80
Legal writing. *See also* Writing
   reasons for importance of, 1–2
   strong, 2
   technology and, 2–3
   to-do section, 81
   transition from academic to, 39–41

Leonard, Elmore, 5
less/fewer, 226
Letters, 175–183
    for arguing cases, 180
    attacking ideas vs. people in, 179
    beginnings for, 178
    blind, 180
    civility and, 179, 180
    copying opposing counsel on, 182
    dates and, 182
    documenting with, 179
    emotions and, 179
    endings for, 178
    fighting words in, 179
    formal closings for, 183
    importance of, 175
    incorporating other documents by
        reference in, avoiding, 182
    justifying bills and, 183
    knowing audiences of, 177
    knowing purpose of, 176
    knowing when and when not to
        write, 175
    leading from the top for, 178
    modern block format for, 180–181
    modern English for, 177
    personal vs. law firm, 176
    postscripts for, 183
    precautions for, 180
    presenting bad news in, 179
    principles for writing, 177
    privileges and, 176
    reference lines, 182
    referring to conversations in, 182
    semi-block format for, 180–181
    single spacing for, 182
    spelling and, 177
    templates for, 176
    thoroughness and, 182
    tone for, 177
LexisNexis, 47
lie/lay, 226–227
like/as, 227
Lincoln, Abraham, 43
Lingo, learning, 120
Links, blogging and, 212
Lists
    breaking up, 118
    designing, 158
Literary sources, avoiding quoting, 24

Local rules, for legal papers, 80–81
Logos, 157
    e-mail and, 196
ly, hyphens with, 238

Manatee County, Florida, Code, 35–36
Married verbs, avoid, 224
Marshall, Thurgood, 56
Master files, creating, for cases, 213
McCreary v. ACLU, 122
me/I, 242
Memorandums. *See also* Briefs
    avoiding *IRAC* format for, 84
    case law in openings of, 84–85
    centering structural headings of, 85
    To Do lists for internal, 134
    informal format, 83–84
    invisible dotted line of, 84
    persuasiveness and, 76
    post-its for, 85
    traditional format, 83–84
    understanding importance of, 45
Message section, e-mail, 192–194
mid, hyphens with, 238
Milne, A. A., 1, 13, 55, 61
Mind mapping, 57–58
Misleading claims, blogging and, 209
Models, finding and working from, 62
Modern block format, for letters,
    180–181
Modern format, for substantive head-
    ings, 104
Modifiers, placement of, 25
Modifying words, placement of, 25–26
Monitors, working on big screen, 61–
    62
moot/mute, 229
Morse v. Frederick, 105
Mudslinging, avoiding, 36
Multiple negative concepts, avoiding,
    28
Multitasking, avoiding, 63–64
myself, 242

Negative concepts, avoiding multiple,
    28
Negative facts, presenting, 93
Nominalizations, 21, 221–222
The Non-Designer's Design Book
    (Williams), 155

Notes, making vs. taking, 58
Numbers, 231–232
  hyphens, 238

Official Reports Style Manual (New
  York), 139
one, avoiding use of, 38
one other/each other, 225
Online advice, blogging and, 208
only, 26
Opening section
  elements of strong, 78
  five questions to answer in, 79
  imagining dotted line after, 78
  lead sentence and, 78–79
Original writing, 40
Orwell, George, 153
Outlining
  from memory, 65
  research files and, 65
  as you go, 65
Outlining View, 81
Overkill, avoiding, 222

Pagan Belez v. Laboy Alvarado, 72
Page numbers, 157
Paragraph breaks, in analysis/
  argument, 111
Paragraphs. *See also* Lead sentences;
  Sentences
  example of working, 114–115
  leading with topic sentence for,
  217
  limiting to two or three, per page,
  16
  signal phrases and, 113
  topics and, 112
Parallel construction
  for analysis/argument, 110
  between bullets, 24
  in subparagraphs, 239
  for substantive headings, 108
  for transition, 129–130
parameter/perimeter, 227
Parentheses, 23–24, 238
Parentheticals
  cases and, 122–123
  proper use of, 123
  prose vs., 120

*Parents Involved in Community
  Schools,* 91, 121, 128
Passion, 34
Passive voice, using, 16
PDFs, reviewing, for design issues, 158
perimeter/parameter, 227
Periods, 232
  quotations and, 239
Plagiarism, 70–72, 138
  checking, 138–139
  correct manuals for, 139
Plain English, 215
  assessing and editing for, 164–165
  coding system for assessing, 164
  examples of deleting legalese and
    rewriting with, 220–221
  principle of, 9
  using, 13–14
  verbs, 221–222
Plaintiff, identifying once for, 29
Plato, 9
Plurals
  for gender, 29
  usage guide, 242–243
Pods, writing, 66
Possessives, usage guide, 243
Post-its, for memorandums, 85
Postscripts, letters and, 183
Precedent, avoiding requests to
  overrule, 116
Prepositional phrases, avoiding,
  223–224
Preventative/preventive, 229
Primary headings, 103
Principles, powerful writing, 9–11
  leading from the top, 9–11
  telling readers what to do next, 11
  using plain English, 9
Print Preview view, 150
  for checking design elements, 160
Privacy, blogging and, 209
Privileges
  communications and, 188
  e-mail and, 188–190
  letters and, 176
Procedural context, understanding,
  44
Procedural history, telling, for facts,
  94

Professional writing, transition from academic writing to, 39–41. *See also* Legal writing; Writing
Pronouns, 242
Proofreading, 147–151. *See also* Editing; Writing
Proximity, design and, 155
Punctuation, 232–239

quasi, hyphens with, 238
Quotations
    cases and, 124
    periods and, 239

Readers
    being kind to, 6–7
    having pity on, 5
    knowing, 43
    principle of telling what to do next for, 11
    understanding environment of, 5–6
Recommendations, 218
Redundant phrases, avoiding, 225
Reference lines, in letters, 182
Reply briefs, in analysis/argument, 117
Replying, e-mail and, 194
Research
    finding and understanding cases, 47–50
    giving global picture of, 119
    organizing, for writing, 62–63
Research files
    creating fact-specific files, 52
    creating subfiles for major topics, 51–52
    filing cases in, 53
    as outline, 51, 65
    writing directly from, 68
Research memoranda
    as impartial surveys of law, 75
    thinking ahead for, 75
Ridicule, avoiding, 34
Right margins, 157
Roberts, John, 88–89, 91, 121, 128
Roman-numeral format, for substantive headings, 104
Routines, creating, for writing, 65–66
Rukeyser, Muriel, 87

Rules, local, for legal papers, 80–81
Rules of procedure, understanding, 44–45

Sans serif fonts, 156–157
    for e-mail, 196–197
Sarcasm, avoiding, 34
Sartre, 185
Saying sentences aloud, 14, 215
Schorr, Ben, 151
self, hyphens with, 238
Semi-block format, for letters, 182
Semicolons, 23, 234
Sendak, Maurice, 33
Sentence-level editing, 14
Sentences. *See also* Lead sentences; Paragraphs; Summary sentences
    avoiding dependent clauses in middle of, 28
    because for beginning, 30
    and for beginning, 30
    brevity for, 14
    but for beginning, 30
    citations in, 137
    familiar, concrete words for, 14
    however for beginning, 30
    originality and, 217
    placing import parts at beginning or end of, 25
    reading aloud, 14
    three-letter words to begin, 24–25
    varying length of, 16
    working from general to specific within, 25
    writing memorable, 15
    writing short, 15
Serial comma, 232–233
Serif fonts, 156
    for e-mail, 196–197
[sic], 238
Signal phrases
    in analysis/argument, 113–114
    focusing on factual results of, 121–122
    for introducing cases, 121
    summarizing, 121
    variety and, 114
Signatures, e-mail and, 196
Skakel, Michael, 78

Slang, avoiding, 22
Social Media for Lawyers: The Next Frontier (Elefant and Black), 204
Sources, crediting, 71–72
Spell-checking, 148–149
    e-mail, 197
Split infinitives, using, 31, 230
stationery/stationary, 229
Statutes
    arguing, vs. law, 116
    nickname, 126
    summarizing, 125
Stevens, John Paul, 20
Stories, 215. *See also* Facts
    choosing interesting words for, 89
    facts and, 90
    identifying clients in, 89–90
    introducing players in, 90
    issues and, 89
    length for, 88
    people and, 89
    placement of, 87–88
    researching clients and, 90
    writing for *next* person reading, 88
    writing interesting, 83–84
strategy/tactics, 228
Stream of conscience, avoiding sharing one's, 38
Stuffy words, avoiding, 220–221
Subject line, e-mail and, 191
Subparagraphs, 239
Substance driving structure, 79–80
Substantive headings. *See also* Headings
    avoiding single, 107
    creating intervening headings and, 107
    first paragraphs and, 106–107
    focusing on facts for, 105
    lettering, 104–105
    liberally using, 103
    modern format for, 104
    numbering, 104–105
    page breaks and, 108
    parallel construction and, 108
    primary headings and, 103
    similar content and, 105–106
    themes and, 103

traditional format for, 104
    using sentences, 108
    using strong titles for, 108
Sullivan, Andrew, 204
summary motion judgments, understanding, 44–45
Summary sentences, for transitions, 128–129
supra citations, avoiding, 141
Surfing, Internet, avoiding, 64
Surnames, using, 29
Syllogisms, for issues, 96

tactics/strategy, 228
Tanbook, 139
Telling your reader what to do next, 133–134
Templates, letter, 176
that/which, 227–228
the (article), keeping, 27
their/they're/there, 228
Themes, identifying, 103
Theme words
    in analysis/argument, 115
    to sound bite statutes/legal theory, 115
there, beginning sentences with, 26
Thinking, writing and, 64
Three-letter words, to begin sentences, 24–25
Times New Roman font, 157
Titles, for papers, 108
to be, avoiding, 27, 222
To Do lists, for internal memorandums, 134
To-do section, 81
To line, e-mail and, 190–191
Tone, selecting, 34
Topic sentences, leading paragraphs with, 217
Tortured constructions, avoiding grammatically-correct but, 23
Track Changes, 151
Traditional format, of memorandums, 83–84
    FICA acronym, 84
Transactional attorneys, tips for, 171–173

Transitions
    avoiding announcing what to you
       will do next and, 131
    leads for, 127–128
    parallel construction for, 129–130
    pattern/repetition for, 129–130
    placement of, 128
    spending time on, 127
    strong summary sentences for,
       128–129
    transferring words from one
       sentence to next for, 130
Tufte, Edward R., 158
Twain, Mark, 175, 213
Typography for Lawyers (Butterick),
    155, 157

Underscoring, design and, 160
Uninterested/disinterested, 227
U.S. v. United Shoe Machinery Corp.,
    188
USA Clio Biz, Inc. v. New York State
    Department of Labor, 72
Usage guides, 31
Use Both Sides of Your Brain (Buzan),
    57–58

Verbosity, killing, 224
Verbs
    avoiding married, 224
    choosing colorful, 19–20
    choosing descriptive, 20
    choosing strong, vs. adverbs, 20
    strong, vs. fussy nouns, 21
The Visual Display of Quantitative
    Information (Tufte), 158
Visual Explanations (Tufte), 158
Visuals, design and, 158
Vocabulary, using, 16–17
Voice, finding one's, 33–34

we, avoiding referral to clients as, 28
well, hyphens with, 237
WestlawNext, 47
which/that, 227–228
White, E. B., 77, 161
White space, 16
    design and, 155–156
    methods of adding, 156

whom/who, 228
who's/whose, 228
who/whom, 228
Williams, Robin, 155
Williams, Tennessee, 203
Words
    avoiding archaic, 22
    avoiding pompous, 21
    choosing, for their sounds, 18–19
    choosing descriptive, picturesque,
       19–20
    choosing familiar, concrete, 14
    commonly misused, 229–230
    formality and, 22
    homonyms, 228–229
    worrisome, 225–228
Working paragraph, example of,
    114–115
Work pages, for writing, 64
Work product, e-mail and, 189
Writer's block, avoiding, 66
Writing. *See also* Editing; Legal
    writing; Proofreading
    avoiding multitasking during, 63–64
    creating routines for, 65–66
    creating work pages for, 64
    directly from research files, 68
    endings first, 67
    finding "flow" of, 63
    first drafts and, 67
    having plans for, 64
    in layers, 66–67
    organizing research for, 62–63
    outlining and, 65
    pods or cells, 66
    principles of powerful, 9–11
    saving deleted material and, 68
    setting aside time for, 63
    surfing Internet and, 64
    talking to yourself and, 67
    thinking and, 64
    work pages for, 64
    writer's block and, 66
Writing skills, lawyers and, 2

you're/your, 228

Zinsser, William, 133

Selected Books from . . .
THE ABA LAW PRACTICE MANAGEMENT SECTION

e Lawyer's Guide to Collaboration Tools and :hnologies: Smart Ways to Work Together
Dennis Kennedy and Tom Mighell
is first-of-its-kind guide for the legal profession)ws you how to use standard technology you already /e and the latest "Web 2.0" resources and other tech •ls, like Google Docs, Microsoft Office and Share- nt, and Adobe Acrobat, to work more effectively on >jects with colleagues, clients, co-counsel and even)osing counsel. In *The Lawyer's Guide to Collabora- 1 Tools and Technologies: Smart Ways to Work Together*, II-known legal technology authorities Dennis nnedy and Tom Mighell provides a wealth of infor- tion useful to lawyers who are just beginning to try ∙se tools, as well as tips and techniques for those ryers with intermediate and advanced collaboration)erience.

ogle for Lawyers: Essential Search Tips and)ductivity Tools
Carole A. Levitt and Mark E. Rosch
is book introduces novice Internet searchers to ∙ diverse collection of information locatable ough Google. The book discusses the importance including effective Google searching as part of a /yer's due diligence, and cites case law that man- :es that lawyers should use Google and other ources available on the Internet, where applicable. ∙ intermediate and advanced users, the book locks the power of various advanced search strate- s and hidden search features they might not be are of.

e Lawyer's Guide to Adobe Acrobat, ird Edition
David L. Masters
is book was written to help lawyers increase produc- ity, decrease costs, and improve client services by ∙ving from paper-based files to digital records. This dated and revised edition focuses on the ways ryers can benefit from using the most current soft- re, Adobe® Acrobat 8, to create Portable Document ʳmat (PDF) files.

ꞰDF files are reliable, easy-to-use, electronic files sharing, reviewing, filing, and archiving docu- nts across diverse applications, business processes, d platforms. The format is so reliable that the leral courts' Case Management/Electronic Case ∙s (CM/ECF) program and state courts that use ҝis-Nexis File & Serve have settled on PDF as the ndard.

ʋ'll learn how to:
Ꞇreate PDF files from a number of programs, includ- 1g Microsoft Office
Ise PDF files the smart way
✔arkup text and add comments
)igitally, and securely, sign documents
ꞋxtractCcontent content from PDF files
Ꞇreate electronic briefs and forms

The Electronic Evidence and Discovery Handbook: Forms, Checklists, and Guidelines
By Sharon D. Nelson, Bruce A. Olson, and John W. Simek
The use of electronic evidence has increased dramati- cally over the past few years, but many lawyers still struggle with the complexities of electronic discovery. This substantial book provides lawyers with the tem- plates they need to frame their discovery requests and provides helpful advice on what they can subpoena. In addition to the ready-made forms, the authors also supply explanations to bring you up to speed on the electronic discovery field. The accompanying CD-ROM features over 70 forms, including, Motions for Protec- tive Orders, Preservation and Spoliation Documents, Motions to Compel, Electronic Evidence Protocol Agreements, Requests for Production, Internet Services Agreements, and more. Also included is a full electronic evidence case digest with over 300 cases detailed!

The 2011 Solo and Small Firm Legal Technology Guide
By Sharon D. Nelson, Esq., John W. Simek, and Michael C. Maschke
This annual guide is the only one of its kind written to help solo and small firm lawyers find the best technol- ogy for their dollar. You'll find the most current infor- mation and recommendations on computers, servers, networking equipment, legal software, printers, securi- ty products, smart phones, and anything else a law office might need. It's written in clear, easily under- standable language to make implementation simpler if you choose to do it yourself, or you can use it in conjunction with your IT consultant. Either way, you'll learn how to make technology work for you.

The Lawyer's Guide to LexisNexis CaseMap
By Daniel J. Siegel
LexisNexis CaseMap is a computer program that makes analyzing cases easier and allows lawyers to do a better job for their clients in less time. Many consider this an essential law office tool. If you are interested in learn- ing more about LexisNexis CaseMap, this book will help you:

- Analyze the strengths and weaknesses of your cases quickly and easily;
- Learn how to create files for people, organizations and issues, while avoiding duplication;
- Customize CaseMap so that you can get the most out of your data;
- Enter data so that you can easily prepare for trial, hearings, depositions, and motions for summary judgment;
- Import data from a wide range of programs, includ- ing Microsoft Outlook;
- Understand CaseMap's many Reports and Report- Books;
- Use the Adobe DocPreviewer to import PDFs and quickly create facts and objects; and
- Learn how to perform advanced searches plus how to save and update your results.

**ʼO ORDER CALL TOLL-FREE:
-800-285-2221**

**VISIT OUR WEB SITE:
www.lawpractice.org/catalog**

Virtual Law Practice: How to Deliver Legal Services Online
By Stephanie L. Kimbro
The legal market has recently experienced a dramatic shift as lawyers seek out alternative methods of practicing law and providing more affordable legal services. Virtual law practice is revolutionizing the way the public receives legal services and how legal professionals work with clients. If you are interested in this form of practicing law, *Virtual Law Practice* will help you:

• Responsibly deliver legal services online to your clients
• Successfully set up and operate a virtual law office
• Establish a virtual law practice online through a secure, client-specific portal
• Manage and market your virtual law practice
• Understand state ethics and advisory opinions
• Find more flexibility and work/life balance in the legal profession

The Lawyer's Guide to Microsoft Word 2007
By Ben M. Schorr
Microsoft Word is one of the most used applications in the Microsoft Office suite—there are few applications more fundamental than putting words on paper. Most lawyers use Word and few of them get everything they can from it. Because the documents you create are complex and important—your law practice depends, to some degree, upon the quality of the documents you produce and the efficiency with which you can produce them. Focusing on the tools and features that are essential for lawyers in their everyday practice, *The Lawyer's Guide to Microsoft Word* explains in detail the key components to help make you more effective, more efficient and more successful.

iPad in One Hour for Lawyers
By Tom Mighell
Whether you are a new or a more advanced iPad user, *iPad in One Hour for Lawyers* takes a great deal of the mystery and confusion out of using your iPad. Ideal for lawyers who want to get up to speed swiftly, this book presents the essentials so you don't get bogged down in technical jargon and extraneous features and apps. In just six, short lessons, you'll learn how to:

• Quickly Navigate and Use the iPad User Interface
• Set Up Mail, Calendar, and Contacts
• Create and Use Folders to Multitask and Manage Apps
• Add Files to Your iPad, and Sync Them
• View and Manage Pleadings, Case Law, Contracts, and other Legal Documents
• Use Your iPad to Take Notes and Create Documents
• Use Legal-Specific Apps at Trial or in Doing Research

Find Info Like a Pro, Volume 1: Mining the Internet's Publicly Available Resources for Investigative Research
By Carole A. Levitt and Mark E. Rosch
This complete hands-on guide shares the secrets, shortcuts, and realities of conducting investigative a background research using the sources of publicly available information available on the Internet. Writt for legal professionals, this comprehensive desk boo lists, categorizes, and describes hundreds of free an fee-based Internet sites. The resources and techniqu in this book are useful for investigations; deposition: locating missing witnesses, clients, or heirs; and tria preparation, among other research challenges facing legal professionals. In addition, a CD-ROM is include which features clickable links to all of the sites contained in the book.

How to Start and Build a Law Practice, Platinum Fifth Edition
By Jay G. Foonberg
This classic ABA bestseller has been used by tens of thousands of lawyers as the comprehensive guide to planning, launching, and growing a successful practice. It's packed with over 600 pages of guidance on identifying the right location, finding clients, setting fees, managing your office, maintaining an ethical an responsible practice, maximizing available resources upholding your standards, and much more. You'll find the information you need to successfully launch your practice, run it at maximum efficiency, and avo potential pitfalls along the way. If you're committed to starting—and growing—your own practice, this o book will give you the expert advice you need to ma it succeed for years to come.

Social Media for Lawyers: The Next Frontier
By Carolyn Elefant and Nicole Black
The world of legal marketing has changed with the r of social media sites such as Linkedin, Twitter, and Facebook. Law firms are seeking their companies att tion with tweets, videos, blog posts, pictures, and online content. Social media is fast and delivers new at record pace. This book provides you with a practi cal, goal-centric approach to using social media in yc law practice that will enable you to identify social media platforms and tools that fit your practice and implement them easily, efficiently, and ethically.

ABA LawPracticeManagementSectio
MARKETING • MANAGEMENT • TECHNOLOGY • FINAN

30-Day Risk-Free Order Form
Call Today! 1-800-285-2221
Monday–Friday, 7:30 AM – 5:30 PM, Central Time

	Title	LPM Price	Regular Price	Total
___	The Lawyer's Guide to Collaboration Tools and Technologies: Smart Ways to Work Together (5110589)	$59.95	$ 89.95	$_____
___	Google for Lawyers: Essential Search Tips and Productivity Tools (5110704)	47.95	79.95	$_____
___	The Lawyer's Guide to Adobe Acrobat, Third Edition (5110588)	49.95	79.95	$_____
___	The Electronic Evidence and Discovery Handbook: Forms, Checklists, and Guidelines (5110569)	99.95	129.95	$_____
___	The 2011 Solo and Small Firm Legal Technology Guide (5110716)	54.95	89.95	$_____
___	The Lawyer's Guide to LexisNexis CaseMap (5110715)	47.95	79.95	$_____
___	Virtual Law Practice: How to Deliver Legal Services Online (5110707)	47.95	79.95	$_____
___	The Lawyer's Guide to Microsoft Word 2007 (5110697)	49.95	69.95	$_____
___	iPadin One Hour for Lawyers (5110719)	19.95	34.95	$_____
___	Find Info Like a Pro, V1: Mining the . . . (5110708)	47.95	79.95	$_____
___	How to Start and Build a Law Practice, Platinum Fifth Edition (5110508)	57.95	69.95	$_____
___	Social Media for Lawyers: The Next Frontier (5110710)	47.95	79.95	$_____

*Postage and Handling	
10.00 to $49.99	$5.95
50.00 to $99.99	$7.95
100.00 to $199.99	$9.95
200.00+	$12.95

**Tax
DC residents add 6%
IL residents add 9.75%

*Postage and Handling	$_____
**Tax	$_____
TOTAL	$_____

**YMENT

❑ Check enclosed (to the ABA)

❑ Visa ❑ MasterCard ❑ American Express

_____
count Number   Exp. Date   Signature

Name _____ Firm _____

Address _____

City _____ State _____ Zip _____

Phone Number _____ E-Mail Address _____

arantee
-for any reason—you are not satisfied with your purchase, you may
urn it within 30 days of receipt for a complete refund of the price of the
ok(s). No questions asked!

Mail: ABA Publication Orders, P.O. Box 10892, Chicago, Illinois 60610-0892
♦ **Phone: 1-800-285-2221** ♦ **FAX: 312-988-5568**

E-Mail: abasvcctr@americanbar.org ♦ **Internet: http://www.lawpractice.org/catalog**

Are You in Your Element?

Tap into the Resources of the ABA Law Practice Management Section

ABA Law Practice Management Section Membership Benefits

The ABA Law Practice Management Section (LPM) is a professional membership organization of the American Bar Association that helps lawyers and other legal professionals with the business of practicing law. LPM focuses on providing information and resources in the core areas of marketing, management, technology, and finance through its award-winning magazine, teleconference series, Webzine, educational programs (CLE), Web site, and publishing division. For more than thirty years, LPM has established itself as a leader within the ABA and the profession-at-large by producing the world's largest legal technology conference (ABA TECHSHOW®) each year. In addition, LPM's publishing program is one of the largest in the ABA, with more than eighty-five titles in print.

In addition to significant book discounts, LPM Section membership offers these benefits:

ABA TECHSHOW
Membership includes a $100 discount to ABA TECHSHOW, the world's largest legal technology conference & expo!

Teleconference Series
Convenient, monthly CLE teleconferences on hot topics in marketing, management, technology and finance. Access educational opportunities from the comfort of your office chair – today's practical way to earn CLE credits!

LAW|PRACTICE
THE BUSINESS OF PRACTICING LAW

Law Practice Magazine
Eight issues of our award-winning *Law Practice* magazine, full of insightful articles and practical tips on Marketing/Client Development, Practice Management, Legal Technology, and Finance.

Law Practice TODAY

Law Practice Today
LPM's unique Web-based magazine covers all the hot topics in law practice management today — identify current issues, face today's challenges, find solutions quickly. Visit www.lawpracticetoday.org.

LAW TECHNOLOGY TODAY

Law Technology Today
LPM's newest Webzine focuses on legal technology issues in law practice management — covering a broad spectrum of the technology, tools, strategies and their implementation to help lawyers build a successful practice. Visit www.lawtechnologytoday.org.

LawPractice.news
Monthly news and information from the ABA Law Practice Management Section

LawPractice.news
Brings Section news, educational opportunities, book releases, and special offers to members via e-mail each month.

To learn more about the ABA Law Practice Management Section, visit www.lawpractice.org or call 1-800-285-2221.

MARKETING • MANAGEMENT • TECHNOLOGY • FINANCE

Join the ABA Law Practice Management Section Today!

Value is . . .

Resources that help you become a better lawyer:
- Up to 40% off LPM publications
- Six Issues of *Law Practice* magazine, both print and electronic versions
- Twelve issues of our monthly Webzine, *Law Practice Today*
- Your connection to Section news and events through *LawPractice.news*
- Discounted registration on "Third Thursday" CLE Teleconference Series and LPM conferences

Networking with industry experts while improving your skills at:
- ABA TECHSHOW
- ABA Law Firm Marketing Strategies Conference
- ABA Women Rainmakers Mid-Career Workshop
- LPM Quarterly Meetings

Opportunity given exclusively to our members:
- Writing for LPM periodicals and publications
- Joining ABA Women Rainmakers
- Becoming a better leader through committee involvement
- Listing your expertise in the LPM Speakerbase

**Members of LPM get up to 40% off publications like this one.
Join today and start saving!**

www.lawpractice.org • 1.800.285.2221

MARKETING • MANAGEMENT • TECHNOLOGY • FINANCE